THE BOOK OF REVENGE

DRAGAN TODOROVIC

THE BOOK OF REVENGE

A BLUES FOR YUGOSLAVIA

Random House Canada

 Published in 2006 by Random House Canada, a division of Random House of Canada Limited. Distributed in Canada by Random House of Canada Limited.

Random House Canada and colophon are trademarks.

www.randomhouse.ca

Library and Archives Canada Cataloguing in Publication

Todorovic, Dragan, 1951–
The book of revenge : a blues for Yugoslavia / Dragan Todorovic.

ISBN-13: 978-0-679-31396-0
ISBN-10: 0-679-31396-6

1. Todorovic, Dragan, 1951– . 2. Yugoslavia–History–1980-1992.
3. Yugoslavia–History–1945-1980. 4. Yugoslavia--Biography. I. Title.
DR1321.T62A3 2006 949.703'092 C2005-906084-0

Jacket and text design: CS Richardson

Printed and bound in the United States of America

10 9 8 7 6 5 4 3 2 1

To the people who make my
world–Ana, Dušan, Silvija and Ana

SLAUGHTER TIME

It is early morning in the late fall of 1963. The fog is lifting slowly. The light is the color of bad steel and the air is cold.

The pig lets out high-frequency cries that hurt my ears. A universal sign for help in the world of sentient beings.

The animal is heavy, more than three hundred pounds, or so I heard this morning. I don't know what it means and if it's good or not, but now, watching this rushing mass through the fence, I can see that the five hundred pounds means power. I don't quite understand why it will all happen to the animal that was a pet until last night, when my uncle went with my aunt to feed it one last time, murmuring quiet words of approval and love. I know only that the men will kill the pig, but I don't know how death looks or what it is.

The lower yard is closed from all sides: the gate towards the upper yard, the narrow passage next to the stable, the one that leads to the orchard, and the big wagon entry from the dirt road. Through the laths on the upper gate I am watching the men slowly close in. The sow that runs panicky inside that narrowing circle is huge, and not because I am five years old. Ten or so dark, tense silhouettes are coming closer and closer, their hands spread wide to fill the space between them. The animal speeds up and changes its direction frequently, but every time it comes close to a gap that looks like an exit, another human figure jumps in to close the passage to freedom.

Two knives and a sharpener rest on a transverse beam near where I stand. The knives are long, with wooden handles, narrow and so old that their dark blades look ragged after years of sharpening against stones. Miladin has left them there after finishing his coffee and *rakija,* so he could fetch them quickly when the time comes.

I feel an unknown fear. Not of what I see but of what is yet to come. I can understand–by the seriousness of men and the rush of women–that this is important business. We all got up before dawn, even we children. Water is already boiling in the big cauldron on the bonfire, and the damp air pushes the smoke low, creating a long, slow curtain that delineates the stage. And, although I'm too young to be in that circle, hunting an animal, I am part of it all. They let me watch on purpose, to harden up, to see how death looks.

Someone is the first to throw himself onto the sow, which loses speed and stops for a second. Others follow and the huge ball of flesh is suddenly on the ground, its legs tied with ropes, two men kneeling on its side, several others holding its snout. The pig is fighting desperately. Miladin, a big, slow, stern man whose hands are huge and the color of soil, and whose face has lines so deep that one could sow wheat in them, picks up his knives.

"Hold it tight," he says as he kneels down on the animal's throat and holds its snout with his left hand. With a quick movement Miladin raises the animal's head, stretching its neck, and plunges his knife into its throat. A stream of dark, thick blood bursts from the wound. I see the knife cutting farther, led by the short, jerky moves of the man's hand. The wound behind the blade has white edges that quickly turn red. Drops of blood cover everyone, and it seems to me that, under that turbid light, everything is dark blue except the pink skin of the animal and the red that shines. Steam is coming out of the cut throat and the pig's screeching slowly turns into a death rattle, going deeper, deeper and quieter. That sound is horrible. I cover my ears tightly with both hands but I can still hear it. The body of the animal is twitching, strongly at first, then slower and slower as the pressure of life runs out of it. Blood gets into Miladin's eyes and he wipes it off with his right hand, still holding the knife, smearing dark red into light pink that doesn't mean a thing.

The animal dies slowly, it lasts maybe two or three minutes, and then it's still. The men are standing up, wiping the blood off their hands and faces.

"It seems to be easy," I think, measuring myself against the grownups. "I could do it all, save for that sound."

1

GAME: BETWEEN TWO FIRES

The rules

Players separate into two groups, facing each other. The distance between groups is about thirty feet. One person stands in the middle. A player from one group throws the ball at the one in the middle, trying to hit her. If she dodges the ball, it goes to the other side, who does the same. If she catches the ball, the person who threw the ball replaces her in the middle.

The reality

The groups keep coming closer, so the ball hits harder, and it's more difficult to dodge. Some contestants take pride in being able to throw really hard and they usually aim at the head. The weakest person in the game cannot throw the ball powerfully enough, so she quickly becomes the target, and then everyone hits her.

The game usually ends with the person in the middle, already beaten and bruised, tripping over and falling.

THE OFFICE OF HIDDEN TREASURES

The courtyard was long, narrow at the entrance, widening into an area paved with cobblestones in the back, where we lived. A wooden gate with missing teeth was the only thing signaling to those outside that someone lived there. For many years the gate wasn't equipped with a lock, and the travelers from the central bus station in Kragujevac–right in front of our home–would come to drink water from the brass faucet protruding from a concrete box close to the entrance. Sometimes they would shit or vomit right next to the faucet, so my father decided to install a cheap, old-fashioned iron lock with one of those medieval big black keys. He was a locksmith in Zastava, the car factory, and he knew everything about locks, so he personally chose that one. And he personally kept fixing it.

To the left of the entrance was the accounting department of some trading company in which only women worked. Sometimes they would let me stamp their documents, and that was a great pleasure for me: sinking the rubber stamp into the dirty tin box containing a thin pillow soaked with dark blue paint, the smooth lacquered wooden head of the stamp in my hand, the short and strong blow of the stamp on the paper and–always the same miracle–the square blue imprint in the upper-right corner of the page. As if I knew how to write. As if I had power.

The job these women did was inspiring to me: they kept entering–in their tidy, miniature handwriting–long lines of letters neatly packed between hand-drawn lines, with numbers at the end of the line. When every line of the page was filled in their black-and-blue hardcover notebooks, they would take the wooden ruler and make more lines for more numbers and signs. It looked like a secret plan, like a map of hidden treasure waiting to be decoded. I never drew, maybe because I was curious and wanted to see everything around me from very close. I loved seeing the smallest details of every structure: the relief of the bark, the first leaves of plants in the early spring, the dust particles on the stone, tiny metal parts inside the lock. I could never draw the outer lines; I could never catch the contours of the object.

I kept asking my parents for cheap small sketchbooks from the paper place on the corner, and when they would bring one, I would draw lines inside and fill the pages with signs that just looked like letters and numbers. I was three years old, and I was very frustrated, because my notebooks never looked like the big ones from the Office of Hidden Treasures.

THE SMELL OF NEWS

Next to the office, farther into our courtyard, was a bunker made of concrete blocks, serving as a trash depository. It smelled bad at any time of year and there were rats in it that always made me run past that place. Next to the bunker were the two cabins of our outhouse. Each had a padlock on the wooden door and looked the same inside: a concrete floor, a hole in it, and on both sides wooden planks with several long nails onto which we pricked the newspaper clippings we used for wiping. My parents would take yesterday's paper, separate it into sheets, fold them several times and cut them with a knife along the folds into tidy, rectangular pieces of equal size. Our asses were always heavy with lead, but we were too poor to travel anyway. The stench coming from the outhouses was horrible—we'd empty them only when the mix of news and feces would come within a foot or so of the top.

Not all the pages were equally useful. We threw out the middle spread, with pictures, right away. The pictures were just areas of condensed lead. And those pictures had politicians in them. It just felt inappropriate, and perhaps illegal. Our asses would be clean like babies' when wiped with the front page: the grand titles of the day, and the few lines below, left no traces on my behind. Also the humorous stuff, with jokes scattered all over the page, tiny titles, and caricatures containing only a few liberal lines and lots of white in between. Sometimes I would flip through the leaves on the nail to find the ones cut from the upper part of the front page. These contained the newspaper logo, usually printed in communist-red, and I loved imagining how the traces of color looked on my skin, probably like the flames coming from the rear end of a rocket. It left me feeling energized.

Through the cracks between the planks one could catch sight of the body in the next cabin, and that recurrent shine of skin, undefined, temporary, secretive and sudden, caused the first sexual feeling I remember clearly. Once I wanted to see more: I waited for one of the young women who worked in the textile store to enter the other cabin, then I stormed into our cabin, took the straw I'd prepared for that purpose, slid it between the planks and carefully moved aside pieces of the newspaper on her side of the wall. I caught sight of the line of her thighs and a quick flash of her pubic hair before she covered herself and yelled, "What are you doing, you idiot!" I waited for her to leave the cabin (she did it fast; she wasn't too curious to learn who was on my side of the barrier) and then disappeared into the house. Over the next few days I noticed some of her colleagues eyeing my confused father with suspicion.

THE LEGEND ABOUT ME

Beyond the outhouse, on the south side of our yard, there was a huge, dilapidated yellow brick wall, the back of the old building in the next yard. That place had just three floors, but to me it looked like the highest skyscraper in the world. Because of it we only had an hour, or less, of direct sunshine in the summer. The wall was fifteen yards long and nothing could grow below it, except for this one bush of ailanthus, always fighting for life. When I was nine, I decided to leave my secret mark there.

I found an empty jar with a metal lid and put Strange Objects in it. The Strange Objects were thingies I would occasionally find while patrolling the neighborhood, stuff whose purpose I couldn't understand but which had to be of great value: a piece of green plastic in the shape of a pyramid cut in half, sprinkled with tiny golden dots, smooth and very firm, resistant even to blows of a hammer; a piece of steel, the length of a finger, with a square bottom and a sharp, slanted top, shiny and of pleasurable weight, the victory obelisk for children of the slums (later I learned it was a lathe knife); a small round tin box with three lead pellets inside (air gun ammunition), and a couple of other things I can't remember anymore. I also left a short message, written in slow and careful handwriting: "THESE OBJECTS ARE LEFT BY DRAGAN TODOROVIC, IN THE YEAR 1967, SO YOU WOULD REMEMBER HIM." I closed the lid tightly and, when nobody was watching, buried the jar under the high wall next to the ailanthus bush. It was ten steps to the east and five to the south from the entrance to our kitchen, the measures that were the solution to the mystery in one of the comics I'd just read. I expected that some day, in the distant future, a construction worker would be digging the foundation for a new building and he would find my collection of Strange Objects. Then the scientists would come and create a legend about me.

Three years later, when we were already living in another part of town, they tore down the building to replace it with a shoe store, and the legend about me was buried by the heavy bulldozers that did the job.

STEELING

On the right-hand side of the gate was a lawyer's office. Inside were two desks at a right angle and a simple bench next to the door. There was a board in the small window–black paint over the mirror–saying "Boško Janićijević, Lawyer." He was a chubby man, with a tidy mustache and hair neatly combed backwards and oiled. My parents considered him a good man, although we never needed his services. Except once: twenty years after the war he sent a letter on our behalf to the seat of the International Red Cross in Geneva, an inquiry about my uncle Dušan Ilić, who had been forcefully mobilized by the Chetniks, the Serbian force loyal to the king, in World War II and subsequently disappeared without a trace. (The answer to our letter came a few months later: they didn't have any record of him, neither on the lists of the dead nor on the POW lists.)

The side wall of Boško's office formed the entrance to our courtyard, together with the Office of Hidden Treasures. They were only a yard apart. At the point where his office ended was our fountain, serving the whole courtyard and a never-ending stream of passengers from the bus station.

Once I stood in the back, partially hidden behind the bush, when a Gypsy couple came in. He was tall and well built and she was young and very handsome. He opened the faucet and let some water flow before he bent over, drank and then wiped his mouth with the back of his hand. Then, without warning and without words, he just grabbed her crotch. She made only a slight effort to defend herself, laughed quietly and told him something in Rom. They turned off the faucet and left the yard. I was too young to understand what happened, but I had a sweet feeling somewhere down there and by that feeling I knew I'd seen something nice, fun and spontaneous, something that brings joy to people.

My father said one day that a man can steel himself and become resistant to cold: if you keep the inner side of your wrists, where you can see the blue veins, under a flow of icy water every morning for as long as you can stand it, your body will become resistant to winter, and in the summer you can lower your body temperature that same way, so you can ignore the heat. When nobody was watching I held my hands under that faucet until my fingers turned blue, rejoicing at how surprised everyone would be when I grew up one day to be a man of steel, resistant to the elements.

A SEED OF BIGGER THINGS

Beyond the faucet was a hovel that belonged to us, a shack covered with tar paper, in which we kept coal and firewood (in the good years, when we could afford firewood–banks didn't approve credit for wood, the way they did for coal). In that hovel we left overnight my shiny new red bicycle with training wheels, and it was stolen the first night. There was no money for another one, and out of despair I never learned to ride a bike.

Next to our shack was Kosta's, better than ours, drier, built from red brick. He was a painter, and sometimes–when he would open it to find something–I could see behind his back the neatly stacked cans of paint, a wooden ladder and dozens of brushes, all expensive stuff. It was whispered in our house that he brought it from his employer's warehouse, then made his private customers pay for it. His salary was miserable, like everyone else's–my parents said–but that's how he could afford all the expensive stuff, like a fridge and electric stove.

Everybody who had anything to do with our courtyard was in a better position than us. The lawyer, the merchants, Kosta, everyone. They had more, theirs was better, we were absolute outsiders. My parents taught me not to be jealous.

"We don't have much, but what we have, we have earned," they would say. "You should be proud of who you are, not of what you have. Dignity, son, dignity is the most important thing. People can take everything from you, but never let them take your dignity away."

Our kitchen was beside Kosta's shack.

We always called that tiny space "kitchen," even when that was the only room we had. It was probably in the hope that someday a room would follow, so the "kitchen" was a seed of bigger things to come. The kitchen was a room of nine by nine feet, containing a table, three chairs, a stove, a bed and a cupboard. Later, when my father gave up his part of his inheritance to his brothers, they got us a washer and we stuck it somehow next to the door.

When I was born, in 1958, they brought me there from the hospital. For the first two years of my life the four of us shared that space: Nana–my mother's mom, who took care of me–Mother, Father and me. The two women slept on the bed, my father on the floor, and I in the laundry basket next to the stove. Then the journalist who had a room in the other house across the yard moved out and my parents and I got his big room. (Nana kept the kitchen to herself.) The other part of the building, overlooking the main street, belonged to Kosta and his wife, Mara, a hygienist in the local hospital, a brusque and rough woman, prone to quarreling. Their space was separated from our room only by a sheet of white-painted glass, and frequently, when Kosta would come home drunk at night, we would listen to their long fighting, and would hear every hit of his hand and every returning bang of her pot against his head. Both of them used to curse heavily, the unspeakable stuff, and in the beginning my parents covered my ears, then gave up.

We washed our laundry in the kitchen. We would fill a large tin pot with water, bring it to a boil on our woodstove, and then Mother and Nana would add bleach and detergent, and fill it to the top with our belongings waiting in the basket that had once been my bed. They would cook it for some time, stirring it occasionally with a rolling pin, and it always smelled bad. It didn't smell like our outhouse but of sweat and machine oil and bleach. It was the smell of the remains of our life. Then they would rinse it in cold water and hang it to dry. In summer a long line of underwear hanging in our courtyard reminded me of the flags on a ship leaving for a maiden voyage. In winter the cold would freeze our underclothes into stiff sheets of body armor that could protect us from anything.

BLACK HAT COWBOY

We had to cross the few yards between our kitchen and the room, then climb up the stone stairs that turned wooden inside the house. The door to our room was the first on the left. From the window you could see the whole yard, and part of the bus station.

Beneath us was a warehouse where unsold newspapers and magazines were stuck for a couple of months before being transferred to the paper factory for recycling. The kind folks who worked there would give me handfuls of old publications suitable for children. My favorite one was something called *From the Lives of Animals,* full of drawings of wildlife with short descriptions of curiosities about them. I was disgusted at how cuckoos put their eggs into other birds' nests, puzzled over why trout prefer cold water and full of respect for the elephants who travel to their cemetery when they decide to die.

And the comics: I fell in love with the comics. There were no other kids of my age in the neighborhood, and in the years before I'd learned to read there was only a limited number of games I could play alone. The comics were my first true friends. I would spend hours staring at the drawings and decoding the stories.

I preferred the Westerns: the lonely cowboy in a white hat and on a racy horse comes into town, where an unsightly guy with a black hat has been doing ugly things—kicking the poultry, looking women in the face and not paying for electricity. (Paying the electricity bill was a monthly topic in our house, followed by sharp and bitter words, so I paid close attention to the drawings, trying to find one where the Black Hat Cowboy was paying for it, without success, and I fully understood the enormity of his crime.) In the meantime the local Indians have been doing foolish things under the influence of the cheap whiskey the Black Hat Cowboy is clandestinely selling them. We see their arrows stuck in the doors of the houses on the edge of town (I was immensely happy that we lived in the center). Then the White Hat Cowboy becomes angry, calls a duel, and the Black Hat Cowboy dies. The townsfolk celebrate (especially those selling the electricity!), and the most beautiful oppressed woman looks the White Hat Cowboy dangerously in the face. He modestly avoids all that and rides into the sunset. On the edge of town the Indians are waiting to thank him for helping them get rid of that bad headache.

I learned to read when I was four, both the Latin and the Cyrillic alphabets. Nobody taught me; I just started one day.

My mother and father would get up before dawn so they could have their first coffee together. While my mother was making coffee, my father would go to buy the morning newspaper on the corner, and sometimes he'd get *Partizanov Vjesnik,* the magazine of his favorite football club. To ease his feeling of guilt for succumbing to his sports passion, he'd bring a new comic and put it on the pillow next to my head, while I was still sleeping. Then they would leave for work, and I would wake up around seven, and stay in bed for some time, flipping through the comics. On those mornings when Mother stayed longer in bed, because she was working the afternoon shift, she would read them to me, while I leaned my head on her shoulder, following the signs she was reading, and must have started relating shapes of signs to voices and words. One morning my mother had a headache and refused to read, and I took the comic book and opened it. When she noticed I was moving my lips, she made me read aloud, and I did.

That was the world in which I grew up. Scared for my health because of the conditions we lived in, my family constantly overdressed and overfed me, and I was a clumsy child, not too interesting to others of my age. The grownups outside our courtyard considered me funny because of my tendency to act older than I was, and they would frequently give me chocolates after my verbal outpourings.

"Dragan, can you recite a poem for us?"

"Sure. Which one?"

"How about the one that Uncle Ilija taught you?"

"Here I go, all dressed in flannel; her pussy's black like a tunnel."

"Bravo! Here's a chocolate."

THE HOLY DUST

The gate to our courtyard was partially hidden behind the small blue kiosk with two porticos that served as a waiting room and a ticket office for the bus station. That kiosk belonged to Lasta, the central bus carrier of the time. Between the gate and Lasta was an area paved with cobblestones, where Gypsy porters would park their carts.

The Gypsies loved me and I loved them. Old Bangeja, with mucus always in the corners of his mouth like some veteran trumpeter, wore an ancient officer's visored cap and a pale, unidentifiable uniform. His name meant "lame"–his right leg was bent, forcing him to limp grotesquely. Bangeja sometimes shared his salami and cheap cheese with me, and we ate from the oily paper spread over the dirty planks of his cart. Abdula was a dangerous dark man of great strength and giant voice who loved to drink and fight. His wife was Rada, a person of disproportionately small eyes buried deep under her lumpy forehead, with her nose broken by Abdula right there, at the station, in front of the delighted passengers bored after waiting long hours for their buses to small Serbian towns. Other Gypsies, whose names I didn't know, hung around because the bus station was their only source of survival.

"Dragan, have you learned any new poems?"

"Yes, I have."

"Which one?"

"'Hungarian Maiden.'"

"Who taught you that one, my shameless son?"

"Rada the Gypsy."

"I'll have a word with her."

"Don't mind your mother if you want to earn a chocolate."

"A Hungarian maiden was riding on a trap, her wet rosy pussy fell out through the gap."

"Oh!"

"Here's a chocolate."

I often went and just hung around the buses, especially on their arrival. I loved the smell of diesel and hot tires, tires bigger than me, the switching-off of the engine, the slow rise of the driver, like after a hard job well done, the opening of the luggage compartments, the panicky bustle of the passengers looking for their bags, the sight of a good-looking, well-dressed woman wiping a few drops of sweat from her forehead (followed by the obligatory womanizer offering help). I loved the dust from the road, layered on the sides of the bus, the dust I touched with my fingers, leaving marks in it before I learned letters. The Holy Dust from the Road. I knew every detail of the bus: the big turn signals on the front looking like the big bras our neighbors hung with pride on the ropes in sun-drenched backyards, the powerful headlights much wider than my head, the grille packed full of dirt and tiny leaves and insects, the six big covers of the luggage compartment, the exhaust pipe into which I would stick my fist when it cooled down. The buses were big houses on wheels to me–their square footage significantly bigger than that of our kitchen–where an enormously interesting life went on.

SMOKING AT FIVE

Across the street from the bus station there was the big Austro-Hungarian building of the municipal court, with a small park in front of it surrounded with chestnut trees and lindens, where I went to play whenever the weather allowed. Although the park was in the center of town, my parents and I never stayed late in it, not even on hot summer evenings. With the long shadows of trees melting into an evening, the prostitutes would sometimes ride their clients on one of the few benches, not paying attention to us.

On our side of the street, opposite the court, was Moskva, the restaurant where my father and I would sometimes go in the evening to order something from the grill to bring home for dinner. No supermarkets opened on Sundays in those years, so we'd also buy bread in Moskva in case we had unexpected guests.

My father sometimes bought cigarettes in the restaurant too. Grandpa Velja had his desk next to the entrance; he sold packs or single cigarettes. When I was five years old, two neighborhood teenagers asked me to buy cigarettes for them from Velja. The old man thought at first that I was buying them for my father, but as I continued buying only two cigarettes at a time, he asked my father about it. Father came home fuming, searched the whole apartment–although I told him I was buying tobacco for those two guys–and found my pipe. It was a fine pipe, made of rosewood, with a carved tin lid. The merchant (I'd bought it in another store, where my father never went) had given me a pouch of pipe tobacco for free, falling all soft over a boy buying a present for his father. I tried once to fill it up and light it, but coughed so hard I never tried again. I kept it as a Strange Object, but it had traces of use when Father found it behind some comics inside the nightstand. My parents were so shocked they forgot to beat me.

Farther down the street was a theater with a small outdoor stage. There I watched the first movie I recall–also the first movie I loved–Disney's *One Hundred and One Dalmatians,* and later another one I considered a classic, *What's New, Pussycat?* Indecipherable communist logic made the distributor combine *Pussycat* with a short educational movie about safe driving, which started with scenes of a negligent couple driving carefree in their car, continued with a scene of the car getting stuck in the railroad tracks, and ended with close shots of the two people dying, screaming inside the car as it was crushed by a locomotive. Cars were rare in those years, and only a few politicians had private vehicles. Those who had one kept it like the few last hairs on their heads, so this educational short wasn't aimed at them. Some functionary probably thought that this lascivious capitalist comedy should be countered with something depicting the cruel reality of capitalism.

"Dragan, I don't feel well today," says Abdula. "C'mon, recite something, cheer me up the way only you know how. I'm thin on cash, but I promise you'll get a chocolate next time I see you."

"For sure?"

"On my mother's face."

"How about 'Mona Lisa'?"

"'Mona Lisa'? I don't know that one. C'mon, gimme that."

"When I traveled to Parisa, I met famous Mona Lisa. Mona Lisa asks for wits, if you wish to see her tits. Mona Lisa looks for gut, if you want to see her butt. Mona Lisa's a little fussy, you can't see her golden pussy."

"You are a great man!"

BEFORE THEY HAD ME

My father, Dušan, had three brothers, all of them living on the mountain Kopaonik, in the parts bordering on Kosovo. The legend running in the family was that in the times under the Turkish occupation a long-forgotten predecessor killed a Turk and hid from blood revenge in inaccessible parts of the mountain. Indeed, the place where my father was born was an excellent hideout: high above and far from any roads, right under the edge of a clearing, on top of the hill offering a great view.

Dušan's family was very poor, as they lived in the place where for centuries only two jobs were available: woodcutting or mining. Born in 1932, Dušan was sent to Kragujevac after the war to attend the Military Technical School, which was free and had its own residence. Well-built, of average height, a mountaineer with impeccable background (a family of peasants and workers; his oldest brother volunteered to join Tito's partisans and became an officer of the State Security Service after the war), he served the army in Tito's guard. After his service he came back to Kragujevac, where he found a job as a metalworker.

My mother, Ana, was born in a relatively rich village, Žabare, in the heart of Serbia, only a few miles from the king's summer house on Oplenac, a vineyard-covered hill. She was the third child. Entering puberty, she developed problems with her spine. Instead of sending her to a doctor, her parents first went to local witches, and Ana was left forever with her spine in the shape of a question mark. She never went back to school. At twenty-four she was sent to Kragujevac to live with her distant cousin. They found her a job and she soon got our kitchen from the local Party Committee, with help from her cousin Ranka, who was a high-ranking Party official in Kragujevac. Ana had to get up at three every morning, because the food stores opened at four, and she was on her feet eight hours or more every day, mostly selling bread, pastries, pies and yogurt. The family would occasionally send a basket of food by bus for her, but that was that–she was on her own.

At the time my parents came to Kragujevac, the city–a booming industrial town of about 45,000–offered hard work and not much fun. They each came hoping to advance to proletariat, not because of the bright lights.

Ana and Dušan never described in detail how they met. The main gathering place for youth in their time was the *korzo,* a stretch of the main street that was the place for the social parade. People would gather on the korzo around seven in the evening and stay till ten or eleven. It shrunk the city to a measure allowing for close contacts, displaying clearly the pool of available partners. So, when my mother once told me, "Your father was very well known in our time," I understood that many girls liked him on the korzo. Anyway, they were introduced to each other, and Dušan started coming often to the store where Ana worked. Soon they became a couple.

In the rare black-and-white photographs from those years I see two beautiful people: the man has wide shoulders, black hair cut in military style–except for a bush in front that makes his forehead look double its height–and a mustache à la Clark Gable, only a little thicker; the woman's eyes are smiling, she is simply but well dressed, and she has full lips and arched eyebrows. Her height can't be more than four feet, because of her bent spine, but she looks handsome. In one of the pictures Dušan is sitting in an armchair, smiling, with a cigarette in his hand, while Ana, with coquettishly crossed legs, sits on the armrest, also holding a cigarette between the fingers of her right hand, although she never smoked and was actually allergic to tobacco.

THE TRAIN LULLABY

When I was born, my grandmother Ljubica, whom I called simply Nana, came to take care of me. She was a big woman, a true hedonist who would go into the tiniest details with her friends about food strategies, food preparation and the joy of eating. The word *calories* was unknown to her, and *fat* meant recommendation. She always picked the best food, no matter what the price ("Health enters through our mouth!"); she loved a good dress whenever we could afford it, and the scarves she wore around her head in the traditional way of Serbian women were only of the best quality.

My parents always worked hard, coming home very tired, and I remember having just a few hours weekly with my mother or my father, almost never with both of them. Sometimes not even that. I spent most of my time with Nana.

Being religious, Nana thought my greatest protection came from God, and everything else–communist resolutions, Party membership–was only a passing fad, laughter in God's court. So one day, she waited till my parents were at work, and then took me to church to baptize me. Trying to minimize the danger to our family, she chose the small Church of the Holy Spirit, surrounded by the buildings that belonged to Zastava–the biggest factory in town–simply because the other one, the big cathedral, was right across the street from the local Communist Party headquarters. She chose her own god, but so as not to insult her daughter's.

As a baby I would sometimes cry inconsolably when my parents went to work. Only rarely could Nana lull me back to sleep; most of the time she would have to carry me to see the trains. The closest railroad was half a mile away, passing between the old bridge–where she would stand, holding me in her arms–and the Church of the Holy Spirit. The first train would calm me down, and several minutes later, with the passing of another one, I would fall asleep.

I don't know what was sedating in all that: the big, mighty machines, the reliable and comforting arch of the old bridge, the view of the river or the peace of the old temple? Maybe all of them together: the anticipation of distance, the premonition of God and the promise of long journeys.

COUNTRY LIFE

Mother didn't have milk to feed me when they took me home from the hospital. They found a peasant woman from a village close to the city who brought fresh milk every morning, since they had no fridge at the time.

When I was several months old, Nana took me to Žabare for the first time. My parents and she were all aware of the unhealthy conditions we lived in and decided to take me where the air was fresh and all the food was from their garden. When Nana brought me back, my mother told me, I was blooming. As the experiment went well, Žabare became my second home. It was only an hour's drive by bus. My grandfather Lila was still alive, but his health was already unsteady. I remember him very faintly, a smiling man with a large mustache who loved playing with me under the apple tree right in front of the steps to the house.

Country life was fantastic. I was not the only child there. My uncle Mita had two sons, Zoran and Bojan, and Boban, the son of the uncle who disappeared in the war, also lived with them. The neighbors next door also had a son, and two children from Kragujevac visited them often. My aunt Gospava would make *palačinke,* thin crêpes, every evening and we would spread homemade jam over them. There was always new offspring to be the pet of the day–a calf, a chick or a puppy. The grownups took me with them anywhere they went: to the garden near the river, to the cornfields and orchard, to swim in the river in the summer. While they worked in the fields, I spent time under a locust tree, watching birds and plants from close up. Every few hours they would take a break when a fresh meal arrived from home: beans, cheese, freshly baked bread, boiled eggs, smoked meat, and they would pick green onions, tomatoes and hot peppers right there, in the garden. I don't think any food can taste better than that eaten on the grass, in the shade of a scented tree, by a hidden spring. With each return to my uncle's I would gain a couple of pounds or so. Soon I became chubby, then fat–not too much, but still.

With the trips to the country, I started living between two places. It was only the beginning. I was never whole in my entire life; I was never one in one place.

A DOG NAMED RUBY

"Dragan, would you like a chocolate?"

"Yes."

"But you have to recite something."

"I will."

"Here's a chocolate."

"I'm not taking that one."

"Really? And why not?"

"It has to be a hundred-gram one, not a small one."

"Right. Okay, here's more money, buy it on your own. Is that fair?"

"Would you like 'The Sun Is Setting'?"

"I don't know that one. Okay–*Setting*."

"The sun is setting, everything goes to sleep. The moon is rising, and the last bird starts to sing . . ."

"What's that? Who taught you that one?"

"We learned it at school. It's a famous Slovenian folk song."

"That's not the deal. Give back the chocolate. And the money."

"Okay, okay, here: A Hungarian maiden riding on a trap, her wet rosy pussy fell out through the gap."

"Right on! And don't screw me again with that garbage they teach you at school."

Our neighbors Mara and Kosta bought a TV set when I was five. The black-and-white model was manufactured in Serbia, and there was only one channel, the state-owned Yugoslav Radio Television.

That big wooden box with shiny buttons was fascinating to me. I could hardly wait for Mara to come home from work each day, so I could go into their apartment and watch the early-evening program. She would pass by our window, tired from work, and I would just follow her upstairs, to their kitchen, where she would turn the set on for me and then go about her usual chores.

It went on like that for several months. This silent child, sitting like a phantom at their table, with his eyes glued to the screen, must have exhausted the poor woman. One evening she couldn't stand it anymore and asked me, "Don't you ever go take a shit?"

I left their apartment, and decided never to return. Mara tried two or three times in the next few days to lure me back, but I refused to even talk to her. I told my parents about it, and several days later my father came home panting, carrying a huge cardboard box. He put it on the floor, saying, "I won't let anyone torture my child." I couldn't believe it when he opened the box to reveal the big wooden cabinet, and neither could my mother.

"But where did you get the money?" she asked.

"I took a loan at the factory," he said. "We'll pay somehow."

He installed the TV in our bedroom, upstairs, partly because there was no place in the kitchen, but also because Mara and Kosta would hear the sound of our new TV through the glass between our rooms.

The main thing to watch every day was the *TV Journal*, starting at eight in the evening and lasting for almost an hour. It was a form of newsmagazine, starting with domestic affairs, followed by the international news, continuing into the sports section, weird stories and the weather prognosis. The news from Yugoslavia was all good news. Marshal Tito visited this part of the country, in that part a new factory was opened, or a new road, Yugoslav workers surpassed production targets by that many percentage points–stuff like that. Frequently they would show a portrait of an overachiever, usually a metalworker or a miner. Even the catastrophic earthquake in Skopje that year–1963–was used to show how Yugoslavia was strong enough to start rebuilding almost immediately.

Except for the first woman in space, who was celebrated widely–the photos of Valentina Tereshkova were all over the media–the world news was bitter. Vietnam was slowly boiling, a bomb killed black girls and boys in an Alabama church, the Great Train Robbery happened in Britain ("How come such trains never pass through here?" asked a guest in our house), Kim Philby was outed as a Soviet spy, Kennedy proclaimed in Berlin that he was a doughnut and refused to cooperate with Communist countries. Then Edith Piaf died, Jean Cocteau died ("I hear he was a candidate for the French national team in soccer," claimed Kosta), Kennedy was shot, Oswald was shot. My uncle immediately named his dog Ruby. My parents and all grownups were on the side of the black liberation movement in the States, and Martin Luther King's speech was translated in full. It was their hope that the United States would change, would become a better place.

The debates the grownups had about politics attracted my attention, because politics was beautiful to me: politics meant national holidays, piglets roasted on a spit, Mother and Father rested and smiling, holding both my hands as we walked though the golden mornings on May Day. Politics meant uplifting reports on national television, going to the country, having cakes and all sorts of sweets on the table. Politics meant red banners on the streets, processions, pictures of the smiling, carefully combed Marshal Tito shaking hands with children and workers. Politics meant days with almost no traffic at all, safe days when one could cross the street without grownups squeezing one's hand till it hurt. Politics meant new shoes, new pants and new shirts. Politics meant our hope, since both my parents were in the Communist Party, and it took care of its own.

It wasn't always good for the health, though. My mother came home once after an all-night Party meeting, and in the morning complained of a headache.

"Everybody smoking in the room, and no window opened, not a single one," she said. "And what was the meeting about? About whether our warehouse supervisor and his employee are having an affair or not. Let them be, why I would care about it."

SCHOOL

I was born in September, the month when school starts. One year I was six and too young for school, and a year later I was the oldest child in my class.

I never wanted to meet other kids. Once they had tried putting me into a daycare, when Nana wanted to spend more time back at her home in Žabare, and it lasted only three days. I cried and went on a hunger strike and refused to sleep in the afternoon. I felt comfortable only in the company of grownups. They seemed to know what they were doing and it felt safe. Other children . . . if they wanted to meet me, why didn't they come to my courtyard to play?

Oddly, I wasn't afraid when the time came for me to go to school. My parents told me we would learn to read and write, and I already knew that. We'd learn adding and subtracting, and I knew that too. So, there was nothing to fear. On top of that, the principal was my aunt, Ranka.

It was a sunny day when they took me into the backyard of the old school in the center of Kragujevac. The teachers stood outside, holding red carnations and smiling at us. It was very noisy, with all the children and their parents, and full of bright colors. The whole backyard looked like a field covered with wildflowers. Parents were crying inconsolably, as people do when reminded that their youth is over.

After some time, Aunt Ranka appeared on top of the stairs leading inside and welcomed everybody. The situation instantly changed: her authoritative voice and serious look consoled parents, but the children started wailing like little ships in a fog. Each teacher started reading a list of names, and we gathered around when called. Then we were marched into the building, class by class.

The corridor before us was dark and cool.

The colors disappeared.

The voices hushed.

The system closed around us.

2

GAME: THE BLIND GRANNY

The rules

One of the participants—the Blind Granny—is blindfolded. Everyone else runs freely around her, and she has to try to catch one of them and then identify that person. If she does, they exchange places.

The reality

The Granny is pushed, even hit by those around her. When she catches someone, that person tries to break free, sometimes forcefully. The game usually ends when the Blind Granny starts crying.

TITO'S PIONEER

Revolution is one lengthy diet. The intake of everything is strictly controlled by the system, including news. Bad news is avoided at all costs, while really good news must wait to be revealed on national holidays. A celebration is immensely better when there is something to celebrate. A new textile factory is about to be opened, which would employ four hundred women from the surrounding area? Don't open it yet, wait for March 8, International Women's Day. An asphalt road to the remote mountain village where a hero of the war against Nazism was born is almost finished? Finish it, but then clean it and keep it closed till May Day. Comrade, we don't have anything ready for July 7, the Day of the Uprising. Paint an elementary school and I'll reopen it. It was painted only three years ago, comrade, it would be a waste. Then I'll lay the cornerstone for the new apartment building next to the library. But, comrade, the city plan doesn't allow building in that area. Don't you worry about that; I'll call Belgrade and fix the plan. You call the TV to bring their cameras.

All the openings looked the same: red tape stretched between two nickel spikes, all the politicians aligned in front of it, cameras on the other side of the tape, a mass of people behind the suits, a military band on the side. A pretty girl dressed in traditional costume holds a small red plush pillow with scissors on it. The most important politician in the crowd, usually a special guest from Belgrade, waits for the hymn to Tito to be over, and takes the scissors, cuts the tape and kisses the girl for no apparent reason. The scissors are always big and made of steel, the type tailors use. The tailors of our destiny.

When there was nothing to be opened or reopened, no corners for waiting stones and no roads leading anywhere, politicians would settle for anything that might look solemn:

a festival of choirs, a concert of revolutionary music, swearing in a new class of soldiers or turning a group of seven-year-olds into Tito's Pioneers.

Communists do not hate freedom; they just worship order. Everyone should have the same ideals and everyone's ideal has to include the current leadership. All cars should be the same color, preferably white, except for the black cars the politicians drive. All singers should have the same repertoire of traditional and revolutionary songs. All tenements should be of the same height and the same color, with the same draft blowing through. Workers should wear blue overalls, children should be in blue uniforms, and everyone should be either at work or at school at any given time. Blue is the color of order (police: blue uniforms and blue cars), red is the color of the revolution. Red carnations symbolize blood spilled on the road to liberation. All is known, all is predictable, because that is the proof that we have the right type of revolution, the one described in the books of Marx, Engels and Lenin. Complaining is dangerous because it reminds authorities that not everything is in order. Every problem can be solved, and if it cannot, then it's not a problem.

Tito's Pioneers was an organization born out of the need for absolute order in all segments of society, including children. What could possibly be more decorative on national holidays than hundreds of thousands of children all dressed in blue uniforms with blue caps and red scarves? It was a promising picture; it was a comforting picture. All those children already in blue: someday they will slip into something more comfortable–workers' blue overalls–without even noticing it.

After several months at school we were all made Tito's Pioneers. It was a lengthy celebration, with choir, brass band and speeches, at the end of which everyone got their red scarf with a profile of a different hero (heroes never look into the camera, because they are always in action, charging forward, and we can see them only from the side; only enemies see heroes from the front) and the logo that said "Pioneers' Squad Andra Marinković." Nobody knew who he was. A lesser hero, perhaps–not big enough to get a school named after him, but not so irrelevant as to be forgotten. Or maybe he was just a Sancho Panza to some Don of the revolution. Our school was saving money for a new building, so we didn't get caps, but the red scarf still fit nicely around my neck, on top of the blue school uniform. I liked it, and so did my parents. When we got home, Nana took one look at it and didn't say a word.

"Don't you like it?" I asked.

"It would look better with white polka dots on it," she said.

Mother closed the window.

NOTHING IS LIKE IT SAYS ON THE LABEL

It was Thursday, and the gathering in our home started around seven. The husbands arrived one by one, carrying bags with food items, tin wires, soldering rods and tubes with some chemicals. My mother and Nana left after making coffee for the guests and offering some rakija, which no one wanted because they needed steady hands. My father removed everything from the kitchen table, except for a small scale, chunks of lead, a strip of lath and a carafe full of water, in case something went wrong. After sipping coffee for half an hour, they got down to work. Everyone pulled out their soldering rods and admired Mile's, being the biggest of them all. Then they plugged them in, untangled their wire, opened the tubes, pulled out their wallets and started carefully unwrapping the cans of sardines they had brought with them.

"I can find the sardine key in the drawer, if you want," I said.

"Shut up, kid, and look and learn–you'll need this when you grow up," said Mile.

"Yeah, learn from the masters, boy," Djura said.

"Wow, you're packing quite a fish this time!" Bora interrupted, looking at Mile's fat wallet.

"Yes, we borrowed some from my wife's family. The kid wants a guitar, I need a new raincoat, and you know my shark: she always wants new shoes, and makeup, and blouses, and skirts . . . Sometimes I tell her she needs three husbands, not one, just to earn for her needs."

"Well, Mile, you do know we're your friends here, don't you? If your wife has needs, we're here to help, anytime," said Moma, stroking his mustache.

"Take a look at your soldering rod, friend. If *that's* your tool, you're the one who needs help," Mile returned.

"Hey! My kid's here," said my father, and they concentrated on their rods, which were already smoking. They started pulling them along the sides of the sardine cans, and I watched as tin slid like drops of silver onto wood. One by one, they all opened their cans and started wiping the lids off while still hot.

"Weigh each can together with its lid, write it down and then use the pot on the stove to empty them," said my father, and they emptied their cans into it. "We'll chop some onion into it later and we'll have dinner when we're done. Now turn the cans over on the paper and let them dry."

They had another coffee while waiting for the cans to cool down and dry well. During that time, everyone pulled rolls of money from their wallets and their pockets.

"Man, there's a lot of money on this table," said Bora. "Too bad we're not gamblers."

"It's a lot to us," Mile said, "but our directors in Zastava take twice this much every month."

"You think so?" Bora said.

"I know so. I have this cousin who works in accounting."

"Fuck the working class, man. Fuck us." Bora bowed his head.

"Thank God for Trieste, comrades," Djura said. Everyone nodded.

The first time my parents visited Trieste was in 1963. They traveled with some friends, spent a weekend there and came back with beautiful things unlike anything I had ever seen. Some of it we kept, and some of it my mother offered to our neighbors and her colleagues, and it sold like crazy. So she started traveling to Italy more often. There was a big open market in Trieste, the Ponte Rosso, with thousands of articles at bargain prices, all that a decent home in Serbia couldn't live without: scarves and handkerchiefs, coats and sweaters, plastic toy gondolas with colored lights and tiny dancers on them, jewelry and makeup, underwear, watches, shoes, mirrors framed in gold, dolls that disappointingly didn't have any sexual organs under their white panties . . . Practically anything she'd brought back would be sold in a few days. She traveled much more often than my father because her main customers were women and she knew what they wanted.

We started dressing better. My new brown pants, made of endlessly soft velvet, and my colorful synthetic shirts started drawing attention at school. My mother started wearing low-cut blouses that emphasized her new eighteen-karat gold chain with a heavy locket, which contained small pictures of Dad and me, while my dad finally got new Italian shoes and fine shirts.

From her first trip to Italy, Ana brought back a small red transistor radio we treated as a pet. My father carried it with him everywhere on Sunday afternoons, so he could listen to the soccer broadcast. One Sunday my mother decided to enrich our cultural life and we went to an afternoon show at the local movie theater, and–to her horror–my father brought the transistor with him and had it on, pressed against his ear, from the first minute of the movie. That afternoon the soccer derby was on, Zvezda playing against Partizan, and towards the end of the second half the men around us started quietly asking about the score, until someone hollered, "Crank it up, man, don't be selfish!" Dad obeyed and the whole room instantly forgot about the movie and started reacting loudly to the moves of their favorite players. Mom swore never to go to the cinema with us again.

At first, Mother traveled to Trieste by train, but later she would take one of the cheap charter buses that would leave on Friday evenings and return on Sundays. These were known as smuggling tours, and Yugoslav customs officers paid special attention to their passengers. Officially, citizens leaving Yugoslavia were allowed to carry ridiculously small amounts of money with them, enough only to sleep and eat, and everything else had to be hidden. The Thursday sessions at our house were the hiding parties. My father invented this technique, so he taught his friends how to do it.

"Okay, wipe them off and make sure they are totally dry on the inside," said my father.

Everyone picked up one of the cloths on the table and did as they were told.

"Now, are you sure you have your money well protected in cellophane?"

They showed their rolls. Banknotes were pressed into cylinders no thicker than cigars, wrapped in cellophane and secured with tape. My father's roll was the thinnest.

"Next thing: put the money into your can, place the can and the lid on the scale and add chunks of lead until the weight is exactly as it was in the beginning," my father said.

"Aren't they supposed to be 125 grams each, like it says on the label?" Djura asked.

"You're naive, comrade. Nothing is ever like it says on the label. Compare your numbers."

"Fuck, you're right, mine was 105 grams," Bora said.

"And mine 95 grams only," Mile said.

"That's too low. Don't go below 100 grams," Father instructed.

One by one they did as they were told, cutting the lead into small pieces and adding it until the scale was balanced.

"Now tear this paper into pieces and fill the cans so nothing moves inside if they shake them. Make it very tight. And then comes the trickiest part: you have to solder like professionals. The line has to be clean and straight, like the one the machines make at the factory. Press your rod a bit against the can, to flatten the bumps, but if you press too hard, the tin won't stick."

Everyone bent over his can and silence descended over our kitchen, interrupted only by subdued curses here and there. When the men were finished, my father inspected their work, and then they rewrapped the cans in paper and cellophane and put them back into their bags.

"Remember–tell your wives to bring three to five cans with them, including the one with the money. More would be suspicious, less would be dangerous. And don't mark the right can–tell them to open all of them when they arrive."

Mother and Nana came back. Mother offered them rakija again, and after each of them downed one, they left.

"Was it good?" Mother asked Dad, who was removing his tools from the table.

"So-so," he said. "But in case someone screws up and you're all caught, I put half of the money aside, for this other plan I have."

"What other plan?"

Father took the loaf of bread Mother had just bought and the ladle from the drawer.

"Watch this," he said, and stuck the long handle at a sharp angle all the way into the loaf, just beneath the ridge on the brownish crust. He pulled out another roll of money, pushed it inside using the ladle again and then squeezed the loaf all over, to mess it up a little. "See? You can't tell from the outside there's anything wrong with this loaf. Now cut it."

Awed, my mother took the knife and cut a few slices of bread from one side. They didn't show a trace of the ladle handle at all.

"The most important part is that you start cutting this bread when the customs officer comes close to you. Like, you're calm because you have nothing to hide, and you're suddenly hungry, and you don't care if you're just passing customs–you just have to eat."

"I could even offer him a piece of bread." Mother's voice was giggly with excitement.

"That's good, that's very good."

"Husband, you're a genius."

"And that's why we can afford the most expensive bread in the world, wife."

They kissed.

BLOODY FAIRY TALE

When the slow river of us children from my school came around the bend, we saw a crowd already gathered below the imposing Monument of the Broken Wing. The stone construction looked like a big letter V, with one side broken, and when we came near we saw little faces carved in the stone. The big stage right under the monument was already full of musicians in military uniform, and there were microphones everywhere, TV cameras, and thousands of people farther down the hill. It started raining, a slow, persistent drizzle, and we couldn't sit on the yellowing grass. They took us to Šumarice Memorial Park to watch the Big School Lesson, the commemoration held there every October 21.

My parents had taken me to Šumarice probably every year since I was born. It was a beautiful, huge park on the northwestern outskirts of town, full of monuments, hidden paths, sudden clearings and birdsong. Every year the local authorities organized May Day celebrations there. Spring comes early in these parts, and by the first day of May everything was luscious green and full of surprising light. Red city buses, free on May Day, would take thousands of people to the area around the hotel built in the heart of Šumarice, where the central stage was set. The program would start early in the morning and last for a few hours, with music, poetry, excerpts from plays, the smell of piglet on a spit coming from all sides, dancing, rivers of beer and drops of Party red all around, on lapels, sleeves, pioneers' scarves, carnations, flags and wild poppies–a communist happening. Street vendors would sell red badges, small flags, ice cream, dolls dressed in traditional clothes, pipes, wooden toys and homemade soda pop colored yellow, red and green. We would all be dressed in our best clothes. Mother and Father would laugh, meet their friends, all workers–heavy industry, faces of steel, lines like grooves, hands clamps–they would introduce me, their friends would tickle me, kiss me, big noisy kisses on the cheek, sometimes they would buy me ice cream, sometimes they would just pass by with a short nod, and I would listen to my parents explaining to each other why that couple was full of shit, and cheapskates, and who the fuck did they think they were, and fuck them. Around noon I would get sleepy, or it would become too hot, or I wanted to be carried, and it would be my mother's or my father's fault, depending on who was faster, a short outburst of argument would ensue, we would take the free ride home to our shady and cool courtyard, and then everything would be fine again. May Day was one of the biggest national holidays, and my parents would stay home at least three days, sometimes even five, bliss. That's how I fell in love with communism.

But one spot always remained foggy. Once when I asked about the park's big monuments of white marble, my parents told me they marked the place where the Germans shot seven thousand men and three hundred schoolboys in 1941, in retaliation for something the partisans had done. A hundred Serbs for each German.

"Seven thousand?" I said, looking through the window of the bus. "Is that many?"

"Yes, it is very many people."

"Are they buried here?"

"In mass graves, yes."

"So this is a graveyard?"

"No, this is a memorial park."

"And because it is not a graveyard we can dance here?"

"Shut up," they both said, and my mother closed the window on the bus.

Our group found a place way in the back, too far to recognize the famous actors, so I just stared at the big monument and listened to the recital blaring through large speakers. A female voice began:

> It was in a peasant country
> On the mountainous Balkans:
> A whole squad of students
> Died the death of martyrs
> In a single day.
> They were all born in the same year,
> They all lived the same school days,
> They all attended the same celebrations,
> All vaccinated against the same diseases,
> And they all died on the same day . . .

It was "Bloody Fairy Tale" by Desanka Maksimović, the most famous poetess of the Serbian language. I started imagining how it would be if my classmates and I were taken from school to a place out of town, to be shot the next day. I didn't like the ending, but I loved the part when they would separate us from the girls: which one, or how many of them would cry after me in particular? We would have made such beautiful victims. We, the boys from my class, standing in front of the barrels; we, the hunted, before some soldiers holding their breath, calming the tremor of their hands, and melting with the shadows around to become invisible.

Toma, standing next to me, said, "Did you know that the Germans never come here, to Kragujevac?"

"How do you know?" asked Duca.

"My aunt told me. My parents work in Germany, and they told her that Germans are told not to travel here."

Toma was my classmate, a quiet guy whose only interest was machines. He talked only about motorcycles, cars and racing. He lived with his aunt and her daughter, Marina, also our classmate, a very cute girl. Marina was the reason all the guys hung out with Toma. He was boring otherwise, and he frustrated us, since his parents kept sending him ridiculously expensive bicycles, roller skates, watches and other stuff our parents couldn't afford. He also liked guns, and knew everything there was to know about the whole arsenal of sport weaponry.

"How come the Germans don't know what happened here?" asked Vlada.

"My mother says that, when time passes, people forget anything," said Mira. "Our neighbor forgot she owed us money. So maybe they've forgotten."

"My dad says that we can forget, but we must not," said Vlada. His father was a history teacher in some high school.

"But there's people dancing here, every May Day," I said.

"That's different," said Vlada. "My dad says that it's because we want to show everyone that we will outlive anything they do to us."

After a while, my legs started hurting, so I found a spot next to a couple with an umbrella, put some newspapers on the grass and sat down. All performers had grave voices, and the military band played slow funeral marches. I got up from time to time, when no one was reciting, to see if anyone was dancing, but in vain. Strange, because I finally understood what this park was about: it was about dying and dancing afterwards.

THE BIG RED BUS

It was 1967 and I was attending third grade. I was still a lonely kid, just hanging around after school, watching travelers at the bus station and reading heaps of comics. I was a little chubby, clumsy, terrible in sports and didn't have much chance of drawing attention to myself. My only comforts were comics and the Gypsies at the station. But I needed other friends, too.

One day, when it was almost the end of the school year and it was warm and sunny, a group of us was coming back from school. Everybody was fighting hard for respect. Some would boast about knowing important people, like football players, and others would tell about their older brothers and sisters and how they had miracles at home, like fifty thousand records or something. Some would just kick your ass for no reason, because being strong was also a path to glory and friends. The stories we heard from our grandparents and parents, as well as the stories we read in our first books, were all the same: Serbian heroes were strong people, stronger than Turks, Germans or whoever else came to conquer us in the past, everybody loved heroes, and the biggest heroes were dead. We all lived in streets with heroes' names, except me–I lived in a street named after someone who was a journalist, so nobody really knew much about him. Bravery was the most valued virtue. If you wanted to have friends and respect, to be loved, you had to be courageous. You had to be Asterix, even without the magic potion, in the world full of Romans.

That day, the debate over who was brave and who was a coward got overheated and someone proposed that we test our courage. How? Simple: the street we were in was narrow and steep and one way, so cars would drive through rather fast. We would stand on the pavement, whistling and pretending to watch the birds, and then, when a car appeared, the tested one would suddenly run across the street. The one who ran closest to the oncoming car was the winner.

Duca ran some thirty yards in front of a bread truck that was already slowing down, so the driver didn't even hit the brakes when he saw him. Danish dashed twenty-five yards ahead of a taxi that went fast; the driver slowed and opened the window and yelled something about Danish's mother, something nasty that we didn't quite understand. Miša and Cagi were almost the same distance from their cars, about fifteen yards. Rabra ran ten yards in front of a fast, small car and really stopped my breath. I thought he was the winner, but he just kept running, as the driver was a guy in his twenties who was so mad that he jumped out and chased him. The driver came back after a minute, spat on the street and drove off. And so it was my turn.

I didn't want to compete. I knew that my parents would kill me if they knew. The other kids didn't even expect me to run; I was only the judge. But something happened during those minutes, maybe the adrenaline of danger, or the challenge was irresistible, or I was desperate for respect, I don't know. The contestants on the other side of the street were already preparing to leave, when I said, "Wait! Watch me!"

They turned in disbelief, and I looked up the street, to see a big red bus filled with people coming back from work. I knew the guys across the street were smiling, waiting to laugh, and I remembered how in a comic book an officer of the U.S. Cavalry told his soldiers not to shoot until they saw the whites of the enemy's eyes, so I waited. I hold my dark blue schoolbag tight, I am in a blue school uniform, drunk with the idea, eight years old but bigger than life, and the red bus is coming closer, closer, close, in slow motion, and I see the driver's dark eyes and his mustache and then I run. I run into glory, I run into the deafening scream of a woman on the street and the terrible sound of rusty brakes and tires screeching on the hot asphalt and into the white sun of legend waiting for me, and I run happy because I'm running towards my friends. And, well, maybe, just maybe I'm a bit too close, since on their faces I see fear, and Duca even closes his eyes, and I realize I'd better keep running. And so I run around the corner, and behind the old court building, and Miša runs past me, he is faster, they're all faster, but wait till tomorrow, when they talk about this in school.

A month later, my only friend was a boy who hadn't been there that day. Those who'd seen it never mentioned my big victory at school, and there was no sense in my talking about it, nobody would have believed me.

Where did I go wrong? Wasn't I a hero? No, I wasn't. That rule was not set before the game, but I should've known it because it was in our genes: the real heroes were all dead. The real and only victor of our game would have finished beneath the wheels of that big red bus.

THE HUNTER

My cousin Zoran was high up in a tree. "Do you think this one would be okay for him?" He held a branch above his head.

"Nah, too thick," answered his brother, Bojan. "How about the one above?"

"Yeah, about right. Even for a girl."

Zoran started cutting the branch with his pocket knife. It was a cloudy, warm day at the end of July, and my cousins were making a bow and arrows for me. I was spending the summer at their house, as I did every year until I turned sixteen. I was almost eight and they were twelve and fourteen. My mother had brought me a sheriff's kit from Italy a couple of months before. It contained a black hat, a star and a plastic revolver with plastic bullets tucked into a black plastic belt. Although it wasn't quite a

Colt Buntline Special, it had a spring to shoot bullets roughly fifteen feet. I practiced pulling out the gun as fast as I could every day till my hand hurt, and I was the fastest pistolero on this side of the Rio Grande. I devoured Wyatt Earp and Doc Holliday dime novels and I longed for a horse and a long ride. After reading the story of the Gunfight at the O.K. Corral, I kept walking around looking for Ike Clanton, but nobody wanted to be him, everyone wanted to be Earp. I tried to egg my cousins into being Indians, without success. Finally, Zoran suggested that we could have a great summer if I decided to become Sitting Bull instead of Wyatt. The advantages were numerous, according to him: arrows flew much farther than my plastic bullets, I could get as many feathers as I wished, there was even some paint left over from the Easter eggs for my face. "Plus, he was a great chief, so everyone will obey you. I'll make you a bow and arrows if you will give me your Colt to play with. Okay?"

The branch fell down at my feet. It was cut from an aspen in front of their house and it was about a yard and a half long. Zoran removed the leaves, trimmed its length and handed it over to Bojan to tie a piece of rope to the ends. They made the arrows out of broom branches, and Zoran even went so far as to stick a needle into the tip of each one and tie a small feather at the other end. So that was that–I handed over my gun belt and ammunition to him.

A few days passed by, and I was already pretty good with the bow and arrows. I had to practice in the orchard, far from the house, since my aunt started asking questions about her missing needles. At first I was hardly able to hit the trunk of a tree, but by the fourth day I was able to shoot an apple on a branch. The arrows didn't fly far when shot from my hand, but when Bojan or Zoran would take the bow to teach me, the broom thistles would fly thirty or forty yards.

One day in August my parents came for a visit. In the early evening my uncle Mita brought my father to watch as Bojan, Zoran and I were competing in the orchard. My cousins made a target of corrugated cardboard, left over from some house appliance purchase, and they moved the target farther away with every hit I made. But I was still better. I learned how to count on the wind, and where to aim to get it right.

As Father and Mita were watching, I hit a bull's-eye from almost fifteen yards.

"He's a natural," my father said proudly.

"A natural," confirmed Mita. "Remember last fall? When he turned off the lights?"

"Yup," said my father. "I remember."

I also remembered. But I wasn't sure whether I should be proud of it. Well, now I knew–I should be, since they were.

It happened a year before. Mita and his family were celebrating their *slava,* Saint Tomas. A lot of guests came that year, and many bottles of homemade rakija and wine were emptied. Now, everyone knows that the success of a celebration is measured by the noise. When half of the guests were already hoarse and the other half gave up on talking altogether, when there was no right note in any song they decimated, and when someone broke the volume button on the radio trying to crank it up even beyond the end point, Mita–already tipsy–decided to crown the whole evening by firing his gun from the steps of his house. The guests loved the idea, too, so he sent my aunt to bring the gun.

But he didn't like the guests liking his idea, and so he decided that I should fire it. The women were appalled.

While they were semi-okay with him shooting, they though the idea of me doing it was an invitation for trouble. To calm them down, Uncle Mita promised to hold the gun so I wouldn't turn it the wrong way.

And so the two of us went outside, and several men followed, carrying their glasses. It was prematurely cold, a clear October night, and the sky looked like a satellite image of a metropolis. Loud folk music was still playing on the radio in the house. Mita cocked the gun and put it in my hand, then put his hand around mine.

"Where do I aim?" I said.

"Wherever you want, just point at the sky," he said.

And so I did. "Close your eyes, kid, the cartridge could pop back at you," said one of the men. I did that, too.

"Now?" I said.

"Now," Mita said.

I pulled the trigger. In a flash, three things happened: there was a loud bang from the gun, a strange sound like *zing* came from the darkness, and the music stopped. Everyone went silent. Some woman screamed briefly inside the dark house, but it sounded more like an appropriate thing for a woman to do at that moment than real alarm. "What happened–," "There's no power–," "The fuse blew out–," said shadows around us.

My uncle looked at me, wild pride in his eyes, and then slowly turned to them.

"No, gentlemen," he said. "It's not a fuse. My nephew has just shot the wire. His first bullet, ever, and he shoots a thin wire. In the dark!"

Everybody went nuts. There was slapping on the back, congratulations, yells, joy, laughter. Someone put me on his shoulders. Women brought candles, wine was poured into glasses, and nobody went home that night. Nobody could, even if they wanted–there was a live wire somewhere on the ground. I stayed awake, sitting at the head of the table with Mita, rubbing my forehead from time to time. Whoever was holding me on his shoulders had forgotten to bend over when we were entering the house.

Two weeks after our little competition in the orchard my parents came to visit again. My father said, "I have a surprise for you," and he pulled out a long narrow box that had "Made in Czechoslovakia" in large blue letters printed on the side. I held it in my arms, not knowing what to do with it. "Well, won't you open it?" said my father. I put the package on the ground and knelt by it. The cardboard was thick, so somebody handed over a knife. The first thing I saw when I cut the side of the box was a polished wooden handle. My heart started beating pretty fast. Slowly, before my eyes, a brand-new air rifle appeared.

"Since you are a natural, I thought you'd need this to advance," said my dad. Beside the rifle was a tiny rounded plastic box with a hundred pellets inside, and a bunch of paper targets. I took the rifle into my hands–it was just the proper size and weight for me. "It's a .177 caliber," he said, "and the pellets are hobby pellets, designed for speed. I was thinking of buying you a rifle that our factory makes, but it's too heavy and ugly."

In the coming days I forgot about everything except my weapon. I would wake up really early, around six thirty, and skip breakfast, taking my rifle and my targets to the orchard to practice. I would not leave the rifle for a second during the day. At night, I would put it on the bed beside me.

My parents went back to Kragujevac on Sunday evening. My mother wasn't so happy about the rifle, but my father was really satisfied.

Three or four days later, in the late sunny afternoon, we were sitting around the old wooden table, the whole of my uncle's family. My aunt served us some warm palačinke and homemade jam, and the more we ate the lazier we felt. We were inside the summerhouse they called *trem,* which was open on three sides, with a corn crib as the fourth wall. A decorative vine grew over the open sides and made the whole space shady and very comfortable. At one point a small crow landed on the vine. My uncle looked up and said, "I really hate these crows. They are black and ugly and they're good for nothing."

I would have done anything for my uncle. So I lifted my rifle and aimed at the crow. The little black pearl of the bird's eye was turned at me. I lowered the rifle a bit and pulled the trigger. There was a short sound of the small chunk of lead hitting the bird in the wing. It let out a scream and fell into the backyard, the one healthy wing flapping helplessly.

"You've hit it!" said Zoran and ran outside to check it out. I couldn't watch it. My uncle saw my fear, and called to his sons, "Just throw the bird on the road."

I didn't sleep particularly well that night. Bloodied birds flew over the sky and haystacks burned everywhere I looked. The next morning I continued to practice with the targets. But aiming at living things was much more interesting. I tried apples, and then plums, and after several hours I completely forgot about the bird. After a while I saw a sparrow fly through the orchard and land on a branch high on a cherry tree. The light was behind it and I could barely see its white neck against the backdrop of dark green leaves. I slowly lifted my weapon and aimed at the tiny white feathers. Watching anything through the sight gives you a sense of power. The stretch of the barrel, that cold comfort of touching it, holding your breath, calming the tremor of your hands and melting with the shadows around you to become invisible. It takes you to a place where you are not a kid but a hunter, provider.

I pulled the trigger, and the bird fell into the grass. Hesitantly I went to find it. The bird had just a tiny spot of blood on its neck and it was dead. I lifted it by its legs. There was nothing dirty about it, because sudden death is clean. I wasn't frightened. I was the Hunter.

OUR NEW FREEDOM

One day my father came home from work early, smiling wide.

"Come outside to see it!" said my dad, and we did: in front of the gate stood a small white car, brand new and shiny.

"Dušan, I can't believe we finally got it," said my mom.

"Hop inside," said Dad, opening the door as if it were the gates of a palace.

It all made sense now: all those previous months of saving every *dinar* were preparations for buying the car.

We bought the car in 1967. It was a small model, a Zastava 750, white with seats covered in cheap red plastic. Yugoslavs loved it so much that they gave it the nickname Fića, a diminutive of Fiat, the Italian car factory from which it was licensed.

The doors of the Fića opened from the back, very dangerous if they unlocked during the ride. The seats were uncomfortable and the dashboard was sparer than the front of a radio: there was a light switch, another for wipers, a ridiculously large speedometer and an ashtray. The shift handle was long and clumsy, the gas pedal was just a piece of naked metal, and the heating switch was a piece of bent iron on the floor.

My father was a slow and careful driver, yet we kept hitting things: a curb when turning to the right, the old gnarled tree under which we parked in the next courtyard, the wooden pillar in front of the bus station. I remember that on this last occasion the bored travelers gathered merrily around us trying to understand how it was possible to hit the pillar so precisely, with our left front tire, when there was at least thirty feet of open space around us. There was no damage, except that the pillar (and the whole ticket office with it) bent a little.

My parents kept going to work on foot. The little white car stayed locked during the week in the neighbors' yard, where my father would visit it every day, cleaning the glass and the nickel fenders. He and I would scrape the dry bird shit off with our fingernails, washing the surface afterwards several times with a soft Italian sponge. I stayed away from the car when my dad wasn't around, since I had the impression–judging from my parents' long talks and from his treatment of the car–that it was an object we'd bought through sacrifice, an object of absolute pride.

On Sunday mornings we would drive to Žabare. Since hitting the pillar, my dad had introduced a security measure–Mom and I would get into the car only after he drove it to the street. It was a trip of only twenty-four miles, but Mom would bake a cheese pie or a cake, and would fill a big Italian wine bottle with water, Dad would load several more bottles of water into the trunk–in case the car overheated–and then we would head out of town, down the old road to Belgrade. I was nine and I was absolutely drunk with wind through the open windows–only if the temperature was over eighty-five, otherwise the draft could kill us, my mother insisted–at the fantastic speed of forty miles an hour. Sometimes, on beautiful May mornings, when we were going to stay for two or three days in the country and when we were all in a great mood, Dušan would step on it, reaching fifty miles an hour. I would bounce up and down in the backseat, hitting the ceiling now and then, and Ana would lean forward worriedly, look at the speed dial, and say, "Slow down, Dušan, slow down, stop racing!" He would immediately slow down to thirty-five and start teasing Ana. I wasn't sure, but I always thought there was some sex in their ritual.

Maybe once a year, we would go south to Kopaonik, to visit Dad's brothers there. It was a ride of a hundred miles and it would usually take us three and a half hours, with a few stops, always by the public fountains built in memory of someone who died young, in the valley of the Ibar River. After climbing up the dusty hidden roads to the house where my father was born, my parents would behave like Sir Edmund Hillary and Tensing Norgay–not so much for the height we'd conquered but because of the car that took us there. After having some cold mountain water with sugar cubes–the poor man's balm for weary travelers–we would climb the bald hill above the house and just sit there on the grass. The view extended forever, like our freedom. We could reach it all.

MEN ON THE MOON

They reminded us at school, and again on the evening news, to set our clocks so we wouldn't miss the live broadcast of the landing on the Moon. When the big old alarm clock screamed at us it was still night, and my dad got out of bed to press the power button on the big wooden box in the corner. Trembling with anticipation, I was absolutely certain that the broadcast would turn into a space gunfight at some point, with us, humankind, coming uninvited to a planet already inhabited by some other civilization. In the days before, I had been practicing recognizing colors based on the gray shades on our TV screen: the dark, warm gray was the color of blood in Westerns, the cold gray was the deep green of leaves, the silver was bright yellow and the neutral was sky blue. Then Mother wiped the screen, all grays became a few shades lighter, and I had to start all over again, but if the extraterrestrials were green–as everyone in my school expected–I would be able to recognize the blood on their chests when our boys hit them.

After a few introductory remarks from the Belgrade studio, there they were: Neil Armstrong and Edwin Aldrin leaving their footsteps in the gray dust. It was exciting, for the first fifteen minutes or so. I kept staring at the rocks around them, behind them, waiting for an alien to come out and tell them it was a private planet and would they be so kind as to leave immediately, thank you. But nothing of that kind happened; we just watched close-ups of Armstrong's boot prints, two men in white suits killing time waiting to embark on their plane home, and listened to the translation of their manly talk with Houston. When it became clear that the aliens would not do anything like they did on my favorite series, *Lost in Space,* I fell asleep.

We talked about it the whole day at school, everybody coming up with some detail nobody else saw or heard. Every step that day was "a small step for me, but a giant leap for mankind."

It was evening when I asked Nana about her thoughts on the Moon landing.

"Enough, already," she said, seriously. "I understand that you believe in such things–you are a child, you will grow up and know better–but you two," and she turned to my parents, "you can't just believe what your Party tells you. You think God would let them come that close to him? I bet they spilled some dust in some building in America, and took two fools to jump around, and you believe their propaganda."

"Mother, it doesn't make sense what you are saying," my mother tried. "This is not our Party saying Americans are on the Moon, this is live on TV, and the Americans are broadcasting it so the whole world can see that they are smarter than the Russians. Now, you know we don't like Americans much because of Vietnam, but we don't like Russians either–they tried to make us their slaves in 1948. So, our Party doesn't have anything to do with this."

"Everything you watch on that box is a lie!" Nana was red in the face. "I don't know why you threw money away on that crap. When you watch Tito opening new roads, you think the roads are really there? The new factories popping up like mushrooms? The new mines, new everything? What, it was just waiting for the Communists to come to reveal itself to them? If the gold was in there all this time, how come nobody ever dug it out? You think everything smart comes in your time only? We were stupid for having a king, but you are smart for having Tito? If you're so smart, how come you don't see he's just like our king?"

My mother closed the kitchen window. That was the bad window: we couldn't see anyone coming, and when we did, it was already too late; they were a few feet away from our door, well within earshot.

"Mother, don't get angry," Ana said. "I can't understand why are you taking it to heart, this whole thing with the Moon."

"Because. Because you act crazy. I feel sorry for this child. He will grow up with your lies. You can choose to believe whatever you wish, but don't poison him."

"But Nana, they really are on the Moon," I said.

"See?" she asked my parents, then turned to me. "Son, that spaceship, that they claim took them there, it has to be big, right? Go out, and look at the Moon, and tell me what you see, all right? Go."

I went outside. It was dark already, and the Moon was almost full, shining a little to the west. My father, then my mother, reluctantly came out and joined me. We stood there, in front of our kitchen, staring at the craters washed with cold, bright light. We couldn't see the slightest dot on the surface. The Moon looked like a long-forgotten battlefield, as always. I went inside.

"I can't see the ship, Nana," I said.

"Aha," said Nana.

SANDWICH SLAP

"Children," said our teacher, "I want you to tell your parents that this excursion is very important. We are going to visit Višegrad, Tjentište and Dubrovnik. All three places are important in the history of our country, for different reasons, and this trip is part of our educational program for this year. We are traveling through Bosnia and Croatia, so it will be a lesson in geography, as well as in history. If some of you have financial difficulties at home, let me know tomorrow, so we can think of something. But keep in mind that this is an obligatory excursion, and if you don't come on Saturday morning here to travel with us, you'll have to have a doctor's excuse for your absence. No fooling around. Class dismissed."

"My mom says Dubrovnik is beautiful," said Mira. "She and my father were there last summer on some trip with their factory, and they say it's gorgeous. I hope we get to swim, the weather in September is still nice on the coast."

"What's the use?" said Vesna. "More than half of the class can't swim."

That was true. Kragujevac had a joke of a river, a narrow creek really, except once in twenty years when it would go wild and flood the city. There was no swimming pool either, and the lake in Šumarice Memorial Park was full of mud and rushes.

"Are you absolutely sure you're leaving at six in the morning? It sounds a little late," said my mother. "I don't want us to come there, in front of your school, with everyone gone."

"That's what the teacher said, Mom," I responded.

"Let the kid be," said my father, "he should enjoy this one. At least they're not taking them to that asbestos mine, like they did last year."

"What's wrong with that?" she said. "The children should see the life of workers. They should see how their parents spend their days."

"They were just scaring them into studying, so they wouldn't end up digging asbestos," he said.

She threw him the evil eye. "I will prepare most of the food on the previous night, but I'll make the doughnuts that morning, so they'll stay warm till Višegrad, at least."

"Mom, I can't take doughnuts. The others will laugh at me."

"And why not? Doughnuts are good for growth."

I knew it. Every time I protested and she wanted to have the last word, she'd pull this final argument: good for growth and full of vitamins, no matter what it was.

"I'll also prepare some cheese pie, some meat pie, some pastry, several sandwiches and pack a couple of chocolates, just in case."

"Wife," my dad said, "it's only eight hours of travel, including all the stops."

"They'll be bored after a while, they will need food to keep them quiet," she said.

"That's right," Nana chimed in. She was currently at 243 pounds, according to the big old scale in the pharmacy on the corner, the only scale that could take her weight

without falling apart. "Make him something with lard, like *salčići*. Bacon helps, too. I know myself–when I can't sleep, bacon lulls me like that."

"That's a good idea," Mother said.

"But Mom, I'm already fat, and if we go swimming there, I'll sink like an ax . . ."

"You're not fat, you're just a healthy kid. If you don't eat it all, share it with the other children, what's wrong with that?"

"Nothing, except that everyone will have tons of food, they always do."

"See!" She turned victoriously to my father. "You want his teacher to think that we have no food for our only child? You want us to be the worst? Instead of babbling here, you better go to the store and start buying some stuff, there's only two days left."

"Okay, I'm on my way," said my dad with a sigh and started to put on his shoes. He turned to me. "You want to go with me?"

"I need minced meat, phyllo pastry, eggs, cheese, chocolates, butter, lard and more sugar. And also, buy some bananas and two big bottles of that orange juice he likes," Mom said as we were leaving the house. At the gate, we heard her voice across the whole yard: "Don't forget some sausages and salami for sandwiches!"

"And baaacooon!" we heard as we turned the corner.

The old red bus was swaying left and right on the narrow, curvy Bosnian road between Goražde and Foča. Sava the driver, a burly man in his early fifties, maddened with our constant yelling, running between the seats and throwing the food our mothers had packed for the long trip, decided to get to Tjentište as fast as he could. Some girls were throwing up in the back and one of them came forward to ask Sava for another black plastic bag. He handed it over with a vicious smile.

Our teacher sat beside him, eating some cookies Vesna had given her. Vesna was not quite the best learner but was very ambitious, and she always had something for the teacher.

The teacher finished her cookie, took the microphone and stood up. Sava slowed down a bit. The teacher tried to talk, but there was no sound from the speakers, so she hit the mike a couple of times with her thumb and said to the driver, "Sava, how do I turn on this–"

Sava flipped the switch.

"–MICROPHONE? OH, oh, right. Children?"

Nobody was paying attention except the few of us who sat in front.

"Children! Attention! Rašić, stop banging Marić's head against the window. Where is Tomić? Perić, don't sit on Tomić; let him get up and sit properly. Mira, did you finish throwing up? Then bring that bag over here; we'll dispose of it. Where's the other one? You threw it out the window?"

Sava the Irascible took the microphone. "Children, don't be pigs! When you throw things out the window, they can hit another driver and cause him to crash and die. We don't want any new dead people here. This is Sutjeska National Park, a place where many people have already died and we are going to visit them, as I'm sure your teacher will tell you now. So, I repeat: do not throw anything out the window." Sava handed the microphone back to the teacher.

Someone in the back threw a glass bottle on the road; there was a faint crash and the sound of brakes behind.

Sava grabbed the microphone back: "If I catch you doing that again, no police or teacher will protect you, you understand? I'll pull your ears off your empty head!" The bus swayed dangerously. Sava wasn't looking ahead and narrowly avoided the coming car. The other driver honked as he fought to stay on the road. "Fuck your mother, too!" Sava yelled through the window, and the mike fell between the seats. I bent over and handed it to the teacher.

"Children, you remember we learned about a national hero of our socialist revolution, comrade Sava Kovačević?" continued the teacher. We all hid behind the seats. Sava the driver lit a cigarette. Another one was already burning in the ashtray.

"Right. In half an hour . . ." she turned to the dashboard to check on the speed, then continued, "fifteen minutes, we will arrive at Tjentište, to visit the magnificent monument to our brave fighters who, outnumbered and underarmed, unselfishly sacrificed their lives so comrade Tito could escape with the members of our military headquarters. The German offensive aimed at catching him and shutting down our fight for freedom." She paused to look around the bus. Everyone ducked even lower, trying to become invisible. "It will be the highlight of our excursion. So, who can tell me about comrade Sava?"

Except for the revving of the bus, there was no sound. Everybody was looking out the windows to avoid eye contact with her. I could hear Sava in front of me chuckling with pleasure. I thought he said, "Pussies!" but I wasn't sure.

The teacher was still trying to catch someone's eye, but to no avail. She rolled her eyes in exasperation and her eyebrows looked like a raven in flight.

"Well, we have no heroes on this bus, it seems. All right then: Marko!"

Marko stood up, fell back to his seat, stood up again, bumped his head against the window and said, "I feel sick, Teacher."

"Well, I feel sick, too." Pause. "Sick of you! You think I cannot see you in the mirror fooling around? I told you all when we stopped in Višegrad that I have a terrible headache, I asked you all nicely to be quiet–but no, you have to yell and fight. When you grow up, if you have brains at all you'll hopefully have headaches like I do, and then you will understand. Marko, we have a lot of black bags here in front, so if you feel nauseous, just come over here and ask for one, but in the meantime answer me: who was comrade Sava Kovačević?"

Marko gulped. "Well, comrade Kovačević was, I mean, he was a hero, and all that."

"Sit down, you dumbbell!" the teacher said. Sava the driver reached with his right hand for the volume control. "Zoran?"

"Teacher, comrade Sava Kovačević was a great hero of our revolution, he fought bravely and if it wasn't for him Tito would be dead today here on Tjentište," Zoran blurted out in one breath.

"Hold it!" she said. Everyone turned towards her this time; we really didn't have a clue where he went wrong. "Tito is the greatest son of our peoples, we all know that people sacrificed for him without hesitation. Although hero Sava did give his life for Tito we must not forget others. Many people died here so Tito would stay alive!"

Vesna raised her hand.

"Yes, Vesna?"

"So we have many heroes who died here, Teacher?"

"No, we have only Sava in this particular place."

"And why weren't the others heroes?" asked Vesna.

"Well, they fought bravely, but were not heroes."

"How does one become a hero, Teacher?" asked someone from the backseat.

"By fighting bravely, and doing unselfish things for your country."

"But you said they all fought bravely here, that's why there's that big monument we are going to see." I recognized that voice from the backseat. It was Perić, looking unusually tall. He must have been still sitting on Tomić.

"Yes, they did," said the teacher, holding on to her seat as the bus sharply entered another curve, "and they did unselfishly sacrifice their lives, but hero Sava was the bravest of them all. He killed the largest number of enemy soldiers."

"So, whoever kills more is a bigger hero?" asked Vesna.

"Approximately, but not only that."

Zoran interrupted: "Teacher, how did they know who killed the most? Was someone counting?"

"No, but some partisans lived to tell about Sava's courage to the very end."

"What happened to them?" asked Zoran.

"What do you mean?" said our teacher.

"They didn't want to give their lives for Tito? Were they jailed afterwards?"

The teacher gave up holding the seat and started gesticulating wildly. She was yelling again. "What are you, a moron? I'll talk to your mother when we return. She will be ashamed of you. She, a respected doctor, and look what a crazy son she has!"

Raising both hands was a mistake. As Sava the driver was trying to miss a goat that suddenly stumbled up on the road, the bus swayed left, then right, and then the teacher, with a pretty loud bang, fell onto the steps.

Twenty minutes later, limping on her right leg, a minor bruise on her cheekbone, the teacher led us up the stairs towards the imposing monument. It looked like a narrow passage, symbolizing the canyon of the Sutjeska River. The real canyon was just a few hundred yards away on the other side of the road. We dispersed all over the hill around the monument. There was no traffic close to us, the hills were green, and the air–coming down from the surrounding mountains–was cool and perfumed.

"Can you imagine? They were in this valley, and the Indians all around them, in the mountains," said Rašić with awe.

"What Indians?" Vesna had overheard him. "They didn't fight the Indians, you moron, they fought the Nazis." The few girls close enough to hear started giggling, but Vesna wasn't satisfied. "Guys, did you hear what Rašić just said?" she yelled.

"Shut up!" Rašić told her.

"He said that Ind–" Rašić threw his yogurt container at her and white liquid poured down over her blouse and skirt. "Pig!" she screamed, and ran ahead to complain to the teacher.

"Serves her right," said Marko with a chuckle. "She shits a lot."

"Rašiiiiiić!" yelled the teacher. The mountain returned the echo, making that long "iiiii" sound like bomber approaching. He crouched behind my back.

"I'm done. Brother, am I done. Build a monument for me, too, will you?" He stood and moved slowly towards the teacher. We hurried to watch.

The teacher grabbed his left sideburn and pulled it hard. "Is this how one should behave in a place like this? This is the sanctity of our revolution, a place where blood was shed for our freedom, for us all, and that includes a monkey like you, Rašić. Unfortunately, it includes you! You think that our comrades who died here fought so someday you would be able to spill yogurt on your comrade? You think that is funny?" She let his sideburn go and started pulling his ear. His face twisted in pain.

"Those like you deserve the worst! Vesna, come here, child. Closer. Now, wipe your blouse and your skirt against him. And you, Rašić, stand still." Vesna was hesitant, so the teacher pulled her closer and started rubbing her against Rašić. "You see how sweet it is, Rašić? You see now how good it is to have yogurt all over you?" She slapped his face and he jumped away from her. "I'm not finished with you! Later, when we go to the hotel for lunch, I want you to clean both yours and Vesna's clothes. If I see one spot, just a single spot, you'll repeat the year. I'm fed up with you!"

Rašić's face was pale on the one side and red on the other where she had slapped him. He massaged his ear. Vesna stood next to the teacher, her face red, and I caught her glance at Rašić. He saw it, too, looked confused for a second, then smiled back at her.

"Gather around me before the rest of the school arrives," the teacher demanded. "On May 15, 1943, the enemy started a movement of large troops in this area, aiming at surrounding and liquidating the core of our partisans. This later became known as the Fifth Offensive. The enemy started the offensive with 127,000 soldiers. They engaged many airplanes, several artillery regiments and a large number of tanks against our partisans, who numbered only 22,000 fighters, among them 2,900 women. At six to one, the enemy expected an absolute success."

She paused to inspect the influence of her words. You could hear only crickets and the wind.

"The battle lasted one whole month. Hand-to-hand, the partisans fought like lions against the enormous enemy power. One whole month. They fought for every step, every stone and every foot of this mountainous area. Slowly closing the circle, the enemy surrounded our fighters in this valley. Together with Marshal Tito and the members of the headquarters of our army, there were hundreds, thousands of wounded from the earlier battles, since our central military hospital traveled with them. So, finally, towards the middle of June 1943, it all came down to this: surrender, and thus end our fight for freedom against the hated enemy, or make one last, total effort at breaking the circle around us. So Marshal Tito gave his orders: We must break out at any cost!

"The only way out, the only area that was not closed yet by the enemy, was between Lover's Grave and Košut. The fighters of the Second Platoon of the Third Battalion of the Fourth Montenegrin Proletarian Brigade took the task of defending that narrow passage through the canyon of Sutjeska towards the Zelengora Mountain. Sava Kovačević, the legendary machine-gunner, led them. Their orders were simple, but it was the most difficult task in the world: defend the passage to freedom for twenty-four hours. And they did it, at enormous cost–only a few of them survived. Among those who fell bravely on Lover's Grave was the hero Sava. The legend says that, even wounded, he held the point all by himself, spraying the enemy to the last second with the bullets from his machine gun. He had a chance to save himself. Other fighters–to whom he was already an idol–offered to replace him, but he refused, and instead told them to save their own lives."

Even Rašić, with the yogurt all over his shirt, stood very still. Next to him was Vesna, still slightly red in her face.

"The cost of the battle of Sutjeska was enormous: 7,500 dead partisans, among them 600 women. Never in the history of war have so many women fighters died in one place. Between these mountains the flowers of our youth were fighting shoulder to shoulder: Serbs, Croats, Muslims, Montenegrins, Yugoslavs, Jews, Macedonians, Albanians. We even had four Germans and ten Italians fighting on our side. Thanks to all of them, you have your future. Never forget that!"

She pulled a handkerchief from her handbag and blew her nose. Sava the driver, far in the back, ran a comb through his hair, and then wiped his eye, pretending that a hair had fallen into it.

"After the war," she continued, "the canyon of Sutjeska was pronounced a national park. Remains of the fighters were buried in the memorial crypt–beneath us, right here–and this monument was built. It is a masterpiece of our renowned sculptor Miodrag Živković."

She paused for us to admire the monument above our heads.

"How can we repay them? By never forgetting what they did, by never forgetting that they fought for our freedom, against the hated occupation. That they fought shoulder to shoulder, back to back, all brothers and sisters, all heroes of the same mother: of our motherland."

Some of us wiped our eyes secretively, behind others' backs.

"And we shall sing now, children. We all know the song of the hero Sava, we learned it in the second grade. Rašić, come here, don't be afraid, stand by me, child, and sing with me."

He apprehensively went closer. She hugged him, and started singing:

From the end of Bosnia, down to the sea
The whole country knows of him,
His glory traveled everywhere–
Commander Sava.

We joined for the chorus:

Roars, thunders Sutjeska,
Blood flowing through it,
Commander Sava's division
Fights the bitter fight.

She continued solo, her voice now soaring among the hillsides:

What's that murmur on Sutjeska
In this late hour?
Dead lies next to it
The glorious commander.

Waving her hand, she brought us back for the grand finale:

Hey-hi, Commander Sava!
Hey-hi, fights to the death!
Hey-hi, glorious commander!
Hey-hi, gave his life!

We stood in silence, watching the mountains around us. I hoped a Nazi would appear, so we could tear him apart. The teacher let us stand there for a few minutes, and then led us uphill, towards the motel surrounded by woods.

The big hall of the motel echoed with our noise. The whole caravan was gathered inside, all six buses, and the teachers were trying to straighten out who's going to the washrooms first, who's entering the dining room, who hit whom for no apparent reason. Everyone brought their food from home–it looked like the evacuation of a minor town–hordes of children with cardboard boxes milling around. Someone started a doughnut fight, and pastries of all shapes and sizes were soon flying around.

We entered the dining area and took tables next to the small stage in the corner. Another place for dying and dancing afterwards. I was seated with our teacher, Sava the driver and three other children. A waiter brought our juices and coffee for the grownups. Everyone had something to say, and soon we forgot about the teacher and Sava. I ate two small sandwiches, a few doughnuts, drank my juice and went to see my friends from the other buses. But they were in the same shape as we: some of them hungry, some of them tired, some had vomited for hours and had yellow faces. I soon returned to my table.

In the meantime another teacher had brought his chair to sit with Sava and our teacher. From time to time he would look towards his table, then yell a short command that would make the children sit quiet for a minute or two. We all feared him. He was a math teacher we simply called the Mathematician, and he was known for his special technique of punishing: the notorious Sandwich Slap. If someone was making trouble, he would take him in front of the whole class, say a few derogatory words and then pretend that he would slap him. The victim would blink, but there was no hit. The Mathematician would repeat the pretend slap several times, causing fear to grow. Then he would finally execute the blow–with both his hands at the same time. We discussed it amongst ourselves at school. Some of us said that he did this to avoid a brain injury–your head can't swing the other way if both hands slap you at the same time–while some said that he just enjoyed torturing us. I never wanted to go too deep into this. I was too afraid to act up when he was around.

So I sat quietly and listened to their conversation, pretending that I was admiring the napkin.

"There's nothing like a good massage for a headache," said the Mathematician to our teacher. "I could give you a good one tonight, in Dubrovnik, colleague." He winked at Sava.

"Er, no, that will not be necessary, thanks," she said, blushing just a bit. "I took two pouches of Combined already, so it will fix it by evening, I'm sure."

"Combined" was the trade name for the favorite painkiller. Pharmacies would mix some ingredients and pack the white powder into small white paper pouches. There was no official name for it, just Combined Powder. Thanks to my mother's frequent headaches, it was part of the food chain in our house.

"The children are killing her, comrade," said Sava the driver. "They are such pigs. I admire you for being able to withstand that pressure day by day. I would go nuts, I'm sure."

"She's too gentle with them, I keep telling her," said the Mathematician. "You let them have it from time to time, they'll remember. Then they're fine. The stick was made in heaven, as they say."

"True," said Sava.

"Not true," said our teacher. "Did your parents beat you?"

"Mine? My mother would break her wooden ladle against my buttocks every time I did something stupid," said the Mathematician. "She even knew this peasant at the market who made them, and gave her a special discount. I'm telling you, my parents beat me like I wasn't theirs."

"Yeah, mine beat me too. I guess they were nervous after the war. They'd lost everything," said Sava.

"It must have been terrible for you," said our teacher.

"No, I'd say mine was a happy childhood, all in all."

One of the children from the Mathematician's class came to our table. "Comrade teacher, can we please go outside to play a little on the grass? We have finished with our lunch, so we thought–"

"I told you a thousand times you're not supposed to think, just listen. If everybody else is sitting here, you will, too. Go back to your table and it'll be better for you if my eyes don't see you again." The boy went back and the Mathematician said, "Okay, I see that mine are restless there, I'd better go sit with them or I won't be able to find them later. Colleague, in case you change your mind about that massage, my room in Dubrovnik will probably be right next to yours." The Mathematician got up and went to his table. Our teacher exchanged glances with Sava.

"Some manners," she said quietly. "So, yours were rich before the war, weren't they?"

"Yes, actually, but I didn't want to elaborate in front of him. And one can see that you come from a good family too . . ."

"My father said he had to learn to curse after the war so he wouldn't raise suspicion. My mom, though, refused ever to learn that. I guess I'm more like my father."

"I have to ask you something, if you don't mind." Sava hesitated for a second.

"And what is that?" she said, coquettishly turning her eyes to him.

"Well, you teach history, right?" He quickly looked around to see if anybody was listening. I pretended to be very interested in the centerpiece on the table: a shabby broken vase with a single dried flower in it. “Tell me, is it difficult to be teaching their history when we know ours?”

She looked around but didn’t respond.

We arrived in Dubrovnik at dusk. Half an hour before getting there, everyone in the bus moved to the left side, climbing on top of one another, because we were coming from the south, and the coast would first appear on the left. Some of the girls complained half-aloud about being touched, and a couple of boys got slapped, so the teacher didn’t need to intervene.

The road was winding through the mountains above Dubrovnik. Coming out of a curve, someone said, “There it is.”

The sea. From the road above it looked like something alive, a giant fish breathing slowly, its sides blue and green, with a red overcoat from the setting sun. It was the first time any one of us had seen it. There was a solemn silence in the bus for a minute or two, and then someone else said quietly, “It’s huge!” We felt as if we had come to the end of the world.

“I could swim across it!” said Perić.

“You could swim over my dick,” said Tomić. Sava the driver giggled. The teacher turned threateningly towards them. “Mind your language,” she said, but it was clear she wouldn’t take further action. Some girl in the back, from another class, started crying.

“What’s wrong with her?” asked the teacher.

“She says she’s afraid of the sea, comrade teacher.”

“Don’t be stupid, children, we’re not crossing it, here’s where we’re staying overnight,” said Sava. “That below there is Dubrovnik.”

Only then we noticed houses and buildings tightly packed by the coast. They all looked like they were waiting for the one closest to the water to fall, so they could jump into its place.

"See that small peninsula over there, to the south?" said the teacher. "That's the old Dubrovnik. The island across from it is Lopud, and we are staying over there." She indicated one of the high-rises on the bigger peninsula. "We'll be visiting the old town tomorrow. Tonight we'll stay in the hotel, get some rest, and after dinner we'll have a meeting. Don't even think about sneaking out of the hotel tonight. If you do, you'll get caught, and then you will be expelled from the school immediately. Besides, Professor Beko–you call him the Mathematician–will be patrolling tonight, just so you know."

Vesna raised her hand. "Comrade teacher?"

"Yes, child?"

"Can we at least take a walk by the sea with you, before we go to sleep?"

"We'll see."

As Sava was steering through the narrow streets, we stared in awe at palms and strange plants with sharp leaves. It reminded me of the sharp edges of Tarzan's land in Burne Hogarth's drawings. Everything looked luxurious beyond belief. Our hometown was a city of factories and schools, decent but unsmiling, while Dubrovnik seemed built for pleasure. The hotel was a blue-painted building, a little off the main road, with a large parking lot behind it and a big terrace in front, facing the beach. They separated us inside: we boys got rooms in the back, while the girls got the sea view. All the teachers, of course, were on the girls' side of the hotel. We were four or five to a room, but it was my first hotel room ever, and I thought it was enormous. There was a telephone on the table (none of us had phones at home, so we had nobody to call), and the bathroom had a double sink and a massive tub.

After dinner, they gathered us, all seven buses of children, in a conference room on the first floor. They repeated that we were not allowed to go out of our rooms at night, that the curfew was ten sharp, and that in the morning we would go visit the old town. The Mathematician said, "I am sure you all know by now that I will be patrolling tonight. You know what that means: don't even think of doing anything. But if you think I'll be at watch only so you don't come out, you're wrong. This is a dangerous city, you don't know people here, and tourists come from all over the world, so nobody really knows them. I'll have double duty: to keep you inside, and to keep the strangers outside. This especially goes for the girls: if someone tries to talk to you, dial 0 and ask for your teacher, any time of night. You hear someone knocking–don't open the door, call the teacher. Someone yelling–don't open the door. Only if you hear the voice of one of us, your teachers, will you open the door. Is that clear?"

Frightened whispers swept the room, and the meeting was over. The girls from the higher grades went giggling upstairs, followed by very loud boys. Our teacher collected us and asked us if we still felt like taking a walk by the sea. "We won't stay long," she warned us, "and if we decide to go, then everyone must go." We agreed, and she took us outside, into the mild night smelling of agaves and iodine.

We passed by the patio, full of smiling, tanned people chatting and drinking. The orchestra was playing lounge music in the back, and a blonde chanteuse with a miniskirt and a sizable cleavage was slowly moving to it. These people were so different from my parents and their friends. There was something lascivious in the very way they just sat there, enjoying the music and the night. Back at home everyone was mostly tired, and overworked, and too poor to have fun.

We took the narrow path to the beach, walking in pairs in front of our teacher and Sava. The head of our small column soon reached the water line and we gathered around.

"Is it true that the sea is salty?" someone asked.

"It's true, children," said the teacher. "Pay attention when you go home and your mothers buy cooking salt: some of it comes from salt mines in Bosnia, but some of it comes from this very sea. Tomić, what are you doing? Don't stand in the water; you'll ruin your shoes. This water can damage them. Okay, Perić, you can lick it, but don't drink it."

"It's so warm, although it's September," Mira said. "Can we swim tomorrow?"

"I'm not sure, depends on the weather. How many of you can swim?" Maybe four or five in the class raised their hands.

"But you said you could swim," said Mira to Tomić.

"Yes, he could in Kragujevac, where there's nowhere to swim, but this here is the real thing," Perić said.

The teacher just looked at him, somehow mellow, not the same person. She turned her head and looked towards the main building, and the lights from the patio twinkled briefly in her eyes.

Sava the driver was standing on a flat stone a few steps from us, smoking, his hands deep in his pockets. He was looking at her. "Let's walk a bit more," he said. "And, children, don't splash one another. Don't be piglets."

So we continued along the beach, always within reach of the hotel lights. Sava and the teacher stayed behind, their talk swept into the murmur of the sea beneath our feet. And of course, everyone was stepping in the water, our shoes now squeaking and spurting small geysers, and everyone was splashing others. Mira tripped and fell, quiet for a second, and then she laughed and everyone roared with laughter, and Perić pretended to trip so he could fall by her. Soon a few more of us did the same, even me. The water was hot, and I suddenly knew the sea was not a mass of water, it was the road to Anyplace. Our teacher wasn't warning us anymore, it was only Sava's voice that would gently repeat, "Children . . ."

Finally, after half an hour or so, the teacher said, "Okay, enough, we are going back to the hotel now. Clean yourselves up a bit, we can't walk like thugs into the lobby."

"Let's not go along the beach again," said Sava. "It's faster if we cut across the parking lot."

We took our shoes off and walked barefoot on the hot asphalt, among the few cars and buses. Some people stood close to the entrance to the hotel, chatting. Mira pulled a wet mass from her pocket and said, "Look at my sandwich. Does anyone want it? It's very salty, I must warn you!" She threw it in the air, and we started fighting for it, and it became a game of catch around the parking lot. Finally the sandwich was in Perić's hands, and he threw it towards the wire trash can by the entrance, basketball style, and he missed. The thing fell into the grass behind the can, a few inches from the men standing there. They stopped chatting and turned towards us. One of them started to say something, but the man next to him laid his hand on his shoulder and said, "Leave it. They are dirty Serbs."

We became quiet instantly. I looked at the teacher, who had turned to stone on the spot, very pale. Sava the driver took the sandwich, put it in the basket and said, "Into the hotel, children, quickly." He put his arm around the teacher and gently pushed her to come with us. I heard the laughter of the men behind us as we entered the well-lit lobby.

"I'll call the police," said our teacher inside, her hands shaking.

"Let's not call the police," said Sava, looking at her. "I've been here a few times, I know what I'm saying."

"I wish I had my air gun with me," I said to comfort the teacher. She looked at me, raised her hand to slap me, and then just let it fall.

THE END OF CHILDHOOD

On a Tuesday morning in November 1970 my mother's crying, down in our courtyard, awakened my father and me. She'd risen early, as usual, and gone to work while Father and I were still sleeping. She wasn't supposed to be home yet. We rushed to the window and saw her, followed by my cousin Boban, entering the kitchen. Boban lived in Žabare, with the rest of my mother's family, and he was the only one of them who had a car. He was supposed to be at work on a Tuesday morning, so his coming to Kragujevac meant that something urgent had happened.

"What is it?" asked my father from the window.

"Nana has died," responded Boban.

"Oh God," said Father. "When?"

Boban wiped his eyes and said, "This morning, around four."

Three months before, she'd had a stroke. She spent a month in hospital, and recovered almost fully. Then she went home, to her village, to enjoy the fresh air and healthy food. We'd expected her back with us soon.

An hour later, we were packed in Boban's car on the road to Žabare. My parents talked briefly about whether to let me see something or not, and decided not to, whatever it was. When we got there, local women were already gathered in the front yard, waiting for us, and as soon as we entered the gate the wailing began: long howls of women in black, piercing, hitting somewhere deep inside, pinning your tear glands with the precision of an eagle. Their wailing listed all Nana's relatives and how we would miss her, some precious moments she would be remembered by, her endless virtues, her beauty in youth and wisdom in old age. Three voices, then five, then seven, nine, all having the same melody, but their cadence slightly apart, overflowing the yard, bracing the old apple tree, rising to the sky, traveling over the village at the speed of sadness, calling for gathering because one of ours has gone, time for tears, time for men to let their beards grow, time for women to put black scarves on, the cry of death, the ancient blues of my people.

After standing there crying for several minutes, we entered the old house. Someone held me back from the side room, where my parents went, and where–judging by my mother's crying and my father's sniffling–Nana was laid. My uncle Mita appeared, and said, "Let him come in. He's a man, and it's his Nana."

I went slowly to the long table in the middle of the room, and they made space for me. Nana was lying, dressed in her best, with a large beeswax candle burning slowly above her head. I recognized some of the clothes. Over the last two years or so, when she received a present of clothes from her friends or us she would put it aside, saying, "This is for my funeral." She was dressed in those now. Her skin was pale yellow, and she had blue circles around her eyes, but what struck me most was her stillness. Nana loved me, and I loved her–there was no chance she would continue to just lie there when I came in. Her stillness was somehow precise. Even stones, even mountains looked less immovable than her. As if she saw something that was immensely beautiful, something that froze her in the very moment she stood before it.

I reached and touched her hand. Her skin was cold and she didn't open her eyes. I started crying.

"Take 'im out, take 'im out, for Chrissake, he's just a child," someone said.

Someone else, standing behind me and holding my shoulders, answered, "He's not a child anymore."

THE BOOK OF REVENGE

Soon after Nana died, they decided to tear down our whole neighborhood, to relocate the bus station and modernize the area. The apartment we got from the city council was a newly added two-bedroom on top of an old building in the eastern part of town, overlooking the cemetery. It was early summer when we moved in. I had my own room and my own desk, we had a real bathroom, and I thought life couldn't be better than that.

My parents would leave in the morning, and I would get up around nine, fix myself breakfast and then sit down to work. Now I had something that looked like an office, and there was no excuse for not trying to discover the Hidden Treasures. Every morning, my meal was the same: ham or bacon, and eggs. That's what Wyatt Earp and Doc Holliday would have while in pursuit of cattle thieves. Yes, Mother filled the kitchen with fruit and cooked food, but Wyatt surely wouldn't have bananas on his saddle.

My parents became worried when I started losing weight. They felt I would be better off if they spent more time with me, which was impossible. They started giving me more money for lunch at school, but I saved that money to buy records, which I had started collecting several months before.

My waist started thinning, my hands–and other parts of my body–extended, and I started feeling an insatiable desire for girls. Clearly, it was puberty. I still wasn't accustomed to my new body, so I just longed with pure, condensed sadness. I didn't even know what I was longing for: sex was an abstract thought related to the pictures of naked women in the soft-porn magazines that were entering the market around that time. Naked models were displayed in a much smaller size than the living girls around me, and they looked like obedient, discreet girls, as opposed to my screaming and kicking classmates.

Growing up without other children in the house made me a recluse, simply unable to share my innermost feelings. From very early on I somehow knew that real men never talked about feelings, and I wanted to become a man like that one day, but I'd never found anything about real men and writing.

At first I wanted to write a novel. I had enormous respect for novelists; I thought them to be the wisest people in the universe. They had to see and live through so much to be able to write the works I admired. But mine was a tiny life. One courtyard, few grownups and a really bad view–that doesn't make for much of a novel.

Then I started making sketches for different stories. They all seemed promising while I was writing them, but I didn't know how to proceed. The stories were about *telling,* and that was something I never learned. So my notebook was full of beginnings without a single ending.

Have I seen enough to be able to write anything yet? I didn't know the answer to that question, but the emotions were already choking me and I had to start somewhere. Reading an art history book, I stumbled upon automatic writing, and began my first trials. At first I couldn't let myself go. I wrote with the notion that my parents might read it someday. It was all polite, and boring, and it wasn't me. Not really. It was a self-conscious diary of a narcissistic teenager, and–like most other teenagers–I was disgusted with myself.

Then, in another book, I found a spy trick that sounded helpful: if you wrote with lemon juice, your writing would be invisible until the page was ironed out. I filled my fountain pen with lemon juice and suddenly I was able to express myself. When I ironed out my first pages I found many errors, but also a new me. And that new me I liked well enough to continue. I enjoyed the metaphorical richness of my new method, too: only under the heat did my words appear. I wrote many sour pages and it felt so sweet.

My parents were happy about my buying so many lemons. Vitamin C can't hurt, they said. They must have had some thoughts about my keeping our iron in my room, but never asked.

After two months and four seemingly blank notebooks, I had a problem: I wanted to go back to some of the previous sections, but I had to make them visible first. Once I did that, I was exposed, and had to destroy those pages. There had to be a better way.

The Romantic poems we read at school were like rhymed stories, and too obvious for my taste, but the modern poetry I found in literary magazines was indecipherable. Some of the new poetry sounded like coded reports from behind the enemy lines. But that was all right: I didn't want to communicate, I just wanted to write my thoughts down. Poetry was safe.

The first poems I wrote were bad exercises consisting of clusters of soft-sounding words, a lacy construction that had the sweet structure of court music and couldn't stand the test of time. By "time" I mean three or four days. Reports from behind the enemy lines? Either I had no enemies, or I didn't know where their lines were.

Although I thought that sadness was a good starting point for poetry, I quickly realized quite the opposite: nothing good would come out when I tried to express myself in those moments. My mother had brought me a beautiful small guitar from Italy three years before and now I started learning to play, so I could leave poetry to my happier moments. My parents wouldn't let me out whenever I wanted; they preferred me to stay at home at night, in my room, under their watchful eye, so I had plenty of time to practice my arts.

Through the open window I could hear the voices of other children playing, making me restless. The world outside had a rotten tendency to go on without me, and my parents' hard "No" to my pleadings for release only made things worse. Very angry, I would return to my room, slam the door, and then sit down and write poetry, or play guitar, waiting for the adrenaline to evaporate. But it never really did; it would only get slower and deposit itself somewhere deep down, coat upon coat. And out of those many layers came a sentence I would utter under my breath every time the laughter from the outside became unbearable, a thought that became my silent promise of revenge: "When I publish my first book, you'll still be playing the Blind Granny." I would whisper it to no one in particular and to everyone whose voice came through the window. I also wanted to make a record, do a concert and give a poetry reading, but a book seemed more permanent, a longer-lasting reprisal for their temporary joys from which I was excluded.

From the window of my room I could see the Lombardy poplars in the cemetery across the street. Their purpose changed with the seasons. In spring, they were watercolor brushes full of light green that would paint the skies in the coming months. In summer, they would become the pillars of this world; transparent clouds would be torn apart when floating over their sharp prongs; the rainstorms never came from that side. The fall turned the poplars into a tall lesson in philosophy, about blood and gold, about armies and deserters; about ideas falling off a myth. In snowy months the poplars were an elegy on the horizon. The idea of a mighty column would get torn into a thousand lonely, impotent branches growing accidentally in the same direction, disjointed, senseless and vain. Pale gray sun rising behind them projected bars on my draperies.

THE POET GOES TO THE MARKET

Around the time we moved, our teacher started bringing a guest to our class from time to time. It was always the same person, Goran Delić, the famous poet. His poems were not on our reading list, but the teacher would always introduce him in the same manner: "Children, our guest today is comrade Delić, the famous poet," so we took it for granted.

He would read a couple of his poems, usually something contemplative that was hard for us to understand, and then our teacher would recommend purchasing his latest work. Those of us who wanted it would raise our hands, he would give us the book, and we would bring the money the next day. He was publishing regularly, two times a year, and his collections of poems were thin paperbacks, hardly thirty pages each, bound in poor-quality card stock and printed in serious black only.

My parents didn't pay attention the first couple of times, but when I brought home his third book they started asking questions. Did I have to buy those books? Yes I did, I lied. Did the school approve it? Not only approve, my teacher brought him in. Is he some important author? Everybody knows about him. They went quiet, but I could see they were not persuaded. And later that night I overheard my father saying in a muffled voice, "Fuck his poet's mother! Do they have any idea how much money we need just to send him to school? It's all the same gang, teachers and poets. I'll find him a job in my factory. Let me see him write poetry *then*."

Why was I buying those books? Yes, I read them, always, entirely. No, I didn't think they were a work of genius. Yes, I would raise my hand partly because it was obvious the teacher would like us to do so. No, I wasn't desperate for good marks at all. But there was something almost mystical about this poet. He was a thin man in his late fifties, wore glasses and had a slightly harsh voice when reading his works, different from when he was speaking. I wouldn't let anyone read my poems if my life depended on it. And he was cool about it–a grown man not only admitting to writing poetry but daring to read it aloud, in front of everyone. He gave me freedom. In my world of one room, eternal struggle, hard work, my father's factory, my mother's getting up before dawn, his books were the only proof of a different existence. I saw, with my own eyes, someone who met the Muse daily, who had breakfast with her, lunch and dinner, who went to bed with her, someone who had his eyes open for brooks and paths, winds and willows, and swallows that flew high over the factory chimneys.

I bought his next book. And the next one. But one evening, at the parents' meeting at school, someone raised this issue, and the poet didn't come again to school.

I hated everyone for this. Wasn't the school supposed to protect us from our parents' selfishness and stupidity? Wasn't the school supposed to just bang on the table and say, "Children need this for their future. Parents, oblige!"

A year passed, and one day in the fall, going to school, I saw the poet on my street. I noticed him only when he was just a few steps from me and–with a sudden freeze in my stomach, as if seeing an old love–I stuttered, "Good day!" He raised his head, looked at me and nodded. Only then I saw bags in his hands, green onions protruding from one, potatoes from another.

The poet goes to the market? A part of my world collapsed so quickly I could hear a bang. So, he goes to the market, where he bargains with peasants, four eggs a dinar, no, three, two dinars for potatoes, two-ten, two-five, they're a little rotten, then you find better . . . He's probably even cooking them himself. He might be waking up at five in the morning. So, the Muse doesn't offer her breasts when poets need milk?

When I came home from school that afternoon, I took his books from my shelf and looked at them again. There was no price on them, so they were not meant for bookstores. Instead of the publisher's name and address, there was his name and "Published by the author" in small print below. Two hundred and fifty copies, each one of them.

The next time we visited our family in the country I took all his books with me and gave them to the local children. I continued to write poetry, but I was ready for the factory.

WIRED

With all the new furniture for our new apartment, my parents bought a telephone, a big, solid machine with a light green casing and a transparent dial on top of the cream-colored circle with numbers. It was difficult to get a line, though; our part of town wasn't scheduled to be hooked up for at least two more years, so the phone was left to gather dust.

But I couldn't wait that long. When Ana and Dušan were at work, I would take the phone off the shelf in their room, take it into mine and pretend to make calls. At first I called our family, asked them about their health, the weather, crops and their plans in general–all very serious stuff. Later I started calling friends from school, then girls, flirting with them, chastising them for avoiding me, telling them about my secret love.

Finally, I went international. Although I had to wait for several minutes for Leonid Brezhnev to finish his meeting, it was worthwhile. I thanked him for signing the declaration asserting Yugoslav independence, and he took it very kindly and invited me to visit his dacha just outside Moscow. Detective Frank Serpico had difficulties hearing me, but he was grateful for my unconditional support. Chairman Mao didn't have any spare blue tunics at the moment, but he promised to send me one as soon as they were back from dry cleaning.

I called God, but nobody answered.

And, finally, I dialed Tito's residence, but hung up immediately.

HEARTS ON THE STREET (TITO IS COMING)

Dear Citizens,

We are very honored to welcome comrade Tito on November 27. It is a great honor for our city and its citizens, but also a great responsibility to make everything happen as it should and as appropriate.

For the above reasons we kindly ask you to adhere to the following:

1. Let's tidy up your balconies and put out as many flowers as we can find. Let's remove everything else from the balconies (i.e., laundry, furniture, bedding, etc.).

2. Let's set a community-cleaning day to beautify our buildings and the space around them. Let's remove every piece of paper from the ground. Let's clean our windows. Let's make big banners for our buildings. Let's raise the flags on every façade facing the way Tito is supposed to pass.

3. On Friday at 9:00 a.m. let's all come out–everyone!–to welcome our beloved comrade Tito. At that time everyone is supposed to come to their place of work or study, and from there the lines of people will go to their prearranged positions. Let's do this in an orderly manner and as a group.

4. Let everyone carry at least a flower that we will all throw on the road 100 meters ahead of the first car in comrade Tito's convoy. On no account should anyone throw flowers on the car in which comrade Tito is driving.

5. While his convoy is passing, let's be cheerful and let's show our joy in welcoming Tito by singing (revolutionary songs), flag-waving (the small ones, distributed throughout schools and factories), and chanting (TI-TO, TI-TO!).

6. When the convoy passes, let's stay a little longer, and let's leave in the order in which we came to our position.

7. No one may stand on balconies or by windows. Windows must be closed. In front of every apartment building there will be a monitor, to observe the building until we return. During that time nobody may enter the building. Lock your apartments when leaving and unplug all electrical devices–ovens, boilers, refrigerators, etc.

8. When leaving and returning, let's keep the grass, flowers and trees intact. Let's prevent any uncivilized or rude behavior.

Sing revolutionary and partisan songs. Show all our virtues and positive qualities. Ensure that others behave as appropriate to the situation. As soon as the procession is over, return in an orderly fashion to your homes, without pushing. Pay attention to children and protect others from being hurt.

Thank you for your cooperation and contribution!

Long live our beloved Tito!

While the red and blue leaflets with this content were still being distributed to homes and institutions in Kragujevac that Monday in November 1970, an outburst of feverish activity ensued. Urgent meetings were called and classes interrupted at school. We were ordered not to leave the schoolyard while our teachers debated behind closed doors, and after two hours of waiting, we were called back to our classrooms. The whole plan for Friday's state visit was already made, and we had to write it down. The instructions were rather detailed: what we should do, and who would do what, to improve the look of our school, especially the tiny area too small to even be referred to as the front yard. We were to be absolutely properly dressed and wearing our blue uniforms at all times in the coming days, and for Friday the uniforms had to be washed, ironed and patched. On Friday we were to arrive at school at six thirty in the morning. Those who were sick would be forbidden to leave their apartments, and especially forbidden to go welcome Tito on their own or with their parents instead of coming out with the school. The classes for the rest of the day were changed, and instead of our regular activities, we had additional lessons in recent history.

At dinner, I learned that there had been a general meeting at the factory where my father worked, and my mother was summoned for a similar thing at her company the next day.

"Why didn't they tell us sooner?" said my father. "There's only four days left."

"For security reasons, I've heard," said Mom. "We have no idea how many foreign spies would love to be able to harm our comrade Tito."

"Do spies need much time to prepare?" I said.

"Shut up and eat," said Mom.

"Anyways, it won't affect us at all," said Dad, taking the leaflet into his hands and reading it. "We have no balcony, and we have no flowers. We've been told to come to work that day at the usual time, and that's what I'm going to do. They said the old man might want to visit our factory without telling us in advance, so we'll all be there."

"I have to close the shop from seven till noon. I'll just open in the morning for bread and milk, and that's it. But we have to make sure that our son is all right." Mom got up to clean off her plate.

"I'm okay."

"Bring me your school uniform."

When I reluctantly did, she inspected it and said, "No need to patch, yet. Maybe I'll just replace the buttons–these two are different."

Dad pushed his plate away and lit a cigarette. "You know what I heard at work about why the old man comes so rarely to Kragujevac?"

"What do you mean, rarely?"

"Well, it's been fourteen years, and we're so close to Belgrade. I mean, he's constantly traveling, he could've come sooner."

"What did you hear?"

"That it's because of Šumarice. They say he doesn't like to be reminded that because of some stupid action of the partisans the Germans executed seven thousand people here."

"What stupid action? They fought for freedom," said Mom.

"I've heard it was something really pointless. There was nothing to gain with that attack, except maybe to take a few rifles. But not many people volunteered to be partisans from this area, and they wanted to mobilize Kragujevac, and to raise the stakes. They didn't count on the Germans doing it. Some even say they did count on it, that it was part of the plan."

"Son, go to your room if you're finished eating."

—

On Friday morning, as usual, I was late. My parents woke me up very early, all of us nervous, and, after they saw that I got out of bed, they left. But I found something else to do, as I always did, and so it was seven when I got to school. I wasn't the last one, though: sleepy children were still arriving when I entered the front gate. Our school looked clean and tidy, the bust of Radoje Domanović in front was cleaned and polished, and the tiny patch of evergreen bushes around it neatly trimmed.

"What's he doing there?" I asked someone, pointing at the janitor standing by the statue.

"He's a scarecrow on duty. Chasing pigeons away so they don't shit on Radoje."

The backyard was a sea of blue uniforms, with the classes already separated and the teachers standing in front of their groups holding big bouquets of carnations. The rest of the janitors were next to the gate, yelling at the ones who came in late, speeding us up, and even pulling an ear here and there. I found my class and slipped into the back. "I saw you!" said my teacher, waving her finger at me.

Half an hour later, the teachers gave each one of us a carnation, and my Aunt Ranka, the principal, gave a short speech.

"Children," she said, "this is a very important day for all of us. This is the day that our beloved comrade Tito chose to visit our city and do us the greatest honor of all. It is not by chance that he's coming to our community. We are a city of proud people, of diligent workers, of smart children, of educated youth. We are citizens of the city that is known all over the world for its victims in World War II. This is the day you will remember for the rest of your lives. When we leave this gate, I want you to walk in absolute peace. No talking! No pushing! Look straight ahead and straighten up! I want you to take this very seriously.

Anyone who starts acting foolishly will be expelled from school immediately, I promise you that! Let us all be proud of you, your parents most of all."

She picked a flower from one of the teachers next to her, raised it high and said, "You each got one carnation, and you will carry it with you. Listen to your teachers and look at them: when comrade Tito's car is about to pass by, your teachers will throw their flowers, and then you throw yours. Not before, and not after! When the procession is over, you will come back in order here to school, and from here you will go home. Is that all clear?"

"Yes!" we said, some of us halfheartedly.

"I can't hear you!"

"YES!"

"Good. And now, let's sing our school hymn one more time." Our hymn was a song by Croatian chansonnier Arsen Dedić, "If All the People in the World," and it went:

If all the people in the world,
Like all the children of the world,
Would decide "yes,"
There would be no war,
And those alone would get a brother,
And all the worries would cease to bother,
Because there would be peace.

After we sang it we formed a line and the first class left the gate. Our position was close to the school, in front of the old church, on the street named after Marshal Tito, so there was no rush.

Other citizens on the pavement stepped aside to let our column pass, and some women wiped tears from their eyes. I guess we did look impressive, so silent, all in blue, with red flowers in our hands. Prompted by the sniffling around us, some of our girls started sniffling, too, even some of our teachers. But we kept our balance. As Ranka hadn't said a thing about kicking and pinching, that's what we did. It was sweet, since the victims couldn't say a word. Our teachers would pull our ears from time to time, also in complete silence. In front of the church, policemen halted the pedestrians on both sides to let through our reel of silent film. The traffic was stopped already, and most of the other organizations were already in their positions. A little farther down the street were students from the gymnasium, not in such order as us, the girls so sexy we stopped our silent wars and started stretching our necks to see them better.

For the next hour or so nothing happened. All the positions were taken, everyone in their best clothes, the policemen turned towards the crowd, their boots like mirrors. I looked up and down the street, which looked awe-inspiring. There were tens of thousands of people, lines of bystanders so deep there was hardly space to pass by in the back. Banners all around us with slogans honoring Tito, the most prominent two being "Tito is the greatest son of our people" and "Comrade Tito we swear to you that we will never leave your path." Windows on both sides of the street were shut, and two men in uniforms stood on the roof of the building across from us.

Sometime after nine, the policemen grew more tense, some of them on walkie-talkies more often now. The people sensed the tension and their chatter quieted to a murmur, as they stood on their toes trying to see the upper part of the street. Then, suddenly, a blazing wave of whispers swept over us, sending shivers down my spine: "He's coming!"

Everyone pushed forward a bit, everyone stretched and stiffened, the policemen like statues, all gestures stopped halfway. The uproar was approaching fast from the direction of Šumarice. At first it wasn't distinguishable; it was just a yell of thousands, just a wall of sound, just distant "thum-thum, thum-thum!" But as the motorcade approached, the sound–like finding the radio station on the band–cleared and I recognized "Ti-to, Ti-to!" I was jumping up and down, everybody was, children and grownups and even policemen, our throats shut down with emotion, hands in the air, flags in the sky, hearts on the street. Someone threw their flower first, then everyone started throwing theirs, we started yelling, a thunder made of our voices, tears rolling down my face, my knees shaking, then two motorcycles appeared, riders in black leather, knights of the invincible army, one car, another, another, another, then the white long car, heavy and slow, like the ship of hope, and Tito in the backseat, with dark glasses, in white marshal uniform, slowly waving back at us in his royal way, billions of carnations in the air, like the red rain that will sweep the world.

PARIS

In May 1973 we finished primary school. I was pronounced the Student of the Generation, having all straight As all the time. As a reward, I got a gilded Russian watch (the Rocket model, of course–how else could a Russian watch be named?), a golden Mont Blanc fountain pen and a book: Vuk Karadžić's *Serbian Dictionary.* My friends opened the dictionary to search for four-letter words, and they were all there, which encouraged us to use it more often.

Every school in my hometown nominated their best students for a trip to Paris, and at fourteen and a half, I was among the youngest of twenty or so students and young workers selected that year. One of Kragujevac's sister towns was Suresnes, a western suburb of Paris, and the two towns exchanged delegations every year. Our trip included two weeks in Suresnes and two more weeks in Normandy, living in a camp not far from the sea, in the same woods where Asterix and Obelix once hunted boars. I wanted to see Paris, but I was much more thrilled about the prospect of living the way my indomitable Gaul heroes did, if only for two weeks. My parents bought me some new clothes for the big trip, all our neighbors, friends and coworkers were properly informed, and some members of the family even contributed a little pocket money.

In the end, we traveled by train, second class all the way, we slept in an ugly dormitory in bunk beds, we saw Paris mostly from the bus, the Normandy coast was cold and dirty, and the undercover Serbian cop, who presented himself as a worker from Zastava, watched over us so eagerly that we all felt like we were in a traveling cage. In the woods there was no trace of Asterix, their sea was gray instead of blue, and the Gaul hospitality was humiliating to us, because they treated us as we were: poor people from a poor country.

The Mont Blanc was stolen from my room by some visitor soon after, and the Rocket worked for almost two years before deciding that Serbian time was immeasurable.

3

GAME: HOT AND COLD

The rules

This game is often played in a large group but can also be waged by two participants. One selects an object, and the other has to identify it. The one who selected the object has to direct the seeker with only three words: cold, warm, or hot. The aim is to recognize the thing, but the seeker can surrender, and then he has to do another search.

The reality

Some people find more pleasure in searching than in directing the game, and they surrender repeatedly. Others prefer to be the invincible masters, and select such an object that even they can't remember what it was. Some even select people to be their objects.

The game usually ends with everyone being fed up with any kind of discovery.

ROSE'S SCREAM

After several years with the same employer my mother gained a reputation for being able to help unprofitable stores make money again, and this resulted in her having to work in a new store every so often. She liked the changes, and so did my dad and I–it was almost like a tour of our hometown. Some locations were better than the others, closer to home and with nicer people in the neighborhood. One day, when I was a child, she came home happy and told us she was being transferred into a particularly nice store across the street from the gymnasium. Nana was still alive then, but for one reason or another, she had to spend a few weeks back in Žabare that summer, and so Mom decided to take me with her to the store every day. To keep me busy, she let me help her, rearrange the chocolates, hand over the warm loaves of bread, then eat sausages and cheese from paper on the overturned crates behind the counter. Around the corner was the big old farmers' market, and so the traffic was rather heavy, and Mom was afraid I might run into the street while she was serving her customers.

There was a woman named Rose who lived in a house close to the store, and my mother asked her to mind me in the store. Sometimes I'd escape, and if she found me on the street, Rose would come close and let out a terrible scream. All the kids were scared of her, and so was I, until I heard my mother telling someone Rose's story, how she had been a very handsome girl before the war, and then the Germans came, and she fell in love with one of them, a young officer, and when the partisans came he was killed and she was jailed, and beaten, and tortured. Those horrible screams that froze the blood in our veins–those were her jail screams, my mother said. After that I was never afraid of Rose, and I would always go back inside when I saw her, to save her another scream.

When there were no customers in the store, usually around noon, I liked to spend my time just staring at the great old building of the gymnasium across the street. It looked stern and imposing, but it was a high school, and I already loved schools. Then we would hear the loud bell from inside the building, and Mom would give me a sign to step back. Hordes of hungry students would run across the street, screaming and pushing one another, and the store would echo with their laughter. They all looked so beautiful to me. Sometimes their professors would come too, older, very dignified people. In gymnasium the teachers had the title of professor. Their students would step aside, my mother would treat the professors very nicely, and she would melt down when they called her by her name. Watching all this during the few weeks I spent there, I decided that someday I wanted to enroll in gymnasium.

Several years later, there I was again, in the same street, before the same building. With my high marks from elementary school I could go to any high school I wanted, and I chose to fulfill my childhood dream. After returning from Paris I found a book on the history of Kragujevac and learned that the First Gymnasium of Kragujevac (its full name) was founded in 1833 as a lyceum. This German type of school, which prepared students for higher education, was a very reputable institution, with a long tradition of excellent professors. It was the same school where some of the Serbian generals who defeated the Austro-Hungarian army in World War I had studied.

I felt as though I was enrolled into faculty already.

JAMBOREE FOR TITO

My new body didn't improve my clumsiness. On the contrary. I was happy during our first few months in high school because the new gym was still being built and we had to play soccer in the backyard most of the time during our athletic classes. Since I proved to be awful with a ball, but had to be included in the game (athletic classes, called physcult, for "physical culture," were required and frequent in both primary and secondary school), our professor put me on goal. Surprisingly, I turned out to be good as a goalie, mostly the result of my fear of the flying ball. Every time someone would come near with the ball I would charge him, if only to stop the player from shooting at me.

The gym was finished by the second semester, so my happy days were over. I couldn't climb the rope, but would get stuck, hanging helplessly, halfway up. I once tried to pass the ball to my teammate during a basketball match, and threw so clumsily I scored from the center. Although I claimed it was intentional, the game was paused for five minutes until everyone stopped laughing. They put me on the beam, and the professor had three spotters below me just in case, but I fell on one of them, almost breaking his leg. Jumping the horse, I missed the whole thing, made a loop and ended on my right thumb, popping a bone in my hand so high that nobody was able to fix it, ever. My professors of physcult even stopped giving me marks. At the beginning of the year, they would write down one ace and keep it for the whole year. My father would come to beg them at the end of the first semester, and then my homeroom professor at the end of the school year, and they would change it to 5, since all my other final marks would be 5s, and they didn't want to ruin my average.

One day, instead of warming us up, our physcult professor told us to line up for a guest to inspect us. The small white-haired old man started checking us one by one, going slowly down our line like a general on parade. He would stop in front of each of us, take a close look at our bodies, make us do several moves that looked like yoga, and then tell us either to get back in line or to step out to the other side. When it was my turn, he told me to join the group of selected.

"Not him," said my professor, "he's hopeless."

"Nobody is hopeless!" snapped the old man, and my professor shut up.

When he was finished, he took us aside, leaving the rest of the class to prepare for jumping the horse. I suddenly loved the old man. Gathering us around him, he smiled and said, "I am Mr. Berak. You know how every year at the city stadium we have our large celebration of comrade Tito's birthday, our Day of Youth? I am the man who does the choreography and who commands the whole operation in our city. Those of you who decide to work with me must listen to me and obey strictly. You will be excused from school for six weeks, and your only obligation will be to come every day to the stadium and practice with me. I know that missing classes sounds good, but we shall work very hard for six hours every day, rain or shine. If you are ready for it, I will take your names and give instructions to your professors, and we start tomorrow."

My parents couldn't believe my story. Then I showed them the official letter.

"They must be desperate," said my father.

The next morning at eight a few hundred high-school students gathered on the side field of the city stadium. Berak was already there when I arrived. He had a megaphone, a stopwatch around his neck and a notebook with a list of our names. After he and his assistants made sure everyone was present, he told us that our crowd was only part of the whole ceremony, that the soldiers were preparing their own choreography, likewise young workers and local nurses. He said some three thousand people would take part, that it was a great honor to be selected for this and that he was counting on us. He also explained that his choreography had sixteen parts, we would start learning it right away and that we shouldn't be fooled by his mild appearance–anyone who was late, disobeyed or fooled around would be sent back to school with a note demanding a bad mark in behavior. A sigh passed through the crowd. It was the general threat above our heads. Once you got a bad mark in behavior, that was that–you were marked as a problem child.

We started learning his moves. They were easy, little more than a mild warm-up, and he gave us a break every forty-five minutes, like in school. The first three hours went relatively well, with everyone trying hard, but then the boredom set in, we started fooling around and Berak began showing his stern face. He started barking into his megaphone more often, and then, after another hour of our misbehaving, he sent two people back to school. This settled us down and we held our concentration for another two hours, after which he dismissed us for the day.

For the next three days we repeated this in the same order: we would start well, slowly lose our focus, and he would send a few people home. But on the morning of the fifth day, someone spread the rumor that those who went back to school didn't get a bad mark in behavior–nothing happened to them at all. One professor was even rumored to have said, "Good that you're back at school and not wasting your time at the stadium." Berak started popping pills, and soon gave his megaphone to one of his assistants and went to sit in the shade. At the end of the day, he reminded us that we should come back on Saturday for further practice on the main field, and on Sunday we would be on the side field, since the local soccer club was playing at home. No one had known we would be practicing on weekends.

Although that Sunday we were quickly sent home, because the soccer fans started whistling and catcalling after the girls, I knew I'd made a major mistake by coming here. I missed school and my classmates, and all around me were mostly jocks. I didn't have any problems repeating Berak's choreography, but I felt stupid. So I decided to ask him on Monday to relieve me.

The next day Berak listened to my excuse, and then sent me back to practice. To sweeten things up, he sent me that afternoon to the dais to be a DJ. We started working with the music selected for the jamboree, some revolutionary song modernized and recorded with a rock band. Watching from above, the picture we were expected to produce–youth in their full strength and grace, in large numbers, acting as one–was nowhere to be seen. I decided there was no way I was going to be there in the end. I had to find a way to be sent back to school.

I started sabotaging from the dais. Whenever Berak would call a break, I would play some rock record and crank up the volume. It was great. They installed enormous loudspeakers and people down on the field felt like they were at a rock concert. After the break I would play the revolutionary song again, turning the volume way down. It worked. Morale dropped, and they felt the whole thing even more of a senseless bore.

Berak was standing below and in front of me, and he did all the moves with the crowd, to lead those who couldn't remember his choreography, and–since he couldn't see me–I started repeating after him, but introducing other moves here and there. Accustomed to taking anyone on the podium as a model, the gymnasts on the field started mimicking me, driving the old man crazy. He stopped the whole thing, gave an angry speech and then dismissed us all for that day.

I continued my little game the next day, but knew I was caught when Berak's assistant came up behind me and pulled my ear. I was demoted to the field again and the assistant took the DJ booth. When practice was over, Berak told me angrily not to come back the next day. Finally!

The next morning I was back at school, but instead of feeling good I felt isolated. My classmates had advanced with their lessons, and I had to work hard to catch up. If I'd stayed with Berak, I would have been excused and my professors could not test me on certain parts of the curriculum, but now that the whole deal was off I was exposed.

That evening I was sitting in my room in a very foul mood reading from some borrowed textbooks. The telephone rang, and when I answered, it was Berak on the other end.

"How are you?" he said. His tone was flat. Well, maybe a trace of fatherly warmth.

"Perfect," I said.

"Any problems at school?"

"You mean with the professors? No."

"Listen, the reason I'm calling is–I think you should come back tomorrow. I was a little frustrated yesterday, but you shouldn't be excluded."

"I don't feel good there, sir. They told you I was hopeless. I am. I'm clumsy. My dad has to ask for better marks from every physcult professor I ever get."

"Your father is exactly the reason I want you back. Did you tell him you're working with me?"

"No. He wouldn't know–"

"He *would* know me. I was his professor in military school. Ask him. He was excellent, one of the best students I had. That's partly the reason why he was sent to Tito's guard. You are his son. Maybe you are better in learning than in sports, but you can't be hopeless. Nobody has ever given you a chance. But that's not all. You are too young to understand, but there is a certain pride with fathers whose sons excel in something they do. I'm sure he would want you to be good in this."

"Did you know who my father was before–?"

"Before I selected you at school? Of course. I know the history of each one of my participants. There's more: you understand that politics affects our lives, and very much so. This thing we are doing is very important in that sense. If you don't come back, I won't do a thing against you, but your professors will suspect something was wrong, and that might affect your future. Then, of course, it might not. In the end, it's entirely up to you. I just called to tell you all this. I know you are a smart boy–you decide."

I was at the stadium again the next morning. But now I was serious about it. I wanted to do it for my dad–the men of our house shall all be Tito's guardians. I practiced at home in the evenings, repeating in my head Berak's rhythmical instructions: "One-two-arm-left, three-four-look-straight, one-two-touch-sky . . ."

A few weeks later, we were on. It was a glorious sunny day, the stadium was full, the speakers blaring partisan songs, the instruments of the military brass band polished beyond a mirror shine. The preschool kids opened the spectacle, then the primary schools performed, and then it was our turn. Each group was better then the previous one, building towards the great finale, which always belonged to the soldiers. So, we were great, the university students were better, the nurses got a warm welcome, the young workers got standing ovations, and the guys in uniforms, with brand-new rifles, brought tears to the eyes of the spectators.

When I met my parents afterwards, they were shining with pride. We took a long, slow stroll through the park surrounding the stadium, then through the quiet back streets leading home.

"Dad," I said when we were entering our street, "did you know that your old professor Berak was behind all this?"

"Who's Berak?" he said. "I never had a professor by that name."

THE POET COMES BACK FROM THE MARKET

The four of us lived in the same area of Kragujevac. Coming home from school, we would drag our feet forever, nibbling the best part of the day when all fears would be left behind, and a good hot mother-made meal would wait at home. The stories of the school day would be told again, each of us adding some new twist until events reached mythical proportions. We would sharpen our teeth against the professors' suits, their greasy hair and manners of speech; we would admire a few of them; we would comment on the newly grown breasts of some of our girlfriends and gossip about someone who'd fallen hopelessly in love. We were classifying our world, separating it into small drawers of memories, chunks always sweetened with some humor.

One day, we'd had a written test in Serbo-Croatian, the last one for the school year. It was an important test, since it would heavily influence our final marks. I'd found a very interesting approach to the topic given for the exam, so I felt pretty good, and I must have been getting on my friends' nerves. They started asking me if it was true that I wrote poetry, which I reluctantly confirmed. A few weeks before, I'd submitted a poem to a local competition, and it won first prize and was about to be published.

"So, how exactly do you write poems?" Bora asked. "Do you need to soak your feet in a basin, like Balzac did, or do you just stare through the window and the verses come?"

"Yeah, and do you suck your pencil while you're at it, and does it make it sharper?" Ratko added. They roared with laughter.

"It's not like that. I usually wait for my Muse to come naked, and then I'm inspired," I tried to joke, hoping that humor would save me.

"I wonder how they pay poets," Mile chimed in. "By the word or by the metaphor? Or do they just count the rhymes? Come to think of it, whatever they choose, you would have to write another *Odyssey* to get rich."

"Yeah, but Homer was blind, and so was Filip Višnjić, and you have good eyesight. You will never be a good poet," Ratko said.

"Here, take this, it will help," Mile said, offering me his pair of compasses. "Make yourself blind, secure your future."

I felt angry and apologetic at the same time. How do you respond when someone is accusing you of something that you love about yourself?

We were passing by the small farmers' market close to the end of our long street, and I suddenly remembered someone from the past: the poet selling his books in our school. I remembered how disappointed I had been to see him with vegetables in his hands, coming back perhaps from this same market. And I realized then that he wasn't afraid to be what he was. His poems were not good enough for the publishing industry, but he believed in them enough to print them on his own. His investment in his books could have ruined him. Standing and reading before the cruelest possible audience–children. He had something to say, and he would say it no matter what.

So I smiled at all their jokes, and said good-bye at the end of the street. But the next day, and the day after, and the day after, and all the days after, I joined other classmates on the way home.

I had something to say. They didn't want to listen. Maybe it was their loss, maybe mine.

OLD WOMAN IN BLACK WHO WALKS AROUND MIDNIGHT

Make and Barni were my new company on the way home and we mostly talked about literature. All three of us read everything we could lay our hands on, and we had already started shaping our taste in books. Make fell for beautiful sentences, for writers whose works offered many quotes. I was devouring Herman Hesse (whose work, only a year later, I would find kitschy and boring); Barni, for some reason, liked mysticism. It was from him we first heard about Alistair Crawley, about black magic, white magic, Zen, Eastern religions and meditation. Make was learning karate and was interested in various concentration techniques, while I was fascinated with Barni's stories, which were full of admiration for Crawley and other mages, and helped me to understand better Led Zeppelin and Black Sabbath.

I found a book in the local bookstore that gave me the basics of transcendental meditation, and soon I started experimenting at home, developing my own techniques, with strange results. I once spent a sleepless night preparing for an important math test; in the morning I did the test quickly, but then I spent another half hour–during the test–with a vision: a mountaintop high above the clouds, a maiden in a long black veil standing on the very edge of an immensely deep abyss, silent wind waving her robes, and her arms extended towards the rising sun. It was beautiful and somewhat scary, and it was before Led Zeppelin released "Stairway to Heaven." Violeta, my bench mate, told me later that she didn't notice anything strange–my eyes were open all the time, and I even answered her questions clearly. Only I couldn't remember her asking me anything. I continued to work on my concentration techniques, not telling anyone about it, not even Make or Barni.

At sixteen, I was able to explain how the laser beam was made, I knew a couple of theories about black holes, I knew in detail the path that sound traveled–from an instrument, to a microphone, to the record groove, to our brain–but I knew almost nothing about people. Those who can't read from eyes, from hand gestures, from body language have to find their own maps, otherwise they are lost. Mysticism became my private cartography, and soon I was using my own techniques to consult my nameless mystical allies about my future. At first I was delighted by how well it all worked, but then I just did it, and stopped thinking about it. I believed that none of it was supernatural, that it was only the awakening of some long-asleep areas of my brain. I soon stopped paying attention to the magic in my life. I knew things were happening, but I was sure they happened to everyone who tried them. There was no reason to consider myself a mystic. And I was learning so many interesting things in other fields that the small miracles became just part of the larger input of general marvels.

At the beginning of our second year in gymnasium, they put me on the same bench as Spomenka. She was a very smart girl, with a disarming smile, natural blonde hair and a great sense of humor. We became good friends almost instantly and I soon started to confide in her, how I longed for that girl, how I disliked that guy, about my hopes and fears, everything.

After two months of this I suddenly realized I was in love with her, but it was too late to tell her, since she'd already started dating another student from our school. I knew Moša through mutual friends. A big guy, he was a wrestler, already representing Yugoslavia in international competitions. He laughed a lot and always had a joke up his sleeve. I already knew that if you made a girl laugh, she was yours, and there was no way she didn't laugh a lot with him.

But something odd happened with Spomenka and me a few days before the big national holiday in November.

We were on the long afternoon break. The dusk was already setting in, and nobody had remembered to turn on the lights, so no one noticed Spomenka standing in the corner by the window all by herself. I was fooling around with some other people and I saw her when I went back to our bench. By the distant light of a street lamp I saw that she was crying. I went to her and she suddenly threw her arms around me, sobbing uncontrollably, and said, "I am afraid. I am so afraid. Please help me."

"What happened? What are you afraid of?" I felt that something strange was going on, something beyond explanation.

"I don't know. I just started having this fear a few days ago, and it grips me hard, and I don't know what it is. I see things, some strange images, and I'm afraid of them."

The hair on the back of my neck went up. I held her tight. She was my love, and I had to protect her.

"Did you tell your parents about it?"

"No. What's there to tell them? They will laugh at me. You know how everyone treats me like a baby."

By that time a few girls had noticed what was going on and surrounded us. Spomenka wiped her tears and told them everything was fine, she had just remembered something sad. Then the professor came in, switched the lights on, and we forgot about it.

A week later, after the holiday, Spomenka didn't come to school. Her cousin Ivan told us she was in the hospital. Our professor, Djordje, deepened my worries later that day, because his face was somber when he said that over the long weekend she had fainted at home and was put into the intensive care unit.

It was the beginning of December and it was very cold. I was sitting alone at our bench, staring through the window at the dirty market across the street and feeling that everything was wrong. And final.

The next day my fear worsened: our professors suddenly became unusually kind, patient and nice, especially those who weren't like that normally. I knew that something bad was coming our way. The children of communism learn to recognize the trading of emotions: you get goodness when it's bad, they treat you badly when it's good, so everything must stay average, leveled, under control. Like with religion, only obligatory. Like heaven and hell, only by decree. And that final decree, I felt, was already written. Every class, each forty-five minutes was a period of waiting for the principal to enter and say whatever had to be said.

It was only a week later, although it felt like a month, and the first snow had already fallen. I worked that night until nearly midnight, all torn apart, then got ready for bed, turned the lights off and went to the window to raise the shades. The whiteness made everything bluish outside. I could see the cemetery between the buildings on the other side of the street. The sky was clear and the night was exceptionally silent. The stars glistening in the eastern sky before me, and little flames flickered in the lanterns on the graves.

I stood still, my forehead against the glass, and I suddenly felt the need to hear something about Spomenka, something more than the vague sentences our professors squeezed out when we asked. I focused on one of the tiny flames and started one of my techniques, narrowing my thoughts until there were only two words in my mind: *Spomenka* and *return*.

In the caves of our mind are thousands of bats we are not aware of. When we start narrowing our mind, the ceiling slowly becomes flat, and those bats have nothing to hold on to anymore. They start fighting, fly around panicking, but they have to get out. When they are all out and the pressure in our mind's cave levels, then, eventually, comes an answer.

The petty, everyday things were the first to fly out: the movies I had watched recently, the books I'd read. Small quarrels. Warm feelings. Secrets learned by accident. Then, one by one, the larger animals went out: my secret love for her, belated, unwanted, in vain, never whispered. My wish for everything to be good fluttered around my mind; it didn't want to leave. The flat ceiling was full of dancing shadows, illusions of safety, but I had to let it all go if I wanted the answer. Finally, my mind was empty.

And then it happened. Very slowly, without any sound in the night, around the corner of the building on the left came an old woman in black. Her steps were insecure and shaky, probably because of ice, if the Old Women in Black Who Walk around Midnight have any problems with ice. I froze. When she was halfway between the buildings, a dark shadow of a bird came low above her head and then flew away. The last thing I remember was a sudden wind that extinguished several little flames in the cemetery, including the brightest one, the one I'd used to focus. The old woman disappeared behind the building on the right.

(I know I wasn't dreaming, nor have the years that passed added to the story, because three nights later I wrote everything down in my diary, and because my recollection of that night is fresh and clear, the way one remembers only one's desires and horrors.)

Maybe it was an answer to someone else, someone standing at some other window, asking a different question. Maybe it was only a blue solo in the long jazz of our lives, but it sounded like a finale to me. I asked for an answer, I got something that was ominous, and yet I accepted it. Was I partially guilty for what came afterwards? Are we all guilty for the deaths of our beloved ones? Is there any way to fold our hands around the little flames of life in the wind and protect them from extinguishing?

Spomenka died five days later of galloping leukemia.

Moša died twenty years later.

JOINING THE PARTY

Several months after Spomenka's death, Professor Djordje came into the classroom during the break and started asking three of us about our backgrounds. He wanted to know our parents' jobs, if they were Party members and for how long they had been–if they were–Communists, how we felt about them being with the Party, and similarly strange things. The three of us, Miša, Goca and I, were the best students in the class. After he finished with the questioning, he told us to reserve time in our calendars for a special meeting of the school's Party cell two weeks later.

"You three will be proposed to become members of the Communist League of Yugoslavia, and on that evening we, your professors, will decide on your eventual acceptance. But even the candidacy is a great honor, so, congratulations!"

Our classmates could hardly wait for Djordje to leave the class.

"This is serious, man. You're going to start deciding on the future of us all. Don't screw up."

"Sir, can I have a bigger apartment? My parents are happy with what we have, but I would like to install a ping pong table, and there's no room."

"I suggest you start wearing that red miniskirt to Party meetings," somebody said to Goca. "They'll vote you the secretary of the cell."

"Yeah, and then you can expel all our professors from the Party, and we're free."

Until that day I had never even given it a thought. My parents being Communists–that somehow seemed a normal thing for grownups. Weren't they all? But I wasn't ready to become one of them. My childhood had just ended, and with the new penis, new body and so on, I wanted to spend at least some time as a youth. Was this an official entry into the world of grownups? It was a disturbing thought, so I gathered my parents for a talk that evening.

"How long have you been in the Communist Party?"

"Oh, I don't know," said my mother, looking at my father, "sixteen or seventeen years, I guess."

"Why did you become members?"

"Why are you asking such things?" Ana stood up to close the window, but then remembered we now lived on the third floor and sat down again. "You didn't do something stupid, did you?"

"No, no, I'll tell you later, it's all good. But what does it mean to become a Party member? Is it good? Does it change anything?"

"It's really nothing, son," said my father. "You just start going to meetings and you have to pay your membership dues to listen to them playing smart, that's all."

"Don't talk like that," Ana interrupted. "If it wasn't for the Party we wouldn't have got our first apartment."

"Big deal," said Dušan. "They give everyone a place to live after a while."

"But God knows how long we would have had to wait for it," she said.

"What are the meetings like? Do you have to decide on anything?"

"Yes," said Ana, "you have all sorts of things to vote for."

"But they prepare it all for you. You just have to listen to them and then raise your hand," added Dušan.

"Can I see your membership cards?"

Ana became truly alarmed now. "Seriously, why are you asking?"

"They are taking him in," said Dušan with a jokester's smile.

"How did you know?" I asked.

"So I'm right? Congratulations, son!" Father extended his hand. "I heard from a friend at work. His son is your age, only he attends the technical school. They made him a candidate last week, and I was asking myself, why not you? You are the best in your class."

Ana was glowing with pride. "His mother's son!" Then she shed a tear. "Dušan, our child has grown up."

Two weeks later, Professor Djordje reminded us of the meeting that evening and advised us to dress properly. "No jeans," he said, "and no school uniforms. Dress nicely, but not too nicely. Somewhere in between. Comb your hair. No sneakers, either. You know, kids, like going to the theater."

"Can we come to watch the show, sir?" asked someone from the back.

"This is not a joke." Djordje could just pretend to be serious. This time he was seriously serious. "It's a great honor for them, but it's also a reward to your whole group, so respect it."

That evening, although it wasn't that cold, my mother made me put an Italian sweater on, the beautiful one she'd bought for me for my trip to France. I had to shine my shoes and wet my hair for the shiny look. I thought I looked like Hitler on his prom night, but she proudly sent me off.

Some of our professors smiled at us to encourage us, but I was nervous as hell. Djordje told us they would first debate whether we should be made members or not, and we had no clue how it would end. We all sat in the large professors' lounge, a place normally forbidden to us; if they sent you there, you could count on major trouble. The tables were arranged in a U shape, and there were three empty seats at the top. Then the principal and two senior professors walked in and took their positions.

The secretary opened the meeting. My palms were sweating. Everybody was silent and unsmiling. This was how I always imagined church, from the stories Nana told me. The secretary proposed the agenda, and I noticed that we came first, followed by something titled "Planning our next excursion" and "Resolving problems of substitutes on the afternoon shift." When he read our names, all the professors looked at us, and I felt that Doomsday had come.

Djordje read the document supporting our candidacy. It actually sounded very flattering, but he was on our side anyway, so the discussion after that was probably the catch.

It didn't comfort me that my parents said they couldn't remember anyone being proposed and not accepted. They didn't know these people.

Then the secretary asked whether someone had additional remarks that would throw more light on our case. One of our professors raised his hand and said a few kind words in our support. Jokingly, he warned me to try not to be late again in the morning, and everyone laughed. The secretary thanked him and asked for further comments. They decided to forever hold their peace, and the secretary called the vote. Everyone was in favor of us becoming members. "Congratulations, children," said someone, smiling at us. "Congratulations, Djordje," said someone else to our smiling mentor. One by one, when our names were read, we stood up and went to receive our small red membership cards from the smiling principal.

Then they moved on to the second thing on the agenda. I couldn't make myself think of "us," the Party cell, although, technically, I was now part of it. When the vote on our next excursion was over (we also raised our hands after Djordje gave us a sign), the secretary turned to us and said, "You can leave now. We are about to discuss the things we started before you became members, so we think we should finish them without you. It would not be fair to bother you with it. Thank you, and congratulations again."

We stood there, the three of us, outside the door, smiling at one another and not really knowing what to do. Through the closed door, we could hear the secretary opening the discussion.

"Well, that's it, then," said Miša.

"I guess. Let me congratulate you, Goca," I said, and stole a kiss. She jokingly pushed me aside.

"Now, now, we're comrades here, we can't push one another like that," said I, and we all laughed quietly, since we were still right in front of the door. At that very moment, someone must have got very annoyed with the current speaker. We heard a wild yell, then another, then the voice of the secretary trying to calm them down, before all hell broke lose. The three of us looked at one another, and ran down the stairs.

LOOKING FOR A LOOKING GLASS

The Communists recognized early the potential poetry had for mobilizing masses. During the most difficult times in World War II, when the Croatian poets Vladimir Nazor and Ivan Goran Kovačić joined Tito's partisans, even Radio London reported it. After the war, poets held a special place in the country's cultural scene. The publishing industry regularly promoted new editions, and poetry competitions popped up like mushrooms even in villages. If Communists love anything, it is greatness in numbers, and encouraging people to write poetry paid off: one had the illusion that the whole nation just sang with love for communism.

In my second year of gymnasium I wrote a rather long love poem ("Then I Know What's with Me Tonight") that was published in the school yearbook. It promoted me as a poet. I soon learned that my classmate Miša was reciting poetry in local and regional competitions, almost always coming back with some award. I asked him where he had learned to recite poetry (he was good; his rendering of Poe's "Annabel Lee" never failed to drown the whole audience in tears), and he told me about the Home of Youth, where they had the Drama Studio. It was close to the gymnasium, but the building looked so gloomy I had never dared to even peek inside.

The Home of Youth was an attempt at democratizing the arts. In every town there was a building with this name and, although its purpose was never clearly defined, the general idea was to give space and means to youth to start dabbling in the arts.

Sometime later Miša asked me if I wanted to help with a production, and I went there for the first time. I was hoping they needed an actor, but it turned out they needed my old Geloso tape recorder (Trieste, 1964) for sound effects, and me to operate it. For the next couple of months, on weekends, while Miša and his partner, Slavica, acted in a dramatization of Dostoyevsky's *White Nights* on the small stage, I sat in the dark, claustrophobic space in the wings, pressing buttons.

But I started liking it there. The people hanging around were witty and intelligent and had the same interests I did. Seeing my enthusiasm, and learning that I could write and play guitar, the director of the institution started including me in everything they did.

In the meantime I continued to write poetry, and I was using the real ink now. My lemon days were long gone, as the gymnasium professors encouraged writing, and taught us how to express ourselves. A few more poems I sent to local competitions won minor prizes.

One day Professor Djordje, who taught us Serbo-Croatian language and literature and was our homeroom professor, kept me after his class.

"There is a new youth magazine just founded in town," he said. "They called me to recommend someone to write for them, and I thought you might want to give it a try. Go and talk to them," he said and gave me their number. I felt a bit intimidated. It was one thing to write good papers in school, but something different to publish in a magazine. A week later I gathered my courage and went to see the editor-in-chief. It was painless, actually. He told me the magazine was called *Youth* and it was meant to be an insert of

Omladinske novine–a bigger, important magazine published in Belgrade by the Socialist Youth of Serbia. Our insert was to be published twice a month, and would be dedicated to news and stories from Kragujevac and surrounding cities in central Serbia.

I was seventeen when my first article was published, and it caused two things:

I read it several times, and discovered that its meaning had slightly changed. Nobody but me had touched it, but the article now had a coat of officialdom that came from appearing in print. A couple of lines of private jokes suddenly sounded cheap and silly. That was my first and most important lesson about the public word.

The second thing happened three weeks later when I got paid for the article: the money was sufficient to go and buy a brand-new typewriter. It was a portable Olympia, in a neat black suitcase on which I immediately placed a sticker with an image of a dragon. That's how I wanted to write–with fire. While my parents didn't pay much attention to my first publication, they were stunned at my typewriter. Nobody earned any money at my age, especially not enough to buy their own equipment. Very few homes at that time had a typewriter. To my parents, such a machine was a tool of bureaucracy, and bureaucracy meant power, long gray corridors of uniform offices where arrogant people worked on making your life hell. Additional proof to them that I'd acquired some of this power was that the magazine offices were in the same building as the seat of the local Party Committee.

Sitting on my desk, the small Olympia simply asked for new works. After I had retyped my selected poems and stories, I started working on new material. The feeling of reading one's writing in print pulled me like a drug, and I became hooked on our editorial work, publishing something in every issue, and sitting long hours at the office every other weekend.

Why did I do all those things?

The tenants of the building where we lived were mainly working-class people, like my parents, with interests and lifestyles mirroring one another. In front of every door were arranged old shoes with broken heels that served as slippers, and old, banged pots with patches of rust where the enamel had fallen off, with geraniums growing in them, spreading their bitter smell. On weekends, women would cook for the whole week, and slow, steady streams of smells would come from under every door and intertwine on the stairs, making them slippery with fat, turning the whole building into a cauldron of greasy food. On Sundays, the husbands would turn on their radios to listen to *Sunday Afternoon,* a popular live broadcast of the Yugoslav soccer league, and they liked their sports loud. You didn't need a radio to know who scored and when: every door, every window and every wall leaked the inescapable yelling of the sports commentators. The occasional screams of their listeners marked every goal. With the radio blaring, the families would gather around the table to have their Sunday lunch, and the smell of sour cabbage and cooked bacon would envelop my world.

There was nothing in it for me and my friends from the Home of Youth. Our parents were mostly the first generation to leave their villages and migrate to towns, where they acquired a basic education and a factory job. Most of them had more than they ever dreamt of, and certainly much more than they'd have had if they'd stayed in their home villages, where every foot of land, every sheep, every cow was as important as they were. Their search was over. But what they found meant almost nothing to us.

I was much more interested in obtaining the new Hendrix album, or in the latest concept Pink Floyd was promoting, or in finding the first print of Neil Young's *Harvest* than in the results of the Sunday soccer games. I already had five hundred albums and a few hundred singles and I spent every free moment learning English so I could understand all those songs that were talking to me. My friends and I debated at length Hesse's "Das Glasperlenspiel" and–although we never came to a universally accepted conclusion whether it was about Tibetan monks or just about people with too much free time–we felt there was more in that search for meaning than we ever got from the media glorifying communist achievements.

And so, on weekends, while our parents enjoyed their strictly controlled freedom, my friends and I would run away to our oases, to the places where everyone spoke the same language. We needed our own mirrors, because those our parents used didn't reflect our world.

OUR FORBIDDEN LOVE

At the end of every school year our professors would select the Student of the Generation from among the graduates. Although we knew about it, and the professors tried to create a certain aura around this title, we never paid much attention. The chosen one would receive a bunch of books, or a watch, his name and picture would get a prominent place in the yearbook, but that was all: no advantages when enrolling at university, no mention in the local media and definitely no improvement in one's love life. This last part was the very reason why we never cared. The title made its bearer sound nerdy, except one year when a gorgeous girl got it. When she returned several months later to give a speech at some celebration, half of the students gathered in front of the building to watch her

long legs in a miniskirt unfold from the red convertible her new Belgrade boyfriend drove. But that was one exception that didn't make a difference.

It became clear in our final year that the title was to be decided between one other guy and me. We both had top marks all through school, and we both were engaged in extracurricular activities. He played piano and attended music school after hours, while I worked for the local youth magazine and published poetry. While he looked like the prototype of a nerd–greasy hair, huge glasses and teeny build–I was funny for different reasons, with untidy hair, a shadow of a first mustache and long sideburns. Looking like this, neither of us had a girlfriend, and we were still virgins–I recognized the same despair in him. His nickname was Era, and I liked the guy, although we never hung out together. He seemed to like me, too, but our love was forbidden: there were Montagues and Capulets all around us–our ambitious professors.

The first semester was fairly quiet, but passions went wild after the winter break. It started with one of Era's professors substituting briefly for one of ours who had fallen ill. The first thing he did when he entered our class was to bring me before the blackboard and start questioning me, driving through the whole year's material. As this was highly unusual, I wasn't ready, but I fought well, and he lowered my mark only slightly in the end. Then my professors heard about it, and–as one of them happened to substitute in Era's class–revenge was swift.

Two weeks later, a recital was to be held at the school, and Era's homeroom professor insisted that Era play a piano concerto. Although it was the time of year when we were going through some important tests, Era had to practice hard for this recital. He played great and, when he took a bow, the whole hall erupted in applause. But some of my professors clenched their jaws and didn't applaud at all. Naturally, to the upcoming festival of young poets only one student was sent–me. I spent four days in some forgotten small town in the north of Serbia, trying in vain to get laid, but the watery-eyed poetess I'd chosen showed no mercy. When I returned, I had to stay up studying for a few nights just to catch up with my classmates.

In the meantime my professors took great pains to stay healthy, and so did Era's. Even those who were considered sworn enemies of fruit and healthy food were seen chewing lemons and oranges during our classes. Barricades were up and all breaches closed.

The students eventually realized they could profit from the situation, and someone from Era's shift stole a bunch of books from my bag during the football game. Some of my friends immediately offered to ambush Era after school and beat him to a pulp. I stopped the whole thing at the offer stage.

In March, the stakes rose with a countrywide competition in math. A few students were selected to represent our school, and, needless to say, both Era and I were on the team. This competition started at the city level, extended to the region, then to each republic, and, finally, in May, there would be the grand Yugoslav finale in Belgrade, where only the twenty best would compete. The books my professors gave me to practice with were absolutely incomprehensible, probably written for postgraduate students. I could at times grasp tiny bits of information, enough to see they were based on something we had indeed learned, but also that there were whole long bridges missing that might have taken me to the place where I could understand it all. Soon I was suffering from feelings of inadequacy, incompetence and general depression, and I was certain that I would fail miserably.

The city level went well, as the questions were easy. The regional level was more difficult, but again, didn't cover anything we hadn't learned. The republic level, at the end of April, was suddenly very hard, as we left the school material and entered the area of abstract thinking. Nevertheless, both Era and I qualified. My professors, excited beyond recognition, gave me a free week to prepare and supplied me with more books. There wasn't a single sentence I could understand. They were definitely written in Serbo-Croatian, but beyond that . . . Of course, when the professors asked about my progress I would assure them I was fine, but–after the encounter with the problems at the previous level of the competition, and knowing that we would be going against the students of the specialized math gymnasium in Belgrade, among other schools–I had no doubt about the outcome. I only hoped my professors would never get to see our tests.

The big day came, and the special early-morning bus took us both to Belgrade. Our professors went with us, so silent and so pale I thought the hypervitaminosis had finally got them. The finale was held at the Faculty of Mathematics, which only increased the pressure. The long corridors and the frightening amphitheater reminded me of a courtroom where I'd come to meet the Inquisition. They gave us a short speech, three hours to find solutions, and sealed envelopes with the problems inside. I opened mine and quickly read the questions. Warm relief flowed in my veins: the problems were incredibly difficult, as in my worst nightmares, but no equations had to be written, and almost no mathematical operations needed to be done; everything required abstract thinking, just like in those books I had been given. I had no chance with this test. My feeling of relief came from knowing I couldn't make stupid factual mistakes–only noble intellectual ones, and these are always easier to defend.

And so I was able to relax. The first problem involved some playing with prime numbers, and I left it for the end. The second started with a long description of a lonely house by a river (which flowed at a certain speed), exposed to the winds from all four sides of the world (blowing at certain speeds, each side differently) and having occasional visitors (arriving at a certain frequency and always in a boat, paddling against the stream). The owner of the house, this lonesome person, wanted to throw a party and invited many friends, from near and far. However, on the evening of the event, a strong storm caught the whole area. The winds increased significantly, not to mention the waves on the river; there were fields of low pressure, inflation in Singapore and a fluctuating exchange rate in Zimbabwe, an escalating arms race and movement of Russian troops on the border with China, one boat broke apart, three female guests got their periods early under the stress and one of the men invited was a spy. The question was, with the menu full of perishable items, would there be enough food for everyone?

The third and last problem described a rubber band stretched around an apple and our being able to push the rubber band slowly around the apple until we shrank the band down to a point. Then the same rubber band was stretched again, this time around a doughnut. Can we do the same trick with the band? If yes, how, and if not, why?

After reading the page through, I turned around to see what the others were doing. I was in the front row, and Era was way back; he waved merrily at me. He had a few apples on his desk, and was chewing one of them. I tried to see if there was a rubber band around it, but I couldn't. Some of the competitors were, like me, still reading the problems, but some were already writing feverishly. These ones all looked like hyper-geeks, probably the math gymnasium students.

I spent the next three hours in a strange mathematical fever, imagining the color of the doomed house, the guests finally arriving in prime numbers, choking on apples from which they hadn't removed the rubber bands.

After it was over, our little team gathered in front of the building. It was a gorgeous sunny day and the amphitheater had been as dark as a cave–we could hardly see. Era and I described the problems given to us, and it turned out we had different questions. My third question made our professors stare in disbelief. "They gave you the Poincaré conjecture? Poor kid!" said one of the women, and hugged me. There were tears in her eyes. Era's second question caused a similar reaction: "The Abelian variety and Hilbert's problem? Murderers!"

The results came back in two weeks. All three leading positions were taken by the math gymnasium guys, and the rest of the list simply didn't exist. But the story about our questions spread among the professors, and Era and I were finally left alone, as if we had been exposed to dangerous radiation and now needed time to rest.

END

One day we just finished school. It was so anticlimactic. Era was named Student of the Generation.

SLIPPING AWAY

My father's health deteriorated while I was in the fourth year of high school. It was mysterious. He complained of dizziness, but only sometimes, and no other symptoms appeared, at least none he was aware of. On some days he would feel quite okay, but on others he would be so dizzy he couldn't get out of bed. He would try to sit and then immediately fall to the side. The doctors in Kragujevac, with all the tests coming back negative, kept pronouncing him healthy, and then one of them called him a malingerer–in communist Yugoslavia the mother of all shames. I started getting frustrated: at eighteen the girls are soft and the promise hard, and the last thing you need is a sickness in the family. I thought it was psychological, and hoped it would go away.

Then again, this thing with Dušan *was* troubling: he had always been in perfect health, never avoided heavy work, never even had a cold. The doctors terminated his sick leave several times, forcing him back to work, and he would indeed go, only to fall at some point in Zastava and be brought home by ambulance. And it kept dragging on like that. He became desperate, crying sometimes and asking us to believe him. We did, of course, and I even started thinking of studying medicine.

When high school ended I wasn't sure what to study anymore. Kragujevac had no medical faculty, so I would have to go to Belgrade. The other faculty that was an option–literature–was also there. Mom was desperate to keep me at home, and to sweeten things up she told me I would drive Dad to doctors, which meant that I would inherit our car. So, at some point, I decided to stay. The majority of my generation was staying in Kragujevac; there was plenty to explore in the arts with my music and theater and writing, and when I thought about everything my decision seemed logical. That left two options–the Faculty of Economy or the Faculty of Law–and so the choice was not that difficult anymore. I'd always thought it was better to study the history of constitutions, Roman law, criminal law and other similar things than to get deep into the theory of capital and fortune making.

My classmates Olivera and Gaga enrolled with me, and we became inseparable. I would drive with them to classes, and–when we discovered nobody was checking attendance–sometimes on sunny autumn days we'd just pass by the faculty building and drive north to the hotel in the heart of Šumarice to have coffee and enjoy the Indian summer. Very quickly we realized how lucky we were to have attended the gymnasium and how high had been the caliber of our old professors. Classes in the Faculty of Law were stultifyingly boring, and strictly adhered to what was printed in our textbooks. I was able to follow some professors' lectures word for word, line by line in the textbooks they wrote and sold–every comma in its place. There was no need to attend those classes.

Some other professors behaved oddly. There was a fat bald guy in his early fifties who didn't even try to hide that he expected sexual services from his female students. In front of a room of two hundred students, he commented on the long legs and exquisite bosoms of some of our colleagues, and invited some of them to drop by his office after class. The whole place looked more like a factory for manufacturing lawyers than a dignified institution. Luckily, I'd also applied to the Faculty of Journalism, in Belgrade, as a part-time student (I didn't need to travel, except for the exams), and was accepted, so I thought I'd just put emphasis on my studies in journalism and try to cope somehow with law. And it was reflected in my results: in December I had the first oral exams in both. I passed the journalism exam with top marks, and failed miserably in the law.

That same autumn I met with the editors of the local radio station. Realizing there was no show for students, I proposed one and got my slot. I named the show *10,* as it was the highest mark in the faculties, and my written proposal included all the regular stuff so popular at that time on Yugoslav radio: interviews with the best activists and the best students, and promoting volunteer work and extracurricular activities. I did this since there was no way I would get a show otherwise, but my real plan was to slowly shift towards something more attractive, less politicized and longer than the original half hour. The local radio was quite rigid at the time. All the male voices were deep, all the female voices friendly (but not sexy–they had to personify a comrade, not a sex symbol), the music was mostly five years old (only the stuff that had stood the test of time), and the jingles sounded like advertisements for the Party congress. I started by creating some nonsensical jingles for my show, bringing in my own music and making my interviews relaxed.

The show quickly gathered steam, and more and more people started calling the station during my half hour. One day, I did an interview with a young actress that was rather informal–we knew each other. It went well for the first couple of minutes, then there was a music break, and when we returned to air, I said, "There are two pairs of legs under the table in our studio. One is long and beautiful, belongs to Branka and will take her far, and the other is short and mine." The producer, well trained in matters of self-censorship, made a face on the other side of the glass, but I didn't pay attention. It wasn't a declaration to be proud of, but it also wasn't something that would cause Party hard-liners to squint. My show was canceled the very next day.

My colleagues from *Youth* gave me space for an open letter to the radio producers. I reminded the station of how successful my show had become in only two and a half months, that I was trying to bring some freshness to the station and that it was harsh to cut the show like that.

To my surprise, they sent an answer, as stiff as their general style. My remarks about the legs were pornographic, they wrote, and they couldn't afford to have a show on their esteemed station that would promote errant Western ways. Enraged, I wrote the next installment of my polemic as a "fuck you, who cares" good-bye.

That was my first clash with the system. I knew it was rigid, but I didn't expect it to crack down on even the slightest deviation. It was an ugly side I'd only heard of. I was bitter–I was hooked on radio now, and there was no other station in Kragujevac. And I was infuriated–excommunication in Communist countries is extremely dangerous for the subject. In our language there was a word invented after the Communists won: *zglajznuti,* slang for "slipping away." Very appropriate, I thought after this experience: it depicted a person skating on the thin ice of unwritten rules, and implied the quick social death from falling into the icy water beneath. The only thing that saved me was that I was still an editor with *Youth*. Otherwise my career would have ended right there, right then.

To make things even more absurd, at the same time someone had nominated me for secretary-general of the Party cell at the Faculty of Law, and I was voted into the position. I had absolutely no clue what to do with it, but after the clash with the radio station I couldn't afford to say no. The only good thing about it was that my deputy was gorgeous, so I tried working with her on a very close basis. When that didn't work out the way I'd hoped, I gave up the Party cell altogether. The Faculty of Law hadn't the slightest appeal for me. I just dragged my feet, passing exams without much interest, hoping the torture wouldn't last long.

LOVE FOUND IN TRACES

I wasn't going anymore to the Faculty of Law and, after being expelled from the radio, I suddenly had plenty of time. My guitar playing benefited from this. Now I was practicing classical music from textbooks for the first two years of music academy in Belgrade, and I felt I was ready for the next step. It was time to go in front of an audience.

While we both were hanging around in the Home of Youth, my friend Stole and I started playing together occasionally. He had studied with the best flute player in Yugoslavia, the old professor Azanjac, and so we both had an inclination towards classical music. One day he told me about this other guy, Mageda, who played guitar amazingly well. The three of us met, tried playing together, and it worked. Mageda and I had learned from the same literature and knew the same pieces written for classical guitar, with additional melodies provided by Stole. Soon I started bringing my own songs to our rehearsals. My two friends liked them, and we began performing our own music. Stole bought a saxophone and we decided to choose a good name and get serious about our band. I suggested the name *Trag* ("Trace"), simply because I already had a good logo to go with it–a red foot, containing the name in psychedelic lettering. I bought some sticky red plastic, cut three logos out of it, and we put them on our small cars. That was that.

We turned out to be an ideal band for Communist rituals. Classical music with a dash of jazz, acoustic instruments, musicians from good families (Stole and Mageda were children of professors, but my working-class background also fit well)–who could ask for more? People liked our name, too: being a new society, Communism was very interested in leaving some trace behind. Soon, we became an obligatory part of all the events organized in the Home of Youth, and then the local authorities started calling us to play at other important occasions.

There was a particular code for such gigs, and it included not only dress but behavior. Our clothes had to be nice but not too fancy. Our bearing had to be energetic but quiet, smart without showing off, dignified in our presumed poverty. In short, when invited to play at political events, we behaved like guilty dogs, our eyes down, our place in the corner, ready to wag our tails at the sound of our master's voice.

One day Stole mentioned some girl called Lana, and Mageda agreed that she was stunning, and then they talked at length about her insatiable sex drive, and how they'd both heard some wild stories about her. The more they said, the more I wished to meet her. I was nineteen. I'd read every theoretical piece about sex I could find, I'd gone through the *Kama Sutra* a few times, even read the ancient erotic Chinese manuscripts and studied the Roman orgies. I was still a virgin. I wasn't looking for a rose, I wanted a nymphomaniac.

Less than a month later a professor from my old gymnasium asked me to help her with a school celebration. She wanted to put together a recital of love poetry and she wanted me to play guitar. She had a reputation for having theatrical ambitions, always trying to put a twist on everything she did, so I accepted. During the first rehearsal she introduced me to a beautiful dark-haired girl with cocoa eyes. Her name was Lana.

I started offering Lana a ride home after our rehearsals; after two weeks we became an item. My worst fear was the difference in our sexual experience, and so–trying hard not to be recognized as a virgin–I played the very cool man of the world. I never knew if Lana bought it or just liked having her personal driver, but when I actually asked her one evening, sitting in my minuscule car, if she wanted us to become exclusive, she said yes. That very second my sexual life began: we had a long, long kiss.

For a month, we stuck at kisses. I drove her to school, drove her home after school, but never dared go further. She mistook it for something else, and became more serious about us. As it happens, her change in attitude prompted one of my own, and soon I discovered that whatever she was, she was a rose to me. My friends tried to warn me about her with discreet remarks here and there, but even the most persistent stopped when they saw I was in love.

And then one evening we ended up in my room, with my parents watching TV in the other room. I made love to her, and her body, perfect as a sonnet, smelled of a forest in the fall. The October rain was drizzling outside, and I was able to move the world, but I didn't since it was perfect as it was.

She didn't notice that it was my first time. All that education had paid off. For one brief moment, maybe she loved me, too.

Love softened me, and I felt the need to share everything. Maybe two weeks after our first time, I told Lana that I'd lost my virginity with her. Her face slowly changed into a mask I couldn't read. I had an idea of what happened, but there was nothing I could do. We were both raised on the principles of macho culture: as much experience as possible is good for a man and strictly forbidden for a woman. I was useless. She couldn't brag about me, about us. The truth I laid before her was suddenly a burden on her shoulders, and her remarks became cruel the way children are cruel.

Finally, in May, her prom was being held in a downtown hotel. It had an underground night bar, and a couple of friends–whose girlfriends were in her class too–and I decided to sit there till the morning hours and wait for our girls together. Around three o'clock, when the other guys picked up their girlfriends and went home, Lana refused to come. I went home alone.

We spent the next two months dragging around, and then she went with her family to the sea. I had to stay in Kragujevac, as the government had imposed a new rule for guys that year–each male student had to spend fifteen days in basic training in the army after his first year of studies. When we came out, Stole and I went to the coast, and I visited Lana. She was absentminded. Desperate, I returned to Kragujevac and waited for her to come back.

One day, her closest friend invited me for coffee, which was unusual. There, in the kitchen of a small, nondescript house on the outskirts, I heard the story: during prom night, Lana had sex with a classmate in the washroom of the hotel, not ten feet from where I had been waiting for her, and she got pregnant. Then she had a secret abortion, and that's why she'd left in such a hurry for the coast.

For the next ten years I trusted no woman and I treated them all with cold detachment. I was never such a magnet to women as during that time.

TITO'S DEATH

We were still enjoying the big cake my mother baked for New Year's, still chomping the last segments of a piglet my father had roasted on a spit, when the bad news came. Tito was ill. It was unthinkable: after so many years of watching him on TV smoking cigars, drinking whiskey and traveling all over the world, the image of Tito was the image of life itself. Some of us believed that the doctors had found a way to keep Tito eternally alive, but they just hadn't told us about it, as it wasn't for everyone, only for the best and brightest among us. And now, when we'd just entered the new 1980, still full of hope, we were hit over the head with this sudden turn. We were too full of wine, pork, cholesterol, sugar and tobacco to be able to cope with it in a rational way. My mother started crying immediately after the somber speaker read the news on national television.

"Dule," she said to my father, "he can't die. We would disappear without him."

"Don't worry, bride," Father said, in the gentlest voice I'd ever heard from him, "the Old Man will be fine."

But we sat in shocked silence for some time, until the telephone started ringing.

Three days later, Tito was out of the hospital, and we were immensely relieved. Smiles came back to our faces.

"Why did you worry so much, Mom?"

"How can you ask such a thing, son? Don't you understand that if Tito died all our enemies would jump on us, like vultures, to take the piece they'd always wanted to have? The Italians would take Istria, Austria would occupy Slovenia and Croatia, Hungary would take Vojvodina away, Albania would enter Kosovo . . ."

"But we still have our army."

"Nothing works without Tito, mark my words, son. Thank you, God, and give him eternal life."

Our happiness lasted only a week, and then came an even worse shock. Tito was admitted to the clinic in Ljubljana, Slovenia, and underwent surgery on the veins of his left foot. Now it sounded dangerous. The doctors were quick to announce that his chances for full recovery were great and to assure us all that absolutely everything that could be done was being done. They said they were consulting the leading surgeons in both the U.S.A. and the U.S.S.R. every day and that they also thought the prognosis was good.

For about a week there was no news about Tito's health, until one evening they interrupted a TV program to announce that his left leg had been amputated because of severe arterial damage.

The music on all the radio and TV stations changed immediately. There was no singing of any kind anymore, only instrumental music, nothing too somber or vivacious. Such music was played only when a catastrophe would happen, or in the days of national mourning. We all lost our smiles.

Tito was more than our president, more than our protector–he was our icon. He had the good looks of an old-school Hollywood actor, luxury all around him and all over him, that exotic accent. Overnight, our icon had lost one leg. The damage was irreparable, there was no turning back. Although for decades Tito had had the same posse around him, and we knew all their names and faces, nobody among them could come even close to having the power to lead us all. Tito's insistence on collective governing in the last years of his life watered down the last remains of the authority held by some of the politicians around him.

We tried to keep occupied, but it was impossible not to sit in front of our black-and-white TV set for the central evening news, which would start every day with a short and indecipherable announcement from the hospital in Slovenia. It would come down to one sentence, usually: "The consilium of Tito's doctors has announced that the medical condition of our president remains serious but stable."

My mother would sigh after that, and then all three of us would stop watching the news, and go to our kitchen to make some coffee and just sit together. As time went on, we went deeper into speculations about who would attack us and how, and who would come to our aid, in case Tito died. Every such conversation ended with one of us saying, "But of course, Tito will get better."

February passed like that, then March and the first half of April. I started realizing that I was immensely enjoying the music on the radio. Since Tito's stay at the hospital dragged on, they eased the restrictions a bit, and now they played whole operas, the whole catalogue of classical music, then the collected works of all the major choirs of this world. They dug out Miles Davis and all the cool or mellow jazz they could find, they found room for instrumental blues and slow, melancholic Russian instrumental music. Satie woke us in the morning, Beethoven and Bach put to sleep those who could sleep, Coltrane kept us company overnight, Dexter Gordon in the afternoon . . . It was by far the best music diet anyone could ever have.

But just when I found the good side of the situation, and was enjoying my parents' closeness, the news grew worse. April 21: "Tito's general medical condition is serious: the bleeding does not stop, heavy liver damage is accompanied by pneumonia, high temperature and cardiac weakness, and kidney function is still not regained." A week later, Tito was in a coma.

On May 4, in the afternoon, all the programs in Yugoslavia were interrupted and the TV screens switched to an inscription that important news was to follow. I was somewhere in town that afternoon, but I hurried home to be with my parents. We just sat there, staring at the gray screen, not talking.

"The president of the Socialist Federative Republic of Yugoslavia, president of the Association of Communists of Yugoslavia and the supreme commander of the SFRJ Armed Forces, the marshal of Yugoslavia Josip Broz Tito, died at 3:05 this afternoon. The central commemoration will be held . . ."

But we couldn't listen anymore. All three of us started crying, fatherless children, helpless, unprotected, all three of us–like twenty other million–leveled to the age of five in two minutes; sentient enough to know that we would live, crushed to the point where we couldn't see how.

Tito's body was taken by train from Ljubljana to Belgrade, one last slow ride. Hundreds of thousands of people stood by the rails, along all three hundred miles, to say their last good-bye to the father of the nation. The leading politicians from all over the world started pouring into Belgrade, awakening immense pride in all of us. Every publication in the territory of Yugoslavia put out a special issue dedicated to Tito's inspiration. I volunteered to be the editor of that issue at *Youth,* and I wrote a farewell article that made my dad clench his teeth in a heroic attempt to keep his eyes dry.

And then, slowly, very slowly, after a week of mourning everything was done, and the illustrious guests went home, and the people started working again, and the flowers dried, and nobody attacked us, nobody came to our aid, the few last articles were published, a few sad documentaries made, and it was over. Yugoslavia was on its own.

4

GAME: PARTISANS AND NAZIS

The rules

The participants separate into two groups, the Partisans and the Nazis. The Nazis first arrest a few Partisans, and then the rest of the Partisans try to set them free and arrest or "kill" the enemy.

The reality

The strongest boys are always among the Partisans. Identification with the Resistance runs high enough for participants to soon forget it's only a game, so the other side gets beaten, spit on and hit with the weapon of the day. The Nazis play halfheartedly, for they know they have to lose. But they do play, because they hope to be the Partisans the next time.

ADVICE

In November 1980 I got a job offer from Belgrade. Ratomir Mirić, one of the best editors in Serbian journalism at the time, called me one day to explain his idea: he wanted me to work as an editor with his magazine *Omladinske novine,* the same publication for which *Youth* was an insert and for which I was writing frequently now. There was no opening on the magazine itself, but there was an opening with the publisher and he wanted to place me there, to become secretary for culture at Socialist Youth of Serbia, which was practically the position of minister of youth culture in the republic. Although he understood that I wasn't interested in politics, he thought we would be killing two birds with one stone–I would get an insider's perspective before I joined his editorial team, and they would get their man in the publisher's office. The salary was beyond my wildest dreams, and something I would probably never be able to achieve in Kragujevac.

"Oh, by the way, I got the whole idea when they gave you an award today."

"What award?"

"The Brave Flower thing. You are now the Best Young Journalist in Serbia. Congrats. Take a couple of days to think it over. Don't let me down, old man. You will rot if you stay there. It's a backwater. Come to Belgrade."

Just two days earlier, after several months of trying, my mother had finally succeeded in finding some connection who'd made it possible to get Dušan an exam with the country's top medical specialists, at the Military Medical Academy, in Belgrade. The first thing the good doctor said when I took my father into his office was, "Except for Parkinson's disease, what else is wrong?" And, indeed, there was something else–Father had diabetes. We were both relieved that he wasn't a malingerer, but we also understood from the specialist's carefully chosen words that Dušan would not only never work again, he would be increasingly confined to his bed.

So, in the same week, I received a curse and a blessing. The curse was like a behemoth: heavy, grotesque and motionless. The blessing, as usual, was there on its flight to someone else. I shared the news with my mother, and she cried. I told my father about the offer, and he said, "You have to take it, you have to go. I'll be all right."

If I decided to accept Ratomir's offer, the job would start in December, so I'd have to move really fast. And I knew that my father was lying to me, that he would not be okay without me to drive him to the doctor for prescriptions, to let him hold my hand when walking through the long corridors of medical institutions, carrying him more than leading him. The more I thought, the muddier the situation became. The only thing that was clear was that the decision had to be mine, no matter how I wished for someone else to just tell me what to do. If I went to Belgrade, my guilt would probably become unbearable. If I stayed, then Ana and Dušan would feel guilty and I would in all probability be very frustrated.

Long walks didn't help. Talks with my friends were useless; they behaved like a cast of characters, speaking from their roles and therefore saying predictable things, and they were all judging *my* options, which was too easy. I sat at my desk, pulled out two sheets of blank paper and wrote "For" on one and "Against" on the other. When after several hours I realized that both pieces were still blank, I knew I had to take more resolute measures. I needed to talk to someone whom I really trusted.

After going through my telephone book, I realized that my best option would probably be my high-school professor Djordje. He knew me very well after four years of fighting with me, and I also knew his sons, so Djordje probably knew even some personal things about me. I gave him a call the evening before the deadline for my decision and told him that I had a huge dilemma to solve, and he told me to come immediately to his apartment.

He must have prepared his sons for my coming, since when I entered they just said "Hi" and continued watching television. Djordje and I went to a small room; he closed the door behind him. I lit a cigarette and started explaining the situation. I tried to be as concise as possible, since I knew that to take him into all the small details would make his judgment more difficult. I also wanted to hear a brief version myself.

I talked for maybe an hour, and he listened with attention, asking short questions from time to time, bringing me back on track occasionally. At one point his wife brought in coffee and some biscuits, but otherwise nobody interrupted us. When I finished, the quiet made the room bigger, the only sound coming muted from the TV in the living room.

Djordje cleared his throat. "Dragan," he said, "I can only admire the morality of your dilemma. Not many modern children would even stop to consider the things you are taking into account when deciding on this. Modern society has distorted the relationship between the generations. But let me get to the point: I think you should accept the offer, and go to Belgrade, because your parents have worked hard to provide the best education for you and your sister, and this offer is proof that their work has paid off."

I had no sister.

I politely waited till he finished his speech, thanked him and left. On the short walk home I wondered what had happened: this man had an excellent memory, he had proved so many times that he remembered tiny details from our shared past, even the ones I couldn't recollect anymore. Was I so unimportant to him?

I started laughing, alone on the dimly lit street. The rain started to pour and I wasn't paying attention. What about the mystical order of things? If the adviser mixed in such a mistake with his advice, should I just take the advice as if it was based on proper input, or was the message from the higher level of consciousness more complex? Crappy input–crappy output, and if the advice was crap, shouldn't I do just the opposite?

And then, just a few yards from the door to my building, I had an answer: if we would all be wounded no matter what I decided, then leave the emotional element out and just judge the technical part. What did Djordje say, that I would prosper in Belgrade? Suddenly, the answer was clear.

I unlocked the door to our apartment and went in. My parents were watching TV with the door to their room open. They knew where I'd gone, and why.

"What did he say?" asked my mother.

"He told me to go. And please don't cry, Mom."

MY NEW SUNGLASSES

One morning early in January of 1981 I found myself in an ugly concrete building in New Belgrade, a mushroom-city that sprang up in the early sixties, with its government and Party buildings and blocks of ugly concrete dormitories that Communist regimes were proudly building all over the Eastern bloc, showcasing them as the fruit of their care for the working class. This whole area was built on marshes filled with stone and sand, and between the buildings were long stretches of barren land. Public transportation was never good, and, although New Belgrade was just across the river, it took me around forty-five minutes to get there from Belgrade's central bus station.

As I sat in the corridor, my shoes and my pants sprayed with slush, my yellow duffel bag dirty from the bus floor, I watched people passing by. Some of them went slowly, reading thick typewritten materials. At twenty-two, I seemed to be among the youngest employees in the headquarters of the Socialist Youth of Serbia.

After almost an hour, someone came and took me to meet the current president and his secretary. The president, some ten years older than I, was a medical student from Belgrade, tall but stocky, his round face shiny below thinning blond hair, his glasses constantly sliding down his greasy nose. I recognized the type: probably a good student in high school, recommended early and made a member of the Communist Party, unlucky with the girls, boring to everyone except those interested in politics. Thousands like him out there, so he must have been chosen by the "key."

Every political function in Yugoslavia had to be filled using the so-called key, meaning that, for each position on the federal level, every nationality and every republic had to have its shot. On the lower level, in each of the republics, different cities would have their go in different years. Also, if the position in the last three rotations had been filled by men, this time it would have to be a woman, and vice versa. Add to this the occupational quota: you couldn't have students only, you had to give a chance to workers, dentists, writers, whomever. In theory, this was a good way of preventing jealousy and making sure that all groups had their voices heard; in practice, pushing democracy to this extreme mocked it. The cadre selected by way of the key was overwhelmingly incompetent, in milder cases just funny, in the worst, destructive to the very cause they were supposed to represent. But the system won either way: if the representative was good, it was because the selection mechanism was fine; if the person performed poorly, she would be more susceptible to orders from above.

Sitting in a leather chair across the table from the president, and listening to him welcome me in bureaucratese on the edge of comprehensible, I was wondering if he was good or obedient, or both.

The secretary, Tomović, was another story. Tall, dark haired, with piercing eyes and a poker face, he had a square jaw and big hands, giving away his factory background and toughness. When we shook hands I felt my bones cracking. He spoke in short sentences, never a redundant word, and his eyes seemed to be cutting through the usual blandness of the situation. While I was trying to decide if I liked the secretary or not, the president finished his fifteen-minute speech. Secretary Tomović just said, "Welcome. You, along with all our new colleagues, will be staying at the Hotel Jugoslavija in the beginning. The driver is waiting to take you there, and back if you're fast. Try to be fast, because we have an important meeting at one o'clock that you have to attend. You'll meet your own secretary, Irena, after the meeting. See you later." And he crushed my hand again.

I was in. My official title was secretary for culture of SYS, my salary was two times higher than my parents' combined wage, I'd just moved to the capital, I had a driver at my disposal and a private secretary, and my future was so bright that I had to buy new, darker sunglasses.

NO TRACES IN HOTEL JUGOSLAVIJA

Hotel Jugoslavija was a five-star affair on the bank of the Danube. It was built and decorated without much taste, but it was imposing, sitting alone on a beautiful stretch of the river, in the area where the concrete buildings of

New Belgrade come close to the old brick houses of Zemun. It had been built after World War II to provide accommodation to various foreign state officials visiting the nearby government buildings. The interior looked much better than its façade. The two huge restaurants, strategically positioned looking out over the river, were luxurious, with marble floors and tables and leather chairs. There was a small swimming pool with a sauna on one side of the lobby and a string of shops on the other. Known as the hotel for diplomats, spies and journalists, it was a magnet for high-class prostitutes. At any time of day or night one could find beautiful girls sitting alone in the foyer or in the restaurants. Their pimps were the receptionists.

I was put in a room on the third floor. The whole floor was reserved for the hotel entertainers and longer-staying guests–the higher floors were less noisy. Mine was a small room, decorated in a brownish palette, with textile wallpaper, a single bed, a radio and a small bathroom. The painting on the wall was a depressing landscape of the same sad valley by the blue river that every hotel manager of this world loves.

The day after I arrived I went out and purchased some theater posters, some postcards and some tape to help make my habitat less clinical. The several books I'd brought with me I dispersed around the room. I hung my only jacket on the back of the desk chair. Now it was starting to look like a normal place. I went to the supermarket nearby, purchased some instant coffee, some crackers and some dry sausages since the room didn't have a fridge. I always got hungry around midnight, and ate while reading, which would put me to sleep. Finally it felt like home, and I took off my sneakers, made a coffee and lit a cigarette. My room had a view of War Island, a long, wooded stretch of land that split the Danube in two. The trees across the river looked naked and helpless against the merciless sharp north wind. The radio was playing some slow music, the lamplight was subdued, and I dozed off in the recliner by the door to the balcony.

In the dream, I was a writer. I was sitting at my desk in my parents' home, typing a novel. On my left was a thin bundle of finished pages, and on my right was a fat pile of blank sheets. The room was warm and lit just the way writers like. There was an Al Stewart record on the turntable, a coffee by my side and a plate of hot cookies my mother must have brought in just recently. My right hand was bigger, yet softer than my left hand. Another odd thing: every time I would finish a page, take it out of the typewriter and put it on the left bundle, that pile would grow thinner, while the blank group would get bigger. But that was okay: I just needed to type faster.

So I typed faster, with the same result. Finally, I had only one finished page on my left, and the blank bunch on the right was so big I couldn't see the door anymore. While I was thinking what to do–I was afraid to type another page, because somehow I knew that everything would disappear then, including me–the door opened. My father came in. He was tall and straight, with no wrinkles on his face. He just stood there and looked at me.

"How are you?" I asked.

"Good. See, I don't have Parkinson's anymore. But watch out for your mother. She is sad. Sadness breaks your wings. Sadness can dry trees out. Look through the window, at those poplars in the cemetery. They were sad a long time."

"What should I do about this?" I said, nodding towards the only remaining page on the left.

"You are doing it wrong. Instead of typing, you should be erasing. Then you will have your autobiography."

"Autobiography? But I'm writing a novel."

"No," said my father, "it's your story, it always is, that's why you have to erase."

"Do you know why my right hand is bigger than my left? Yours are normal, Mother's too."

"Your hand is normal, it's only your middle finger that's longer, that's all."

I looked again at my hand, and he was right. "Oh, I understand now," I said, with a mischievous smile.

"You are wrong. It's not like that so you can show it to everybody whenever you please. It's to put you in danger." And he left.

Confused by his last sentence, I opened the door and it wasn't our apartment on the other side–it was a white surgical room. It was full of people, some naked, some in white robes with surgical masks over their faces. A group of tables stood in the center, and I went to one of those under the bright light and saw that they were making a new man by stitching together pieces of other people who were lying on the surrounding tables and chatting merrily with the nurses and doctors who were cutting them. There was no blood anywhere in sight and the whole atmosphere was relaxed. Then I looked closer at the face of the man in the making, and he was me. His left eye was still missing, but it was undeniably my face.

"What will happen to me?" I asked a doctor next to me, a middle-aged guy with fine hands that held a cigarette.

"Oh, don't worry, comrade," he said, "what do you think this is, Dr. Mengele's office?" Everybody laughed and looked at me. He slapped my shoulder in a comforting manner and said, "See how everybody is smiling here? This is a happy thing. You will become a much, much better man now, and your old self will stay here for other people who need parts of you to be perfect. In the end, we all become better here."

I wanted to ask more, but a gorgeous woman came to me. She had the body of Raquel Welch and the face of my secretary, Irena, and she was a nurse–this I recognized by her small white cap, the only piece of clothing she wore. "Follow me, dear, there's a table ready for you." She took my hand in hers and led me to a table on the side, where a team was already waiting. They stripped me and laid me on the table, and she handed me a huge joint. "Take this," she said, "and inhale deeply." While I was smoking the joint, they were telling jokes around me, laughing and enjoying themselves. "He is ready now," Raquel-Irena said, looking at my eyes. A jovial doctor brought a scalpel to my face. "Your mother needs your eyes," he said. "She cried hers out, and yours are nice and dry."

I woke up in a sweat and went to the balcony to take a sharp breath of wind. War Island was dark.

The next day, when I returned from work and unlocked the door to my room, I stood shocked. Somebody must have stolen all my things. I stepped back to see the number on the door, and it was 309, my place. But there were no posters and no postcards on the wall, and everything was back in the same place and the same state as when I first came in. Even the recliner was as it had been, at exactly 20 degrees northeast. I stepped in and found my jacket in the closet, my shoes in a drawer, and my books hidden between the bed and the night table. My food had disappeared completely, and the posters and postcards were neatly tucked inside the drawer of the writing desk.

Why on earth would they want to erase the traces of me? I unpacked everything again, stuck the posters to the wall, threw the books around, added newspapers, put my shoes under the bed, and then brought a plant from the corridor into my room. There.

The day after, the same: the invisible maid removed everything, including the tiniest particles of dust, aired the room, and, yes, she found the shoes. I sat down and wrote a note. It said that I was supposed to live here, not just sleep, that I was to stay for a longer period, possibly several months or even longer, so she simply didn't have to bother with my room. Then I messed up the place. I left the note on the desk before I went to work the next morning.

And found everything tidied away when I came back. So I wrote a letter this time. I went soft, mentioned my childhood, happy family, my recent move to Belgrade and my new life far from my friends. I described how small details meant much to a guy living alone, how I wasn't trying to ruin anything, just cut my piece of space in the big city. I left a flower on top of the envelope.

No result. The woman's soul was replaced with a vacuum cleaner. My next note was stern, mentioning my high rank in a political organization (I didn't specify), my need for privacy, the sensitive files I was bringing from work, and possible repercussions. The room was even tidier after that one.

In the coming days I visited the reception desk to complain about the obsessive maid, I talked to the manager, and I tried to find out who she was by inquiring with the hotel staff. The only result was that the hotel personnel started eyeing me in a strange way. I probably had the reputation now of an utterly annoying weirdo who hated hygiene.

After three weeks of this silent war, I gave up. I wasn't allowed to leave any traces in Hotel Jugoslavija, and that was that.

COLLAGE

I liked Irena from the beginning. She seemed to be among the few intelligent people around, was well read, an avid consumer of all things cultural, and she came from an influential family. She lived with her mother, her step-father and her half-sister in a big apartment on one of the very few nice blocks of New Belgrade. We got along well, and soon started gossiping about the others around us. She'd been at SYS just a little longer than I, but she already knew the procedures and timelines, and everything else that made my life easier.

Vera shared the office with Irena. She wore tight black leather pants, high black boots, short dark jackets and several layers of heavy makeup, in a style somewhere between professional mistress and teenage rebel. She had icy eyes lined with Egyptian black. We never talked much, partly because we didn't have any business together, partly because I couldn't think of any common topics.

One morning I entered the office looking for Irena, who still hadn't come to work, and I felt I had to try and make some conversation with Vera, in the spirit of camaraderie. We ordered coffee, started some small talk, and I noticed a long line of blue magazine files and black binders on the shelf behind her.

"How neat," I said. "What do you keep in those?"

Happy that I asked, she stood up and took one binder from the shelf. She opened it and slid it proudly across the desk for me to see. There was an A4-sized sheet of paper and on it something that looked like a collage, except that the only thing it could represent was some kind of report. Shorter or longer chunks of some other documents were neatly cut and glued to the page. Even the line spacing between the different chunks was precisely the same, and they were all left-aligned. I raised my head and–seeing a glimmer of pride in her eyes–didn't dare ask what it was.

"Wow," I offered, waiting for an explanation.

"Am I not smart?" she asked, taking the binder back. "For example, this page here was my report for the last meeting of our committee, the one about pioneers. In these magazine files I keep all the reports other people before me wrote. So, when I needed the report from that meeting–and you know how it goes here, they always need it yesterday, as if the country would fall apart–I found some old reports, photocopied the best parts, cut them, put them together and photocopied the new version. It was done overnight. They were all in shock."

"So you just . . . snip-snip?" I said in awe, my fingers imitating scissors.

"No, of course not," she said, all proud, "I use a scalpel. The cut is much cleaner."

"Did they notice?"

"Who would? All the secretaries are here just for some time, then they go to another position. All the members of the committee are in this for even shorter periods. I think it would be a pity to throw these reports away. Someone spent many hours writing them, they contain some very good ideas, not to mention the style. Here, this one is by my favorite writer. I love his stuff! I'm looking for him, I want to meet him." She pulled another file. After few moments she found the page she was looking for and started reading aloud.

"'The future of our children is bright under the leadership of President Tito, but there is always room for improvement. Because the future of our children is our own future, it is our country's future, it is the future of our all hopes. The mornings of May are sunny only if they are sunny for children. The brooks of spring feed the rivers of autumn.'" After emphasizing the last sentence, she looked at me, her eyes all bright.

She put the file back on the desk and lit a cigarette. "Isn't it something?"

"Indeed," I said. "Who was the writer, do I know her?"

"It's him," she said, giggling. "His name is Marko, and I've heard he works now in the building of the Central Committee of the Communist Party of Yugoslavia. No wonder, eh? I wish I was able to write like this."

We were silent for a minute or two. She was savoring the effect her reading left, and I didn't know what to say.

"So, did you ever have to write a new report?" I asked.

"Only once," and she rolled her Egyptian eyes, "when I was still green. It was awful! It took me five days, I almost got sick. You know, I'm not a fast note-taker, so I lose half of the stuff that's been said at the meetings. That's my biggest trouble. Then, one day, I was passing down the corridor, on the other side of the building, and I saw them emptying an office. These binders were out in the hall–they wanted to throw them away. Can you imagine? I mean, we do some huge work here, long hours of writing reports and proposals, and then, when we leave for a higher position, it all gets thrown away. Isn't it sad? What stays behind us? How will someone know we existed at all?"

She thought about it for a while. I was impressed that she kept her eyelids open with all that weight on them.

"I took a couple of files with me, to read them over lunch, and then I realized it was all reusable. I mean, it's the same system, and the problems are not solved overnight. Something bothering us today was already there five or ten years ago, and some other people discussed it. How do we know they didn't have ideas better than ours? When I understood this, and I saw this amazing style–oh, there are some others, not as good as Marko, but different, very precise, so I can use them when I need such a style–I ran back and saved all these."

"Do you know by any chance if the others like your reports?"

"As far as I know, they love them."

"But they don't know the history, right? It's your secret."

"Some of them know, and they think it's very good I kept the old stuff. Some of my colleagues are jealous because they don't have such a collection. I heard only last month that they were proposing that we make a library of our old reports, so they can use it too. Can you imagine? I'm not sharing my stuff with anyone!"

THE LINE THAT WAS CUT OUT

Ratomir Mirić and I were sitting in his office on Boulevard of the Revolution. It was Thursday afternoon, the magazine had gone to print, and it was quiet. I dropped by, as always when I needed to clear my mind of politics and talk to normal people.

"I never asked you one thing I'd love to know," I said. "What brought me here? I mean, I know you said it was the Brave Flower award, but really, what prompted you to pick me?"

"I never told you that, old man?" he said, looking slightly surprised. "Remember when we sent you to Požarevac?"

I remembered. It was a year before. *Omladinske*–read mostly in Belgrade–wanted to increase its profile in other cities and decided to try to publish more material from small towns in Serbia. Ratomir came up with the idea that they would send a team of young journalists and a photographer to a different city every week. He invited me to be on the expedition going to Požarevac, a town east of Belgrade known mainly for teenage marriages and pregnancy, and a big, notorious prison called Zabela. The majority of the leading Party cadres served their jail time there before World War II, debating and translating Marx in secrecy. Now it was a top-security prison for hardened criminals–multiple offenders, murderers, robbers and rapists. When he called me, I immediately told him I wanted to cover Zabela. "Yes," he said, "I thought you would, but there's a catch: the purpose of this whole series about cities is to promote *us.* And people don't want their city portrayed through a jail story, do they? So, old man, you have to come up with some angle on it."

"Listen," I said, "I can't imagine them having a Party cell in jail, the Communists don't go there these days, but they must have some form of Socialist Youth of Serbia organization. You are the magazine published by SYS, so we just have to write something about that."

He laughed. "Well, all right. But we both understand your article can be cut from the report if we decide so."

"Of course," I said.

And so I went to Požarevac as a member of a team of five. I visited the gloomy prison, surrounded by high walls topped with barbed wire, and talked with the superintendent. He looked at me as if I was absolutely crazy, but–since I asked about something that was of a political nature–he didn't dare to just get rid of me. I wasn't allowed to enter the jail itself; instead they brought a couple of guards and one prisoner to talk about his political activities. There was no meat in all that, but I somehow wrote that report, and it was published–in a sidebar, but still.

"I don't know if you can recall, but there was this one sentence you wrote in that report. I remember it clearly. You wrote: 'As we approach Zabela, the houses on the side of the road are smaller and fewer, and the guard dogs in front of them are bigger.' That was your ticket to this. When I read that, I knew you could write."

"But, wait–you cut out that sentence . . ."

"Of course I did, old man. But that line brought you here."

KOSOVO SAFARI

In March 1981 we heard news about student protests in Kosovo. The official report, circulating through the offices in our building and marked "Sensitive," was meager: after a basketball match several hundred students in a Priština college started chanting slogans, calling for a higher standard of living, more autonomy and the reunion of all Albanian countries. This last item was particularly bad, since it meant they wanted to separate from Yugoslavia and join Albania. The author was laconic, and the paper was soothing in a way, suggesting that everything was under control. It went on to emphasize that this was an isolated incident in the Kosovo capital, and there was no danger of the unrest spreading farther.

Irena came into my office after reading it.

"You saw the report?" she asked.

"Yes, I did. Nothing serious, I think."

"Except that it will make our lives more difficult." She sat across from me.

"Why would it affect us?"

"Because you and I are organizing the final celebration of Youth Day in Serbia, and this year it is scheduled to take place in Leskovac, and that is close to Kosovo."

"Why us?"

"Did you ever bother reading the description of your job here?" She started laughing.

"You mean the whole . . . You and I?"

"On top of that, we are responsible for the route of Štafeta through Serbia. Dates, times, names, everything. We need to start right away. Actually, compared to previous years we're already late, but this report will save us–we'll say we waited for the security issues to be cleared."

Štafeta was a ritual, one of many the Communist system developed after the war to replace the old ceremonies and to celebrate the new era, the victory of the working class. Promising youth carried a sculpted baton throughout Yugoslavia, as if it was a long relay race, until finally it would be handed over to Tito on Youth Day, a national holiday honoring his birthday on May 25. The whole idea was to show how the socialist youth of Yugoslavia would devotedly follow Tito's revolutionary path. But this was also the way to tie the president's aging image to the metaphor of eternal youth.

Combining the Olympic disciplines of relay race and marathon was intentional. Every new custom had to fulfill two functions: draw on tradition, and point to the future. This newly created procession would unite the ancient humanistic ideals with the values of the new system, giving false depth and tradition to a system that, in terms of history, was born yesterday. It was like growing a beard on a baby.

The central Yugoslav celebration would always be spectacular, with tens of thousands of participants, luxurious costumes and sets, live on national TV. But the local festivities, held in each of the six Yugoslav republics separately, were not to be left behind–the local politicians would use this occasion to show their loyalty to Tito. The money spent on the Youth Day spectacles in Serbia was exorbitant, and Irena had just told me that I was practically the executive producer.

There was only one tiny problem: Tito had died the previous year, and now nobody knew what we were supposed to do.

The Kosovo Albanians were counting on this confusion. For several days it seemed that the unrest in Priština was under control, but on April 1 an emergency meeting was called in the early afternoon in our building. *Emergency* is a mild word–they were chasing people out of the washrooms and into our conference room. No undersecretaries were allowed to attend and no notes to be taken.

The president of SYS was on a business trip, but his secretary was there. In a somber voice Tomović announced that he had just received a telegram from Kosovo. He didn't reveal the source, but we guessed that it had come from the police headquarters down there. He read it aloud, surrounded by deep silence. It said that earlier that morning the internal enemy had started armed conflict with the police force, that there were dead and wounded among the police and that the situation was very grave. It ended with an ominous sentence: "At the time we are sending this report there are shots being fired on the streets of Priština."

Among us was our comrade Hoxa, an Albanian from Kosovo. He was a quiet, friendly person who spoke poor Serbian with a strong Albanian accent, and nobody ever paid much attention to him. Now everyone tried hard not to look at him. He felt the need to say something.

"Comrades . . ." His tone was harsh, atypical for him. "We should not rush to conclusions. Those students in Priština were manipulated, but they are good young men, and I'm sure that . . ." He stopped. His face was white, his cheekbones bright pink. We waited some time for him to continue, we wanted at least someone to be sure of something, but it looked as if he wasn't going to.

"I want to say something." Nikola Kanda stood up. He was the secretary for security. A black bushy mustache and glasses of a thickness that made his eyes look unnaturally large gave the impression that he wore a mask.

"We can't rely on telegrams in a situation like this. We need to know what is going on down there. The Albanian separatists started their protests by manipulating the students; I hope you all read it in the report I prepared several days ago. The students are in our domain, and we, of all the political institutions in this country, have to have the most reliable information about the situation there. I want to go to Priština and see for myself. Of course, I will send you an update right away, and I will give you a detailed report when I return."

"But the planes aren't flying to Priština now," someone said.

"I know that. I need Tika the driver. It will be safer if it's only two of us. He's the fastest driver we have, and we can get there in a few hours. I'll sleep in the army barracks and return tomorrow."

It sounded like a safari trip: go where the animals are, stay in your Rover, watch them devour one another, and come home to develop the pictures.

"We can't let you go. It's too risky," said Tomović.

"What risk? Both Tika and I will have guns–I keep them in our safe and I'll pick two big ones. I would really love"–he looked quickly at Hoxa from the corner of his eye–"I mean, hate"–he chuckled–"to use them, but we'll be protected."

"No," said Tomović after few long seconds.

"What do you mean, no? You think we should just sit here and wait?" Kanda raised his voice warningly.

"No." Tomović wasn't even looking at him anymore.

Kanda was still standing. "I must warn you that you will be held responsible if we reach any conclusions based on bad reports, wrong in the very assumptions we're starting with, and–" His pitch was unbearably high.

"I said no. No conclusions will be reached here today. We've just gathered to share what we have, and we don't need any extra information from you. You want to go there–take a vacation. Meeting's over." Only then, standing up, did Tomović look down at Kanda. He was a whole head taller than him, and it looked for a moment as though he was going to hit him. Instead, he turned to Hoxa and said, "Let's have a drink in my office."

When I told Irena–who was an undersecretary and not allowed at the meeting–about Kanda's safari idea, she said, "You know what his father is? Some high-ranking army officer, general, I think, who works for the Yugoslav Army Security. Top spy, everything top top secret. Not even Kanda knows much–at least that's what he said–but he seems to be impressed with his old man. That's why he works as a spy here. Did anyone stand up to him?"

"Only Tomović. But in such a way that I felt like kissing him."

"I'm not surprised nobody said a word. Kanda writes reports every month on all of us. Tomović, ha? Maybe there's hope for him."

"There's hope for quite a few of them," I said.

We entered a gray zone that day. Everyone seemed perplexed by the Kosovo events. We would come to work as usual, but most of us were late; we would bring the newspapers with us, drink mugs and mugs of coffee together and try hard to find some topic of conversation, anything but Kosovo. We didn't have our regular meetings for almost ten days. Hoxa was away on business, we'd been told. We didn't know if he'd gone to Kosovo to try to calm things down somehow or if he just wanted to be with his family, but I felt sorry for him anyway.

I used a few days of this confusion to go to Kragujevac to spend time with my parents. I started having migraine attacks. Their coming was always the same: dancing shapes of light would suddenly cover whatever I was looking at, leaving my peripheral vision intact. I couldn't see whatever I wanted to see at the moment but I saw everything else. Half an hour later a crushing headache would follow.

Irena had promised to let me know if someone wanted me badly at work, and she called one morning. "You have to come to Belgrade," she said. "Not tomorrow. Now. I can't talk over the phone."

Four hours later I was in the SYS building, sitting in her office.

"It's getting serious," she said quietly, leaning over her desk. "We had a meeting this morning–I told them you were at the dentist–it was highly confidential. No taking notes again. We have tours of duty now. Kanda made a schedule. We will have someone in charge of our quarters at all times. During working hours we're fine, we just have to be here, all of us, every day, but after hours, there will be a person on duty. That person is to sit in the president's office, by his official phone, and take calls any time of night. The system of codes has been put in place, and you are expected to leave a detailed report about your shift. We girls are excused."

"When is my turn?"

"Wednesday, I think, but Kanda said he will distribute instructions to all of you guys later today. You will have a gun, a car and a special phone at your disposal."

"A gun?"

"A gun. You know how Kanda loves guns. Well, he wants to share the joy."

"What did Tomović say?"

"He wasn't there. And my sources tell me he had some hard times after that confrontation with Kanda."

"How hard?"

"Hard. I told you Kanda's father was some important bullock up there. Hard to the point that we don't know what will happen to Tomović, whether he'll stay here or not."

US AND THEM

My first tour of duty came two days later. The political cadre left around three, the undersecretaries around four, and by five in the afternoon even the bureaucracy was gone. The building felt like a sinking ship. I went to the supermarket downstairs to buy some food and cigarettes, returned upstairs and locked the main entrance behind me. I was supposed to do a quick check of the place, to make sure nobody was hiding, so I took the gun and went out into the long corridor. Gary Cooper in New Belgrade, when all the mice had left and Frank Miller is about to arrive on the noon train from Kosovo. I practiced pulling the gun as I opened the doors with my shoe, but it got boring after two minutes. Then I entered Slavko's office.

SYS had three large groups of employees: the political cadre like me, whose term lasted two years with an option of another two; undersecretaries like Irena, who had a semipermanent position (depending mostly on the goodwill of superiors); and the bureaucracy that was here permanently, knew all the secrets and could make your life extremely difficult if they didn't like you. Slavko was officially an undersecretary, but he'd been here so long that he was treated as part of the inventory. Most of the time he was not in the building, and his colleague would point at the open briefcase on his desk and say he'd be back soon. Sometimes it seemed that the thing had been in exactly the same position for days, but then you'd see his newspaper opened to the crossword, half filled, pen on top. Irena told me her theory: two identical briefcases, one that he would really carry around, and one for alibi purposes only.

Here was an opportunity to check that theory: indeed, I found a briefcase in the last drawer and a newspaper inside more than two weeks old. Then I found on another desk a postcard from the Adriatic coast, sent a week before by Slavko. So that was settled. He had gone for two weeks, which is what Irena had guessed.

I also checked on some other theories: Julija did not shave her legs at work (nothing even remotely resembling a shaver in her desk), Janko did have hemorrhoids (a tube of an anti-itch, hemorrhoid-shrinking cream), and Zoran did read porn hidden inside magazines (a Swedish booklet still inside *Time*).

The Gary Cooper–turned–George Smiley phase lasted two hours. The TV set didn't offer any fun, the news was boring. So I sat down at the president's desk to write my report. They had instructed me to write an hour-by-hour diary, noting everything interesting that happened during my shift. I read some excerpts from previous days, and everyone seemed to adhere to this idea. So I wrote about Slavko's twin briefcases, negated rumors that a certain employee was shaving her legs at work and described the porn booklet in detail. I thought everyone agreed that this whole idea of night watch was ludicrous, so I wanted to give something funny to the person who was supposed to take over from me.

When, at midnight, I opened the door to my successor and saw the bearded face and small eyes of Goran, I wasn't sure anymore that my idea of fun was still okay, but it was too late to change my diary. Goran was Kanda's close friend, a perfect example of communist youth who probably even asked for sex by quoting some Party resolution.

The next day I got a call from Kanda. "I read your diary from last night. Very funny. Ha." And he hung up.

A week later it was my turn again. I was better prepared this time: several comics, instant coffee and two chocolate bars in my bag meant that I was ready to defend the building against any enemy. I did my gun practice between the comics and afterwards tried to open several desks. This turned out to be an easy way to find out who Kanda's friends were–those whose desks were locked. My shift this time started at midnight, so around six in the morning, when the eastern sky was already burning, I opened the report book to read other people's notes. I couldn't believe my eyes: each one of them was dead serious. No drawings of guns, no allusions, no irony, nothing. For the first time I realized that, except for Irena, I had no friends in this sad house.

I put the notebook aside to rethink this whole situation. When I had come to Belgrade, I sincerely hoped that this position would give me an opportunity to do something for young artists of all sorts. I wasn't sure why. Maybe because I knew how lonely it was to spend months in a Serbian town creating something, making it really good, making it fly above the ordinary–only to realize that the media in the Yugoslav capital wasn't interested at all in anything happening outside its city limits. I wanted to do something about decentralizing culture, to give some signal to people like me to persist, to show them that what they did mattered. Such things *were* in my job description.

I tried once: they told me to form a committee to take a good look at the issue. I tried again: no money in the budget for initiatives. And again: the last congress of the Communist Party hadn't proclaimed anything about that area, so we had to wait for clearance from above. I became fully aware that we were children never expected to grow up. It made me physically sick.

On Fridays I would take the bus back to Kragujevac, a two-hour drive in a shaking, fucked-up can, sitting next to people who would never shut up and let me read my books, listening to folk music blaring from the buzzing speakers, getting off at the filthy station, walking dark dirty streets towards the home of my proud parents. I never had the heart to tell them how it really was; I always talked about how high my salary was, how beautiful Hotel Jugoslavija was, how my life was all shiny now.

On Monday mornings, at five, I would run down the same ugly street, by the buildings where my first and second lovers still slept, under the trees that entered some of my poems, near the lake where my father took me fishing a long time ago before he fell ill, trying to catch the same stinking bus, the same farting tin can, where I would listen to the same folk morons wailing for two hours about their lost loves, because they were good for communism, because communism was all about the people. About us, the people, not them, the enemies. We–same; they–different. Our joy, their jealousy. We build, they destroy. Us, brave; them, cowards. Imperialists, fifth column, revisionists, liberals, mercenaries, dogs of war, god lovers, traitors, scum, filth, anarchists, ass kissers, capitalists, exploiters, aggressors, fascists, black shirts, white army, anarcholiberals, technocrats. We–good. After two hours of banging my forehead against the greasy window trying to sleep, with a morning erection the size of a battleship, I would get off the bus at the Belgrade station, surrounded by pickpockets, Gypsies, prostitutes, beggars, and cops in civil suits, take the streetcar to my hotel and–wham!–enter my sanctuary. Why? Was I better than my parents? Was I better than the others? Was I smarter, more beautiful, a better fuck?

There were fewer and fewer things I could discuss with my friends back home; my parents were getting only a tiny part of the truth, only its selected rosy part. I simply lived in such luxury that I didn't dare tell them about it. I couldn't find the way between.

Sitting in the president's office, smoking and staring at the wall, I couldn't believe that the black book showed no sign of life. Or–even worse–if some of them felt like I did, but hid it, they'd decided to remain silent and take part in this lottery we were playing. Some of us will prosper, but who will it be? Oh, how interesting. Wake me up when the revolution's over.

Some delegation from Slovenia was visiting Belgrade, and we organized an evening for them in the Danube restaurant in Hotel Jugoslavija. Attendance wasn't obligatory, but many people went, including Irena, and it was only natural for me to go downstairs. They put together several tables for us, the house band, Bekvadro, played waltzes and golden oldies, and the shine of crystal chandeliers and the whisper of violins took us all to some happier place, where nights were safe without guns.

Around midnight Irena wanted a coffee, but they were serving only drinks, so I offered her an instant coffee in my room. We went upstairs and she showed me how to make a proper Nescafé.

I felt good with Irena. She didn't hide that she thought I was funny as hell with my clumsy manners and my "all out" approach, but she was among the very few capable of reading between my lines. Or willing to.

So we sat there, in room 309 of Hotel Jugoslavija, sipping coffee and gossiping about our colleagues. The door to the balcony was slightly open and the distant murmur of fine music was hanging in the air. She started talking about how she came to SYS, and my thoughts wandered for a while. I watched her dark hair, her brown eyes and her full lips under the light of the lamp, and I realized this was all a terribly sad thing. How much time did we have—not only she and I, but all of us, the whole bunch at SYS? Several months, at most. We had been brought under that one roof from various places in Serbia, picked up by the invisible hand of the regime, put to work under strict control, and when our terms ended, we would all be dispersed again with only memories of our good salaries, this luxury and our chauffeurs. Irena would stay in Belgrade, go to parties at her friends' villas, enjoy life to the fullest. I would probably return to Kragujevac, drag my feet down the dirty streets, trying to create something important, be it a book, a poem or a song. We'd meet, what, twice a year? We wouldn't have mutual friends anymore to gossip about, and few shared experiences to keep us warm.

In the middle of her story I got up, knelt in front of her, and kissed her.

"Wait, wait." She pushed me back gently. "Haven't you heard that you should never sleep with someone you're working with?"

"I know that in theory, but I've never slept with a colleague before. Have you?"

"No."

"Then how do we know it's bad?"

She was silent for some time, looking carefully into my eyes. Then she said, "Try this: 'In these insecure times a hard dick might be the only reliable thing on the horizon.' And then turn the lights off."

Another week passed and I had to take a third stab at guarding the building overnight. There was no gun this time—Kanda took his toy away from me. Good. I opened the black notebook right away. I wanted to put together a crossword puzzle for the guy after me. I was trying for a revolutionary puzzle–every word in it related to our bureaucratic language. After finishing it, I quoted some Yesenin and some Mayakovsky, glued down several photocopied pages of *Das Kapital,* and that was that–the notebook was full. I did the same thing the history books said our top leaders did when they were imprisoned–used their jail time to educate one another by translating Marx, Engels and Lenin and to debate the idea of communism.

At five to midnight, the doorbell rang. I went to open it, and there were two silhouettes outside: Goran and Irena.

"Hi, colleague," said Goran coldly.

"I came to keep you company," said Irena, "I brought some cookies."

"I don't know if you're allowed to be here," said Goran.

"Actually, she's here during my shift, so I'll take the responsibility." I waved her in.

Irena made coffee and the three of us sat in the president's office, munching cookies and talking. At one in the morning I signed the last page of the notebook and handed it over to Goran. "I'm afraid there's no more space, so you better have a quiet night. And there's no gun anymore."

"I need to get something from my office," said Irena. "Come with me."

We had an order to keep the lights to a minimum in the building, and the corridors were dark. I followed her to her office, and she pulled me inside. "I have an idea," she whispered after closing the door behind me. "Let's steal the official car and go for a ride."

I saw her excited eyes in the light of the street lamp.

"The keys are in the desk," I said.

"I'll divert him while you sneak in and take them," she said.

I could hear her high heels echoing through the empty

space as she went to distract Goran. I could hear their voices in some distant office as I took the keys from the desk and tiptoed towards the front door. I carefully opened the squeaky door and headed for the parking. I waited in a shadow till she came, and then we ran to the car, hopped inside and drove away. It was the cheapest vehicle in our parking lot, an old Lada that was falling apart, but the motor, guzzling gasoline, was still powerful. I drove across the bridge and parked in a shadow in the desolate parking lot behind the Faculty of Arts. We made love on the front seat, hungrily, devouring each other, crazy with excitement. Once the wolves were fed, we lit cigarettes and became quiet. I switched on the radio; they played some slow lemonade.

"What will we do?" I said.

"If this falls apart, you mean?" she asked. "I finished this school"–and she pointed with her toe at the dark building– "and it will probably lead me to theater. I'll be producing shows, drink with the actors, gossip with them, sleep with the directors, the usual stuff. What about you?"

"I'll have to go back to Kragujevac, tend to my sick father, get married, serve in the army, have three kids and get a job in the car factory. I'll eat dead pig on holidays, drink cheap wine and learn to love folk music. The usual stuff."

"So we're fine, then," she said. Her voice made me look into her eyes, which were glistening.

I turned the key and the old Lada jumped. We zoomed past the dark SYS building and continued towards Hotel Jugoslavija. We caught the green wave of a traffic light and I put the pedal to the metal, and found a rock station. The asphalt was wet and our faces were wet and the air was sweet and the world was distant. It was past three in the morning and there was no traffic on the long street that curved along the Danube. Hitting eighty-five, the car was slightly unstable, but I loved it–it felt like driving on thin ice. Then Irena, in a very quiet voice, said, "Baba." It took me a second or two to realize that she wasn't telling a story about her grandmother but referring to a dark silhouette crossing the street ahead. The old woman was already in the middle and the street was too narrow to avoid her. I tried slowing down but the car swayed dangerously. I downshifted for better control and hit the gas again. The car roared and we whizzed by only inches from the woman. In the mirror I saw the old woman just standing there, like a monument to chance. Irena started shaking and I slowed to a crawl. We entered Zemun and I randomly picked some street going uphill. It took us straight to the cemetery. I stopped the car and we sat there, crickets all around us.

"Let's go back," she said after a while.

I took her home, and then I went to the hotel and parked the car. I'd tell them I couldn't find a cab at that time of night, so I had to take the vehicle.

There was no trace of me in the room, as usual. I found my bottle of wine below the dirty socks in the closet, opened it, and took the chair out on the balcony. The night was starry and the Danube was murmuring something reproachful. I started shaking and didn't stop till morning.

THE LESS YOU KNOW

After several weeks the situation in Kosovo calmed down–or at least we didn't get any bad news from there–and the work at the headquarters of Socialist Youth of Serbia hesitantly continued. Hoxa was rarely seen, and nobody asked much about him. Irena and I finally got down to working on the Youth Day celebration. She saved us by finding a binder with old files related to Youth Day, and it turned out that many things could be recycled, Vera style: timelines, a list of places and people responsible for various stages of organization, and detailed instructions on how to follow procedures with the police and security. We finished the work in a week, it was approved, and copies of the plan were sent out to local producers. The baton, as usual, would come from Bosnia, circle Serbia for two and a half weeks and end up at the big central celebration in Belgrade on May 25.

"This is your gun, a semi-automatic, and here's a box of bullets." Kanda pushed a piece of paper towards me to sign. "Keep these safe at all times. If you lose any of these, you're in deep shit. Don't fire a single bullet for fun, because then you will have to write a long report about it, and not to me–to the police." He had to give his toy to me again, and he was pissed about it.

As Tika and Bora, two drivers assigned to me, were signing their papers and receiving their pistols, I looked at the big map on the wall behind Kanda: I was supposed to follow the Štafeta for three days through western Serbia, an area along the Drina River, close to the border with Bosnia. I wasn't sure what I was to do with the gun, but the heavy, shiny thing was now stuck in my belt and the square box with twenty-five bullets was in my pocket.

"You know nothing about what we need to do, do you, boss?" asked Tika as we drove southwest towards Drina. I was in the backseat, and Bora was next to him in front.

"Not much," I said.

"That's why you work at SYS headquarters. They usually pick you that way: the less you know, the higher you get."

Bora laughed. He was middle-aged, cross-eyed and always smiling. He'd worked at SYS for several years already, yet nobody knew much about him, except that he was married. Tika was a tall guy, with a square jaw, low forehead and no scruples. His job was to drive us politicians around in a state-owned car, but his true love was racing. He took this job so he could steal car parts and practice for rallies with his scared passengers in the back. The majority of official drivers in Yugoslavia, probably all of them, were spying on the politicians they chauffeured around. Almost every time you rode, the driver would start talking trash about your colleagues, provoking you–unless, of course, you were positioned so high they wouldn't dare. I wasn't, obviously.

"I guess you're right, Tika," I said. "That's probably why we have you, the drivers, who are the informers, so–inform me."

"Oh, we're smart today," he said.

"Smart always, brother, and count on it."

They didn't like it. And that was fine with me. Three days in the same car with these two wasn't going to be fun, but I didn't want to let them have fun at my expense, either.

Bora found some gross radio station with the worst folk music imaginable and set the volume to "throbbing headache." Without saying a word, I took my Walkman out of my shoulder bag and put the headphones on. I could see Bora's crossed eyes in the mirror, and I merrily waved at him, lit a cigarette and took off my shoes. I was always fond of the "beat them with their own weapons" strategy.

Half an hour later, while passing through some small village, Tika switched the radio off. I took my headphones off.

"Seriously, boss," he said, "do you know how it goes?"

"No, except that we are supposed to drive behind the Štafeta and make sure everything unfolds as planned."

"Okay, here's the story. Štafeta is always made in three identical copies. One goes from hand to hand, and that is the one that people see. The other is in our trunk. If someone steals the first one, we are to replace it in under ten seconds. We have the final word in everything. Even the police have to listen to us. If we decide to change the route for some reason, the route will be changed that instant. Also, when festivities in some village last longer than scheduled, we command the Štafeta to go on, no matter what, even if that means we have to go up on stage and take it out of their hands. All traveling must be done during the day. When it gets dark, the Štafeta stays overnight in a city, and a wake-up is organized."

"What's with the third copy?"

"It stays in Belgrade. If the first one is stolen, and we get killed, the third one will be flown in by helicopter."

"Why do we need guns?"

"You never know. Two years ago we had to use them. Somewhere around Kraljevo, while passing through a wide forest, we heard shots, so we stopped the convoy, jumped behind the car and started firing back. Then someone found out that there were some stupid local hunters in the woods. This year, we included those guys in our security system. There's one place in the same area where we have to let the Štafeta travel until eleven at night. The schedule is so tight we have to let it go. Well, you should know–you made it. But we got those hunters on our side. A hundred and fifty of them will be hidden in the woods on both sides of the road."

"What if some of them get drunk and decide–"

"To start shooting anyway? There will be around three hundred soldiers hidden behind their back."

"What happens to the Štafeta in the end, now that Tito is dead?"

"It's going straight to his mausoleum. It'll be taken to his residency on Dedinje."

The next two days were a major bore: sitting in the car the whole day, driving slowly behind the runners carrying the Štafeta, grabbing a sandwich here and there, and speeding up some overzealous local politician. Then, on the morning of the third day, I discovered that the ammunition box had disappeared from my bag. I searched my hotel room and found nothing. Bora and Tika advised me to report it to the local police. Being almost sure it was Tika who'd stolen it while I was sitting with the politicians at the long dinner the night before, I decided to keep quiet. If someone was pulling a prank, nothing would happen when we returned to Belgrade. If I was wrong, well, then I'd know.

The next day, in Belgrade, Kanda made a grave face and told me to write a report on the disappearance of the ammo, but nothing ever happened afterwards. Nothing formally, but I didn't like what had happened, because a trick of this type, when pulled on you, always meant you were beyond being taken seriously. It always meant you were on your way out.

I didn't have time to worry about it, since my job was still far from over. Irena and I had only scratched the really difficult part–production of the Serbian celebration.

BEYOND SERIOUS

The celebration of the Štafeta was always the same communist kitsch: thousands of young bodies jumping mindlessly in the stadium to the music specially written for that occasion, to the lyrics of some scribbler, according to the script of a group of opportunists, in front of an audience that didn't have better things to do. But we still needed composers, librettists, choreographers, writers, performers, scenographers and a director. When I returned to Belgrade, Irena already had the whole list of names. None of them were familiar to me, but she assured me that she knew all of them personally. She even sent the names to Serbian police headquarters for security clearance, and they approved the list after some delay. So we rented a bus and drove all together–everyone except the choreographer, who was already there–for five hours south to Leskovac to start working on the show. We had less than two weeks left.

After settling into the local hotel, and having the first quick meetings with the local officials who would work with us, we discovered there was not much to do in the evening except frequent the local joints and stuff ourselves with greasy local food and cheap booze. Instead, we improvised on the roof of the hotel. That was how I got to know the team that Irena had selected. Chatting, with glass in hand, I learned about their artistic background, and I slowly realized that their portfolios were–blank. The scenographer, a thin small woman, had done some work in Belgrade theaters, but the rest of them had almost no experience. The director, a bony bald guy in his mid-thirties, had done only a couple of amateur productions in provincial theaters and had no experience with large-scale shows like ours. I had deep trust in Irena, so this seemed odd.

A tall, gray-haired guy in his early fifties, in tight jeans and cowboy boots, appeared briefly on the roof, shook hands with everyone, introduced himself as our choreographer, Beli, and then whispered to me, "Room 511. In half an hour. Be alone." Then he disappeared.

Half an hour later, slightly drunk and thoroughly confused, I knocked at his door. He appeared with only a towel around his waist, his hair still wet.

"Don't worry, I won't fuck you." He let me in, stuck his head out to see whether anyone had followed me and locked the door. I decided to stand next to the heavy crystal vase on the side table, just in case.

"Are you insane?" he said without further ado. He looked me straight in the eye for a second and said, "You really don't know, do you?"

"Know what?"

"Who selected these people up there? Was it you?"

"No. Actually, I was rather busy, so my secretary found them all."

"You seem like a decent guy, so I'll cut the crap. They're druggies. I know from my connections in the police. They've had their eyes on all of them for some time now. The reason why they're still free is that they are all children of important people. Your director is under suspicion for pushing heroin. Your dear secretary may have her own interests she didn't tell you about."

Several voices argued in my head. One of them was saying something about running away.

"A friend of mine, a police inspector, told me they approved your list because they wanted to have them all in one place, the whole ring. The police will let you finish this, of course, but how will it look in the end? I suggest you don't sleep at all, I suggest you breathe down their necks the whole time. If they screw this up, you will go down, understand?"

I still couldn't find a single word.

"I'll help you. I'll give my friend a call, and when you go to Belgrade, tell him I sent you. At least they will know it wasn't you. Okay?"

"Thank you, Beli, I don't know what to say."

"I'm helping you just because you seem like a nice guy, okay? By the way"–and he pulled a cardboard box from his travel bag–"I just came from Switzerland two days ago and I brought with me more cassettes than I need. They're good, TDK, sixty minutes. Wanna buy? Only fifty bucks, pack of ten. You can give me the money later."

I took the box and went back to the roof. The talk was subdued, somehow ethereal. I saw Irena kissing the director in the corner. After he went inside, I walked over and looked in her eyes.

"Sorry, old man," she said. Her irises were wide, as they are when in love, or when drugged, or when standing in the dark, as we were.

I got really drunk after that, and didn't remember much the next morning. There was some glass I'd broken by squeezing it hard with my left hand. And there was blood somebody had been washing off my hands. Irena and the small woman took me to bed, and I tried to make love to both of them. They told me to shut up and sleep. Or maybe none of that happened.

The next day I got a call from the secretary of the local city council, inviting me to lunch in Leskovac's best restaurant, on a hill overlooking the city. They would come to pick me up at noon.

At noon, in the car in front of the hotel were Tika, Bora and Tomo, a fat man in his fifties. He was an official of the city council, and by the way everyone saluted him I understood he was important. We drove uphill to a house painted white, with a large grill outside and a sheep's skin, still bloody and hung up on a post in front of the entrance like an ad for fresh meat.

We ordered from a suicide menu: everything was full of

fat. Leskovac was reportedly a backward community with patriarchal values and a strong tradition of Turkish food. Without asking, Tomo ordered rakija for all of us. It was the beginning of May, the day was sunny and hot, and nobody gave a damn that I wanted some mineral water to cure my headache and wash the awkward taste of last night from my mouth. And the dancing lights were flickering before my eyes. Testosterone was all over the floor here and if you were not careful you'd slip and fall directly onto someone's fist.

Scratching his balls, Tika looked towards the city below.

"So, Tomo, bro, what's there for us in the evening? Where should we go? Is there anything to fuck?"

"That's all we do, bro. Drink and fuck."

"Where can we catch some young pussy? Cafés?"

"Wherever you want. They fuck like thin pigs here."

People drink and fuck in all backwater towns, there's not much else to do. They do it like thin pigs here, they fuck like pikes in Topola, they fire in Niš and they knock in Zaječar. And when all this is over, we'll all get drunk and fuck.

"What's wrong, little Dragan, our rakija is not to your taste?" asked Tomo.

"It's too early, Tomo, and I had way too much last night. We will have to work hard today. We have a lot to do and time is short."

"Oh, *that,*" said Tomo. "You're not taking it seriously, bro, are you? We'll do it with our left hand, don't worry. Besides, who cares? The kids will jump up and down, as they always do, and the old man is dead anyway, so he won't get angry if it's not nice."

"No, it's not that," said Tika. "Our little Dragan is an intellectual, Tomo. He fucks through proxies. He puts together a team for everything, even that. Sometimes his team can't get it up, but that's another problem."

Laughter. I was way beyond serious.

THOSE TIRED EYES

I decided not to call Beli's friend. Whether Beli was provoking me with his story or telling the truth, I didn't want to know. And I didn't care if I went down with the whole thing. Irena had betrayed me. I just didn't care.

Five days later I traveled from Leskovac to Belgrade to submit the plan of the whole operation to the central office of the Serbian police. I met one of the bosses of the special interventions section, a gray-haired fellow of worldly manners. All the younger policemen around us were tiptoeing, confirming that he was very important.

I pulled out my stack of papers, with names, places, plans, numbers, and my gray-haired friend just waved his hand nonchalantly, ordering, by a short quick roll of his eye, one of the policemen to take the heap away. No, the two of us were way above that. He ordered whiskey for two, although there were seven people in the room. He offered me his Marlboros and lit my cigarette with his golden Cartier lighter. He gently caressed my hurt pride and I felt important again; he was my friend. Our whiskey arrived with coffee for all and we chatted.

After half an hour spent in this pleasant, relaxed atmosphere, the five policemen around us stood up without any visible sign from him and left us alone.

"I respect highly what you do," he said. I didn't have a clue what he was talking about. He stood up and went to the window with the glass in his hand. His thoughts drifting briefly, he played with the rocks in his whiskey, staring through the light curtain yellowish with tobacco smoke. Bogart of *Casablanca*, with the tinkle of ice cubes substituting for the piano in the background.

"Dragan, people like us are misunderstood. Others look at us from the side and they think it's easy for us, as we have it all. They don't realize how difficult the work behind our façade is. They don't see all the rooms in our heads and what's going on in them. What do you do in your spare time? Write, as far as I know . . ."

I nodded.

"I write, too. Poetry. And what do people think? A cop, his is a dirty job, he beats people, he spies on his friends. He is trash. And about you: a journalist; he knows everything, he knows nothing. A scribbler."

I wished he'd cut this, and he did–right on time.

"For that reason, people like us have to stick together." He was still at the window, his back to me. "What is our power? Information!" He spun on his heel, perfectly underlining this sentence. His blue eyes of a tired old Siberian husky had seen all the evil of this world and they understood it. He hugged me with those eyes and I felt that it was okay to tell him everything. Tell him how I was afraid those so-called authors in Leskovac were a gang of idiots without a single artistic idea, how the show was only a senseless waste of several hundred millions. The only thing holding me back was my inbred mistrust of the police.

"Information is what keeps us. That's my philately: collecting information. And not only about the enemies of our system–about everything. Because all of it is floating and mixing, like this cigarette smoke, and you see this now, and that then, but it's all part of the same picture. My policemen here are good, but not good enough. They can't melt in with the masses. As soon as they appear somewhere–as civilians, we don't wear uniforms, ever–it's as if they had a sticker saying 'cop' on their backs. That's because of their vanity. They think they are important. Our look comes from our brain, and people can sense it."

He sat next to me, his eyes fixed upon mine. I couldn't avoid his stare because it would have been a betrayal of all the related beings of the universe. We are unrecognized artists, we are the elite that knows, we are brothers in arms. The question, if there was one, would come soon.

"You go places; you meet writers, actors, other journalists. You sit at panel discussions on political issues; you've even been moderator on some of them. You sit at the meetings at the Association of Socialist Youth of Serbia. None of these places is safe. You can't even imagine how many there are among us who want evil for this system. I can never understand that: this state has given an apartment, a salary, a car, a person can do the things he's interested in, and yet some devil makes him work against the system. Now, when we say 'system,' ordinary people think, 'It's an apparatus, it's not me,' and that is a huge mistake. If even the tiniest wheel doesn't function well, we all feel it. I'm not saying that our system is weak, that it can be easily destroyed, but it's one fine mechanism and it needs protection . . . I need you."

He was obviously well prepared for this meeting; he knew my biography inside out. But what led him to the conclusion that I would be material for his line of work? I had never betrayed anyone. On my list of principles, loyalty to my friends was among the highest ranking. Well, exactly. How stupid of me: loyalty was the key. But he misread it. I was never loyal to the system, never to an institution. I always felt that systems, organizations, come and go. What stays are those few good people you gather along the way.

There are no seducers–there are only people who heard "yes" too often. This man before me was a master of seduction. So how many like me, before me, had said yes to him? Were my friends among them? And if they were–now spying on me–wouldn't it be perfect self-defense to do intelligence work for the same master?

I could see secret agent Dragan One-Million-and-Seven receiving a badge of honor. He was more beautiful, more able and immensely more powerful than me, a member of a secret brotherhood of chosen ones. He traveled around the world, did the dangerous things that belong to the night and the blade, and he won, wins and will win . . . And then he goes out to celebrate, but wait, there's nobody with him. He can't look anyone in the eyes; he doesn't belong to himself because he has a center to report to till the end of his life. He is isolated, poisonous.

"You don't need me," I said. "The fact that you can read my file doesn't mean that you know me."

I tried to say this calmly, but he saw that my cheeks were flushed and read that as the end of our conversation. He invited the other policemen into the room, gave some orders, we shook hands, and I was escorted out of the building. Those tired eyes of an old husky stayed forever behind the yellow curtain.

I was out.

My status changed from that moment on. After returning to Leskovac I became the target of ominous jokes, and–not speaking much to Irena anymore–I had no one to tell about what went on. Someone would call a meeting of the team without telling me; an almost naked teenage girl knocked at my door one night to ask me if I was able to fuck at all; at dinnertime, after a few drinks, I would listen to tasteless remarks that all came down to this: I was a loser who couldn't recognize what was good for him.

We did finish the work on time. The celebration of the Štafeta in Leskovac that year was the same communist kitsch as always: thousands of young bodies jumping mindlessly in the stadium to the music specially written for that occasion, to the lyrics of some scribbler, according to the script of a group of opportunists, in front of an audience that didn't have better things to do. Only, this time, I produced it.

When we returned to Belgrade, I was informed that I had to move out of Hotel Jugoslavija. Fast.

EUROPA

I took a vacation that summer. Miša the poetry man, Paun (Professor Djordje's elder son), Nagip and I planned a trip: InterRail offered a second-class ticket that would allow us to travel anywhere in Europe for a month. We had addresses of cheap hostels, we purchased new backpacks and we saved some money. Miša and Paun wanted to travel to Paris and London first, while Nagip and I wanted to go to Switzerland and Germany. All of us wanted to visit Amsterdam, and then we would stay for a week in Barcelona. Not being able to keep in touch during the trip and coordinate our timing, we set three dates in the second half of the month for our meeting in Amsterdam. There was a hostel that belonged to the Salvation Army, or some equivalent Dutch organization, in the heart of the red-light district, close to the Amsterdam central station. Friends told us it was only a relatively safe place, and advised us to take knives with us.

Nagip had an Arabic name and looks, although he was born in Serbia. He belonged to a rare nationality who called themselves Goranci, and insisted on their differences from their neighbors, the Kosovo Albanians. With his dark eyes and his always unshaven square chin, he had the type of face that makes cops suspicious. When we started our voyage, he told me that he wanted to buy a machine for making ice-cream cones. His father, who had left his family when Nagip was seven, ran a lucrative business selling luscious ice cream in the center of Kragujevac. I suspected Nagip thought he might bridge the gap between his parents if he could make something his father needed.

But Nagip didn't speak any foreign languages. So, in Germany: we visited a store selling high-end appliances at thousands of deutschmarks, I asked for the cone-making machine, Nagip nodded and tried to make the shape of a cone with his hands. It looked as if he was depicting a bomb, they stared at us, and they called security. In Switzerland: we visited a store selling high-end appliances at thousands of Swiss francs, I asked for the cone-making machine, Nagip nodded and tried to make the shape of cone with his hands. They stared at us, told us to leave, and then a police patrol stopped us on the street, asking for IDs. On the train in between: we stood in the corridor talking about the cone-making machines, and then security came and asked for our passports. Somewhere between Munich and Hamburg a six-pack of giants in black leather showed us their German Security Service badges and searched our backpacks. My black beard didn't help either, I suppose. It made me feel safe: if we looked dangerous enough to have six giants come at us, we wouldn't need our knives in that hostel in Holland.

We arrived in Amsterdam in the late evening. The hostel was in a narrow street close to Oude Kerk, the oldest church in the city. It was a three-story building with large rooms of fifteen to twenty beds each. Men and women had separate floors, and you were not allowed to stop on the opposite sex's floor. The bathrooms looked like those in army camps: doors hiding only your private parts, and two guards who kept peering over the top of each cabin so you couldn't masturbate or take drugs. The main entrance was locked after midnight and opened again at seven in the morning. But it cost ten guilders a night when a Big Mac cost four and a half. Nagip and I took two beds in the corner, and kept our backs to the wall.

Morning in the red-light district looks like morning in a giant theater on the day of a premiere. The rehearsals are over, a sense of expectation hangs in the air, the trucks keep bringing requisites for the show, the stone-cobbled streets are clean and wet, and the canals and the windows of the prostitutes' rooms are sun-spangled. I went downstairs first, rolled a Drum and leaned back against a tree by the canal waiting for Nagip. A group of Hells Angels drove by, headed for the tattoo parlor around the corner. Three blondes on a boat waved at me, laughing, and I waved back. A Rasta came by and offered me some coke, or ganja, or watches–underneath his coat was a whole traveling store. A small Thai restaurant had an ad for Angel Cakes in the window, but next to it was a picture of their real specialty: small rounded loaves spiked with marijuana. A giant red penis cast in bronze stood in front of the Casa Rosso erotic theater across the channel. Al Stewart's "Year of the Cat" was playing loudly in a brown café down the street.

Something happened to me, right then, right there. All those bastards in Belgrade: why should I waste my time on them? If you stay too long within the four walls of your worries, that space tends to get smaller and smaller, until you choke to death. If you travel far enough you will always find some cities, some vistas, some mornings that can set you free. I'd just found mine.

Miša and Paun arrived on the third day. By then I felt so different I almost didn't expect them to recognize me. We went to Barcelona and watched the sunset in the harbor, under the monument to Columbus, and saw the monument to Franco, and the pigeons shitting on it. And every day we would take the train to the beach in Sitges, where Dali used to swim. And every afternoon we would go back on the same train, and Spanish women would sometimes spread their legs to flash us. An old conductor cried and hugged us when he realized we were from Yugoslavia: he had fought in the Spanish Civil War shoulder to shoulder with our countrymen. Nagip never found the cone-making machine.

Europe was in my backpack when I returned to Kragujevac.

HOW WOULD THEY WRITE IN AMSTERDAM?

Late that summer of 1981 I was given instructions to travel to Knjaževac, to attend the traditional Festival of Youth Culture. It was an insignificant event, where older Communist cadres would go to get drunk and chase easy TV women, but it always had good coverage. Well oiled after a week of mostly free food and paid expenses, journalists lied through their teeth glorifying the festival. In return, the budget for the festival was always generous and the performers loved going, because a bad review was unknown there.

And it was another of my defeats: Irena and I had proposed new solutions for the festival a few months before—mainly, to make it happen in a different city every year. Our ideas were refused on the pretext of money, although our documents showed savings over the usual cost.

I didn't want to go there that summer, but I had to. Kanda and Irena were going, too, as well as many others who worked with us at SYS headquarters. Irena and I were rarely communicating now. I expected some explanation from her on what was happening in Leskovac, and she felt she owed me none.

As I expected, nothing worth mentioning in the artistic sense happened, and everyone drank and ate a lot, and chased one another. But on the closing day, Irena came into my room, slightly disturbed, and–after some persuading–told me that she couldn't sleep the previous night, because Kanda had come into her room and sexually attacked her.

After she left, I called Ratomir Mirić. During my work with SYS I sometimes wrote for his magazine, but neither of us was happy anymore with that cooperation: he expected me to lobby more for him, although I was so busy with my own little wars that I couldn't, and I was pissed off at him for throwing me into the pressure cooker that SYS was. I said that I wanted to write a critical article about the festival, and try to create a storm that could bring some change. He agreed with this, and so I sat down and wrote a sketch for the article.

I didn't refine it much when I returned to Belgrade. I couldn't see a way to polish it, other than the usual communist approach–constructive criticism–but that was something I had tried with no luck. And, since coming back from Europe, whenever I would sit down to write something, I would ask myself, "How would this article be written in Amsterdam?"

So I wrote it as they would in Amsterdam. Ratomir cut it as they did in Yugoslavia, and gave it a small space in the corner of the umpteenth page, but he left a sentence where I alluded to Irena's incident with Kanda–no names or descriptions, but there was enough there for both Irena and Kanda to recognize themselves. The article was published on a Friday, and I was in Kragujevac over the weekend. Irena called me there. She sounded sad, I guess because she understood why I wrote it.

The next week at work was ominously silent. Nobody talked to me about that article, although Irena told me everyone was discussing it in hallways. On Friday, the new issue of *Omladinske* came out, publishing a letter against me, signed with a false name. It was a full frontal attack, a call to lynch. Irena told me Kanda bragged about writing it. I went to Ratomir's office and threw my press ID from *Omladinske* at him.

FINISHED

The following week I received a piece of registered mail, sent care of my parents in Kragujevac. It had a pink slip inside: conscription. I was to be in the army camp in Sombor in less than two days: less notice than usual in war. I traveled home, shaved my beard off after five years, and my father, trembling with Parkinson's, got out of bed crying and hugged me long, long. My friends reacted with confusion. Clearly, I had some troubles with the system, which shouldn't be discussed. They focused instead on traditional army jokes and teasing. "Don't forget to apply hand cream regularly so your dick doesn't get sharpened like a pencil." In fact, they tried so hard not to ask me anything that I could only hear the question they avoided: "Are you finished?"

5

GAME: WHOM DO YOU WANT?

The rules

Contestants separate into two groups about fifteen yards apart and face each other. Each group holds hands. One group calls, "Yelechkinye Baryachkinye, whom do you want?" The other group yells a name. The selected person runs as fast as she can towards the other group, hits the living wall and tries to break it apart. If she does, she selects a person to take back to her side. If she fails she stays with the new group. The game ends when all contestants, except the one that nobody wanted to take back, are on one side.

The reality

The challenged group always calls for the weakest player to attack them, and the attackers in turn always aim at the weakest spot. Although the groups try to put the stronger contestants next to the weaker ones, there are those with whom no one wants to hold hands. Most runners launch a karate blow at the time of impact.

The game usually ends with someone being hurt.

SITTING DUCKS

Ensign Mile Tintor opened a new pack of cigarettes. His fingers were yellow and full of knots, like trees growing in badlands. His mustache was black and bushy, tips turned a little towards each other. If you drew straight lines down from both, they would probably cross at the center of his universe–the head of his dick.

He took a long sip of beer, which almost emptied his bottle, wiped off the foam with the back of his hand and pointed his bloodshot eyes at me.

"I don't know if I can tell you that," he said. "You understand it's top secret?"

"Of course I do," I replied, raising two fingers towards the waiter sitting in the corner, by the furnace. He got up, brought two half-liter bottles and dropped them on our table.

"Wait," said Tintor, "take this one back. You know I never drink from green ones."

"He can have it," said the waiter, nodding in my direction.

"What the fuck is with you, buddy?" said Tintor. "Nobody in their right mind drinks from green bottles. Beer shouldn't look like lizards." The waiter took the bottle and left. The back of his white jacket was soiled with coal dust and something red. "He's new here," said Tintor, looking after him. "He came only three years ago."

It was snowing again. The winter of 1981 was sharp as an officer's sword. The small joint on the outskirts of Sombor was warm, but the plains of Vojvodina outside looked threatening and depressing. It was getting dark. Tintor had taken two other soldiers and me with him to bring some equipment for the recital of revolutionary poetry to be held at the barracks that evening. On the way back, he sent those two off with the stuff and took me with him for a drink. I wasn't his favorite, nobody was anymore, but he hated drinking alone, and he didn't mind me. After two hours of talk about where to find prostitutes, and how to recognize a promising widow, I'd asked him what our garrison was supposed to be doing here in the far north of Serbia.

"I'm not supposed to know this, so you never heard it from me, okay?"

"Absolutely."

"Here's the deal: if the enemy attacks, since we are stationed in the fucking plains, they would almost certainly come with hundreds of tanks preceded by planes that would bomb the shit out of us, right? We have tanks, but they are stationed farther south. And this is technically an airport, but we don't keep the planes here, it's too close to the border. Our troops farther south need forty-five minutes to react to a sudden attack in numbers sufficient enough to give them trouble. Our task is to survive for forty-five minutes."

"But . . ."

"I know–there's a city, there are factories, there are people, everything. I know. But we are not supposed to defend anything. We are supposed to keep the enemy busy for forty-five minutes and then we are free to die. Fucking plains. If this was my Krajina, with all the hills around, with rocks sharp as an ax, we could fight for months. In the plains, you are a sitting duck."

Keep the enemy busy? Buy Belgrade an hour? For what, for the politicians to flee the country as they did when Hitler invaded?

MANTRA

When I arrived at the gate of the Sombor garrison that first night, it didn't look big from the outside: a wide gate for vehicles and a small one for pedestrians framed with three stone posts in the front. A small house lurked behind the barbed wire, and a line of trees concealed the yard. They took me in, asked my name, searched my bag, stole my cigarettes, gave me a bad haircut, and then some lizard took me to find a place to sleep. "Lizards" were the new soldiers, so named for dragging their bellies through the dust while being trained.

The camp was three miles from Sombor, a city of around fifty thousand people, less than an hour from the Hungarian border. I was happy to get this post. When I took my draft order to the army recruiting center in Kragujevac, a guy there looked into his books and said, "Oh, the emergency case. You did something wrong, killed someone, or what?"

"What do you mean?"

"Well, my boy, you have a powerful enemy somewhere high up. We got special calls ordering us to send you to very bad places. Some general, I think. You're lucky I hate them, so we'll send you to Sombor. It's the air force, so it's a little easier, the city is full of liberated women, and you'll look good in a blue uniform."

By the time they showed me to my bunk bed, the lights were out. I took off my newly acquired uniform, hung it up and climbed into bed. It was September, and it wasn't cold, so the windows were open, and it was quiet outside. I started listening to the breathing of others: it was shallow and spotty. Nobody was sleeping. I counted the beds: there were fourteen of them. Twenty-eight scared men. Slowly, the stench of the garrison crept in: male sweat mixed with the musk of genitals, some chemical–probably something against lice–and the heavy, omnipresent smell of weapon oil. When I was eight, I would sneak into my cousin Boban's closet, open the small bottle of walnut oil he used to comb his hair and apply it generously to my scalp. I thought it was a well-kept secret, until I realized they all knew it every time, partly because I looked greasy, partly because I smelled. But that was the reason I stole his oil: the odor was masculine and stern, like the punch of a middleweight. Now it was here, all around me. The weapon oil definitely had walnuts in it.

My life started rewinding, slowly at first, but then faster and further. It didn't feel the way they say it feels when dying; it seemed more like trying to hold on to something from my past to get me to the other side of night. No matter how hard I tried to grab at something, and keep that thought, everything was just too slippery, everything had just too much of that stinking oil on it.

As the minutes passed, nobody in the room tried to talk. A quiet, sad fart would come now and then, stifled under the harsh military blankets. The stink was getting worse in spite of the open window. It was two hours later, at least, when I noticed that several guys had fallen asleep. Their breathing was deeper and rhythmical, and some of them were weeping in their dreams. The guy below me started calling his mother, another man across the room called some female name, then another one. Soon, at least six or seven of them were calling the women in their lives. They were seeking softness in that hard, sharp military space: concrete steps, concrete floors, iron beds, metal closets, armed guards, barbed wire, rifles in the corridor.

I pulled the blanket over my head and started repeating my own name, quietly, whispering, the way prayer is said, or a mantra. That put me to sleep, late, late in the night. I dreamt that nine naked girls knelt with their backs towards me. I knew their names by the shape of their buttocks, but each of them had the map of Siberia tattooed on her back.

PERFUME OF REALITY

The surreal atmosphere of the army makes you angry and bitter–of course, that's the whole idea–but women are the bridge to reality. Yes, there is that environment, full of masculine odors, testosterone, machismo and brutality, and that indeed makes you very sexed up. And yes, the notion of woman is reduced to the level of prey, because the whole brainwashing applied against you is about being Goliath, including a hard penis. But I really believe that the biggest part of the longing for women in the army comes from their being the only way back to reality.

Two weeks after coming to the garrison, we pledged our allegiance to the constitution in a large public ceremony that brought our families and friends from all over the country, several thousands of them. Now officially soldiers of the Yugoslav Army, some of us were allowed to go to Sombor and celebrate with our guests. Those who were married were allowed to spend the night with their wives.

Some soldiers whose families couldn't make it were still rewarded with permits to go to town. They were easy prey for prostitutes, of course. One of them came back just before ten, when everyone else was already in bed, holding his right hand high in the air.

"Come, lizards, and smell heaven!" he exclaimed.

"What is it, you wiped your sister's ass?" asked someone.

"Okay, you won't get to smell. Come, come!"

After a minute or so, the first curious guy approached and smelled his fingers, and smiled. Then we all smelled. Pussy.

"I brought it back just for you, comrades. Keep that in mind and return the favor next time you're out."

The oddest thing was that nobody laughed or made a rude comment. It was almost solemn: men getting out of bed, one by one, going to smell his fingers, their faces melting into befuddled smiles.

Nobody wept that night in their dreams.

THEATER

It was several days past my twenty-third birthday when I became a soldier, but all around me were eighteen- and nineteen-year-old men. I postponed service for three years while I was a student, and then another year when I became a government employee. They started calling me the Old Man. The first couple of times I protested, but then I saw that it gave me certain privileges. At four thirty in the morning, while the others would have to run five full circles around the stadium, I was allowed to run one and then stand aside, huffing and puffing. Playing a Tired Old Man was much easier than running. While the rest of my group jumped across high obstacles and ran their noses through the yellow grass crawling under the barbed wire, I provided sage advice. The corporal, younger than me, a guy from Krajina, didn't object. He would offer me a cigarette and we'd sit on the grass under the clear September sky and talk about girls, life and other things we didn't understand. Even the officers closed one eye at my acting, although I knew they understood what was going on. When the officer in charge of political education asked for volunteers to teach political science, I decided not to raise my hand, although I was the ideal candidate, and he knew it from my dossier. I'd had enough of politics, and he seemed to understand.

I started perceiving the army as yet another form of theater. I let my mustache grow, and the officers liked it—they all had them. I gained some weight, to emphasize my Old Man status, and they liked it even more—some of them had sizable bellies.

—

Ahmed was a thin man with a face full of freckles and yellow teeth. His vocabulary was limited; he probably used a few hundred words only. He'd never gone to school, never learned to read or write, and spent his entire life as a shepherd in the Bosnian mountains. He was twenty-one: it had taken them three years to find him in the mountains to serve him the draft. Other siblings went to school, the sisters had gotten married, but from childhood on, Ahmed spent nine months every year in the hills surrounding his village. He was a good man, never nervous, never aggressive, always ready for a laugh, even at his own expense. The number of jokes the rest of us invented on the theme of Ahmed and his sheep alone in the mountains would have been sufficient to drive others from their skin, but not him.

Once, during a break, we started telling jokes. The jokes that Serbs told were insulting to Bosnians, Bosnian jokes insulted Slovenians, Slovenian jokes targeted Macedonians, but Ahmed's story was different.

"A hooker enters the dick store . . ."

"What store, Ahmed?"

"The dick store. Where they sell dicks."

"Why would anyone sell their dick?"

"Nobody is selling their dick. But they sell dicks."

"For how much?"

"Wanna hear the joke or no?"

"Okay, okay, go on."

"A hooker enters the dick store. And she says, 'What dicks do you have today?' And the guy says, 'What dick do you want, madam? We have Serbian dicks, we have Croatian dicks and we have Muslim dicks.'

"'What's the difference?' asks she.

"'Well, the Serbian one is short and thick, the Croatian is long but thin, and the Muslim dick is circumcised.'

"The hooker thinks, and she thinks, and she says, 'I'd like a Serbo-Croatian dick with a Muslim head.'"

The whole group started rolling around on the grass, some of them laughing at the absurdity of the joke, some of them at the rural length of Ahmed's vowels.

"Tell us another one," someone said.

"I don't know another one," said Ahmed.

"Try to remember, man!" said the corporal. "I'll give you a cigarette if you do."

"I'd love it, Corporal, but I know only this one."

"What do you mean?" I asked. People tried to interpret his words even when he meant something very simple.

"This is the only joke I've ever heard, Old Man," he answered. "Until today."

Janez, a thin, blonde Slovene from Ljubljana, and Željko, a Croat from Zagreb, were constantly together from the day they met. They both loved German music and often laughed at other people's poor manners. There was a whiff of white supremacy about them, and something pathetic I couldn't pinpoint. Frequent whispering in the presence of others certainly didn't bring them closer to the rest of the company. I expected them to be the targets of cruel soldiers' jokes, but the majority considered them too boring even to bother.

Muhamed was a dark, strong Albanian, of very few words. Deep lines around his eyes made him look much older than his nineteen years. When our names were read aloud on the second day, we learned that his family name was Hot. There was a roar of laughter from some five thousand people in the field, but he stayed calm. In the following days he avoided everyone, answering every question in a laconic way, and standing alone during every break. Only several weeks into our stay, when he found some Albanians in another company, did he relax a little. At least we saw him laugh with them sometimes.

Miladin, a Serb from close to my hometown, stole everything in his way–a cigarette here, a matchbox there, a stamp, a shoe polish, pen, postcard, audiocassette, anything. Although we tried several times to find mutual territory and become friends, it just didn't work. Even weather talk was impossible.

"This rain in the plains is somehow worse than the rain we have at home," I said to him one day, standing under a tree on the side of the training field, trying to avoid the cold gray drops. He was playing with a lighter he had probably just stolen. "We're going to drown like rats."

"It's a good rain," he responded. "Good for corn. The grapes will not be great, though, it's going to be a bad year for wine."

I was interested in learning more about Ahmed and Muhamed–their stories would make for a good piece. I kept trying to get them to open up, but it didn't work. I wouldn't last a week where they survived. In Belgrade, where I'd moved around the political labyrinth, they wouldn't understand anything. Janez and Željko came from a milieu similar to mine, but they were soaked in some kind of upbringing that prevented us from communicating.

The officers in the garrison were an unhappy bunch, here for the benefits or because they were too lazy to learn anything else except yelling and shooting. Maybe five of the hundred or so were really in love with their jobs, their pride evident in their posture, their impeccable uniform and their mustaches trimmed with telling precision. But they were castaways, in their own way. Watching bad officers with good connections being promoted ahead of them, their ideals got crushed. These professional soldiers were hoping for war to show their courage. But there was no war in sight, not yet.

The only good thing for me in Sombor was that I started feeling safer than I'd expected. Some garrisons were known to be dangerous places, but Sombor was huge, and the whole system was in slight disarray. In such circumstances, it's easier to get by unnoticed, and that's all I wanted. I decided to try to stay in that garrison after the three-month drill was over.

YOUR MAMA'S MILK

Every garrison had something called a Soldiers' Club, a unit where artists of all kinds would gather to prepare cultural activities for the rest of the soldiers. Soldiers' Club was considered a shelter from the strict regime, a place that would even allow its members to work on their own improvement during the fourteen months they were supposed to stay in the army.

I discovered the Soldiers' Club in our garrison early, and started hanging out there–it was the only hope I had of staying in Sombor. Their commander was Ensign Cvijetić, an extremely polite and warm man with a great sense of humor and enough vanity and possessiveness to protect his unit from the higher command. One day Leka introduced me to him, and he asked me about my past and–when I told him selected parts–asked if I wanted to stay in that garrison. He didn't guarantee anything, he just said he would see.

Leka was a young actor who'd just graduated from the theater academy in Belgrade but had already done a few noted roles in theater and film. When we first met, he was reading Sun Tzu Wu's *Art of War.* Since I knew the book, we started chatting about it, and soon became friends.

Leka was a dark-haired, handsome, dynamic person, with true charisma. He hated communism with a burning passion. His family in Šabac was very rich before the revolution, and lost everything when Tito came to power. When we were alone, he would distort Tito's name, pronouncing it as Tutu, Tata or Tntn, mocking the robotic obedience and opportunism that surrounded us. It was a micro-mutiny, a portable revolt.

Shortly after I met him he was ordered to organize a big recital honoring the Day of the Republic. He decided that all of us who took part in it had to polish our belts, our boots and the stars on our caps until they were blindingly shiny. After we'd applied hundreds of layers of shoe polish, lacquer, acrylic and whatnot, our uniforms had turned into caricatures. The parody was so obvious I was expecting some officer to give us real hell, but it didn't happen. Leka also included in the script verses of officially prohibited poets, such as Radovan Zogović, and that went unnoticed, too.

What Leka was doing then was the same thing I had tried to do: dance on the edge of the prohibited. It was the choreography of one step forward, three steps back. Do something bordering on the forbidden, and then—when you attract their attention—retreat and stay calm. "They" were the eyes and ears of the system, the thousands on the payroll of the State Security Service. The stakes in the army were high, since we were technically under the jurisdiction of the military courts. Military trials were not open to the public. So if you hit an army jail, you'd stay there.

I had already taken my one step forward, and ended up here.

Two days before our drill was over and the lists with our transfer destinations were finalized, I was called before Ensign Gvozdić, a minute man with a disproportionately large voice. He had the sharp hand moves of a dictator, and the patience of a firing squad. And his name meant "iron man." What a choice I had: the meaning of Cvijetić was "small flower."

"Cvijetić called me to recommend you," Gvozdić said. "I'm in charge of the warehouse where we keep the training mines. We have to teach you dickheads how to avoid and remove them. Not much work to do, but I don't tolerate lazy soldiers, and everything has to be in perfect order, because some of those things can hurt badly, and some could kill. Are you lazy?"

"No, comrade ensign."

"Are you a mama's boy?"

"No, comrade ensign, I left my parent's house some time ago."

"I have only two soldiers under my command. The other one has been here several months already, and you'll listen to him, although he's not your superior and he's younger than you. Can you stand that?"

"Yes, comrade ensign."

"Get in good with me–I'll be the best for you. Act stupid–and you'll piss your mama's milk. Understood?"

"Yes, comrade ensign."

"Then I'll take you. Cvijetić will borrow you from time to time, but don't expect to hang out there with his pussies. Dismissed."

Several days later I transferred my things to a small room with only five beds. The warehouse to which I was assigned was on the northern edge of camp, next to the old railroad tracks. It had its own bathroom and a small office, and the job was so simple a child could do it: count the landmines when you're lending them, write the numbers down, verify they're all returned. Gvozdić would come by occasionally, always unannounced, stay a couple of hours, then leave. There was plenty of time for reading, writing, playing guitar. And I could take a shower any time. What else would one need?

TO THE STARS WITH STARS

Miki and I met one day in the canteen. When he told me he was from Kragujevac, I was glad–memories get rusty if you don't share them. A tall guy stood next to him, whose name was Čeda. He was from Belgrade. Čeda told me right away that he loved punk music, as if it was his ID. It probably was: in the army, our identity reduced to badly pronounced family names, there wasn't much to differentiate one from another. A tiny mark, be it a strange hobby, an odd accent, a funny hand gesture, or even a preference for the arts–was enough to make you stand out. That's why Miki told me immediately he worked as a lab technician in the military hospital in our garrison. Čeda happily slapped his back when Miki said it. I didn't have a clue why–maybe because one needed connections here the same way nothing functioned without them on the outside. But I didn't expect to end up in hospital, especially now, living healthily as never before–even the migraines that had tortured me had miraculously disappeared. Before leaving, Miki said, "Anything for my countryman," and winked.

Several days later, Čeda found me in the canteen. We talked a little–Čeda was interested in some rare records I had at home. Before he went back to his dormitory, he brought his lips close to my ear and whispered, "Miki makes great cocktails." I didn't pay much attention: I always preferred my alcohol straight and recognizable, and hated sweet or mixed drinks.

In town one Sunday afternoon, I met Čeda and Miki in a café behind the Army Club, and they invited me to join them. They drank beer, but their eyes were shiny and they were exhilarated about something. I thought I'd interrupted them and offered to leave, but Miki said, "Don't worry, we have enough for you." He put his hand into his shirt and brought out a pouch with the generic pain reliever, the Combined Powder. In the past ten years it had been disappearing from the market, being replaced with commercial pills, but some people still preferred it even though it had enough acid in it to drill a hole through your stomach and keep drilling to the soles of your shoes. Miki pushed the paper towards me.

"I'm fine, thanks. I don't have a headache," I said.

"Yes, you do," said Čeda, and they both exploded with laughter.

"If you weren't fine, I wouldn't be giving this to you," said Miki, wiping tears from his eyes. "You'll be much finer with this. Mix it with your beer."

Cocktails? Military hospital? Lab? Of course.

"What did you mix?"

Miki acquired the solemn look of a proud but humble scientist, and said, "I'm still experimenting with this one. The last one was too strong, so I brought it down in some ways, but I boosted it with one new thing."

"Strong?" Čeda rolled his eyes. "I couldn't climb into my bunk, man. They had to push me up. This one seems to be perfect, at least so far. I mean–I've had hash more violent than this."

I held my beer below the table and emptied the pouch into it. It foamed up and sprayed my pants, but when it came down, I still had two thirds of the beer, and the white powder was fully dissolved. They were right: after the first few sips I felt wonderful.

"We're not sharing this with anyone, okay? There are only so many drugs I can remove from the fridge without them noticing. If you have some good friends you want to treat, I can make my regular cocktail for them."

"How good is the regular one?" I asked.

"Nothing remarkable," Čeda said. "It speeds up your drink, whatever it is, so you save money, but you don't go up."

"Up is only for the best, my man. You don't reach the stars unless you know the stars," said Miki, and we exploded with laughter.

THE FALL OF POLAND

Life in the Yugoslav Army was based on a simple exchange: you had to offer something other people could use if you wanted to be respected and well taken care of. But being a writer, or a journalist–really, what good was that for anything? Journalism was useless in the garrison, since there was no publication of any kind. Writers smelled of intellectuals, and that's the second worst thing in any army–after desertion. So I had nothing to offer to the officers. But for the other soldiers, I had the shower.

The mechanism of the army is similar to the mechanism of prison: there is a uniform–which, like in prison, is a stinking piece of thick cloth, an ugly envelope for instant recognition–there is barbed wire around you, there is isolation from the opposite sex and, of course, there is no freedom. Like in prison, soldiers try to find some small things that would give them back some dignity. There was nothing one could do about the barbed wire, but slipping through it–if only to walk to the first joint, have a shot of brandy and return in less than half an hour–felt like a victory. The only real problem was bathing. Soldiers were allowed to take a shower only once a week, in organized groups.

During the first few weeks after being transferred to the warehouse I took showers so often my skin began to hurt. Even murderers don't bathe that frequently. When other soldiers started asking me to let them remove the stink, the only thing I asked in return was for them to be secretive about it. Soon, I had the whole Sect of Tidy Soldiers on my side. We would sit in the tiny office in the warehouse in the evening; someone would always bring some food his mother had sent, and there was something to drink.

The Iron Man must have heard something about it, since he dropped in for a surprise inspection around eleven one morning. Everything was going smoothly in the warehouse, so he seemed happy. He brought a newspaper with him, and–while he waited for the coffee I offered–I took a look at the news. On the front page in big letters: "GENERAL YARUZELSKY PROCLAIMED A STATE OF EMERGENCY IN POLAND."

I took it like a personal blow. The Solidarnošć movement in Poland was a beacon of hope to the people of Yugoslavia. For months we'd been following developments in Poland: the appearance of Lech Walesa, the mustachioed shipyard worker from the north with charisma and the will to fight for reforms, the strengthening of his workers' movement and its widening into intellectual spheres of society, the impotence of the Polish Communists before this new threat. The situation in Poland seemed to offer a recipe for bloodless regime change.

Suddenly, everything was over. The Polish Army decided it had had enough and banned all political parties, including Solidarnošć. I dropped the newspaper, slammed my fist against the desk and started cursing at the top of my voice. The Iron Man was shocked. "What, what?" he said.

"Did you read this?" I said. "A stupid general shuts down democracy! Too stupid to understand that even his bloody army would be better off in a democratic society. No, let's just suck up to the damn Russians! Stupid jerk!"

The Iron Man waved at me: "Hush, you idiot! You never know who's listening here!"

I shut up, realizing that I'd had an outbreak of anger at a professional soldier in front of another professional soldier.

"Yes, I read it," the Iron Man said. "What can you do? You and I don't decide on that. Better watch out for your own ass. Haven't you learned anything yet?"

The coffee was ready. I poured it into two cups, and he gave me the back half of the paper, the one with crosswords and the sport section. We read in silence.

"Light a cigarette if you wish," he said after a while. "Although it's forbidden here, ya hear me!"

ROOM IN TOWN

On a gloomy Saturday afternoon that winter I went to Sombor alone. I had waited in line for an hour that morning to call my parents from the only public phone in the garrison, only to discover that the telephone numbers in my hometown had just been changed. There was no automated message. After four months in the army I felt there was some symbolism in that: I was cut off even from my mom and dad.

The winter wind in Sombor always came from the north and could shave you in three seconds. The city was desolate. I went into a restaurant and had a decent lunch and a coffee while reading the newspapers. Before taking a cab back to the garrison, I stopped to buy some chocolate and wine to take back to the guys. That's when I saw the note, handwritten on a small piece of paper and taped to the window of the supermarket. "Room for rent. Ask Makarik, upstairs, on the left." Without thinking I went upstairs and knocked. A woman in her early seventies, very thin and bespectacled, opened the door.

"You came for the room?" She looked at me, confused. I was in uniform.

"Yes, I did," I said, and just stood there. I wasn't sure, actually.

"Come in," she said, and stood aside. "Coffee?" she asked, adding quickly, "I live alone and I love having coffee with someone, so . . ."

"Yes, please," I said, although I'd just had one. The apartment was one of those built before World War II, with high ceilings and that quiet feeling of stability. Everything in it was old but impeccably clean.

She brought two cups and sat across the table. "I didn't expect a soldier," she started. "You are not an officer, are you?"

"No, ma'am."

"Then why do you need a room?"

"Well, I sleep in the garrison, but I often come to town, on business . . ." I felt stupid. What business? She must have thought I wanted to masturbate in peace. "Actually, I need a room to feel normal again. I can't come often. When I do come, it will be just for a few hours. I'll be very quiet. I might sleep over sometimes, but very rarely. And I don't have much money, I'm not rich."

She looked straight into my eyes, then said, "Well, let me show you the room first."

It was a great room, with two large windows looking at the small square in front of Hotel Freedom, partially hidden behind a tree the locals called *bodyosh,* claiming that it grew only in Sombor. There was one wide bed, a coffee table with two armchairs, and a TV set in the corner by the window. The glass door was covered with a sheer curtain, and I had to pass through the living room to get to the bathroom, so there wasn't much privacy.

"There is no other room?" I asked.

"I sleep on the couch in the living room, but I don't hear well and I sleep tight."

"I'll take it," I said. Half an hour later I was back on the street again, with a key in my pocket.

ON THE SAME SIDE OF THE STREET

I didn't tell anyone about my room in town, and I would lie to everyone when I decided to go there.

Once in my room, there was nothing special to do, just remove the uniform, lie on the couch and read. Sometimes my landlady and I would have a coffee and a decent chat–that was all. But it felt like a third life, my life.

The first life was what was left after Belgrade, with my parents at home in questionable health, and my future uncertain. I hoped some of this would resolve itself on its own.

The second life was army life: dried out, scheduled, boring, brainwashed, flat, slaving in the dungeon of a paranoid communist regime. Sometimes I could hear the quiet cracking in my head, like thin branches in deep-winter freeze, the sound of billions of brain cells dying of neglect.

The weekend after I rented the room I falsified a permit to go home to Kragujevac, where I collected some of my clothes. Afterwards, when night would fall while I was visiting my room, I'd put on my civilian clothes, my cap and glasses, and go for a walk. I restricted myself to darker streets, which in Sombor were many, and avoided getting too close to other soldiers. I couldn't afford to be recognized. If they caught me out of uniform I'd end up in military jail, with a lengthy extension of my service.

One night, I turned the corner and ran straight into Ensign Tintor. "I'm sorry, sir," he said–after a couple of seconds in which I was sure he recognized me–and proceeded without looking back. My pulse increased to a disco beat. I ran back to my room, changed and took a cab back to the garrison, expecting Tintor to do a sudden inspection and hoping to get there before him. But he never mentioned it. We met on the same side of the street.

THE END OF FLOWER POWER

Promising warmth was in the air that spring evening, and I was carrying a triple album I'd just bought in the record store–a live recording by Azra, a new group from Croatia. I had nowhere to play it; it was just a plastic bridge to reality. I decided to cross my new bridge and have dinner in a pizzeria in the center of town. The place had recently opened, and it was a hot spot for the locals.

Waiting for my order, I was reading the list of the songs on the back cover, when a striking blonde approached me. "Hey," she said, "we all love Azra. Would you sit with us, so we can take a look at your record?" Another girl and a bearded young man with Lennon glasses sat at her table. His name was Zok, the girl who approached me was Nina, and the third was Lola. Her hair was the color of old gold and her almond eyes had an expression of someone older than her age. The conversation was dotted in the first half hour, but then Lola quoted something from one of Azra's songs, Nina joined, and Zok and I responded. Suddenly, we had a code, and the good thing was that it came not from a three-minute record but from a triple album. Late that night, I went to sleep at Mrs. Makarik's with a smile on my face.

Zok and I became friends fast. He lived with his mother and was one of the very few men of his age who stayed in Sombor. The highest education one could get there was secondary school, so almost everyone went south, to Novi Sad or Belgrade, to study. Zok was a gentle character, of quiet voice, intelligent and well educated, although he got his education mainly through a self-imposed reading list and hated academia. We started hanging around whenever I was in town.

Sure, part of the reason I loved being with Zok was that good-looking high-school girls were always around him. They didn't know what to do with themselves, and neither did he. Together, they just dragged away the long days of life in a small town.

For several days in the summer I wasn't able to leave the garrison. We had been warned that a group of generals from Belgrade would soon visit for an important yearly inspection, and our officers said there was no joking with this thing. The barracks were purged of porn, alcohol and less-expensive drugs. Finally, they came one night; we marched for twenty-eight miles, returned by trucks in the morning, the garrison got good marks, and we were free again. I called Zok the same afternoon to tell him I'd survived the long march, and he promised to throw a party that evening to celebrate.

I arrived at ten in the evening in my civilian clothes, perfumed and ready to take the center stage. On the way there I had already cut the corners off the long-march story to alter it from being a drag into a clear proof of my discreet superiority. I had even practiced the look of a veteran before the mirror. Zok told me he'd invite girls, and it was always great seeing Lola again.

When I entered the living room in Zok's house, all I saw were several guys who drank beer and stared blankly at the wall, pretending to dig the incredibly dark music coming from the stereo. I asked someone what was playing, and he said, "It's The Suicide, man," as if I didn't recognize Janis Joplin.

"Good," I said, "just this morning I realized I was already fed up with flower power."

A horsefly entering the room would've caused more reaction, so I sat by the window and started reading the sleeve notes on the first record I'd found. In less-oppressive regimes it's called masturbation in public.

After some time Zok came out of a side room.

"So you invited men only," I said. "Should I come out of the closet now, or do we wait for midnight?"

"No, no, there are girls, but they're all in this room with me," he said. "One of them learned today that her father is gravely ill and now everyone is low."

He returned to the room and closed the door behind him.

I counted geraniums in his garden, checked all the lit windows on the surrounding houses hoping for a free neighborhood striptease, and then pricked my ears in case someone at the party showed signs of life. The chunks of conversation I overheard while the needle plowed the blank grooves between songs made sleeve notes sound like Dostoyevsky, so I opened another beer and started browsing the records on the shelf. I was hoping for something silly, some German disco perhaps, or a polka record. The party was in desperate need of subversion, but there was nothing a normal person would play without a gun pointed at their head. German progressive rock, Polish jazz, industrial noise, stuff like that.

After an hour, since Zok wasn't coming out, I opened the door and saw an unknown girl crying on the couch and Zok and the other girls just sitting in silence around her. Behind my back another Suicide song started: a monotonous synthesizer riff interrupted with occasional screams. Zok had played it to me when he got the record from the States. "Frankie Teardrop" was a story about a guy losing his job, coming home and killing his wife and kids. I thought that "Frankie" was pure aural torture, but that song had cult status among Zok's Sombor friends. I noticed how some girls gave significant looks to one another when they heard it over my head at the door.

"Somebody care to dance?" I said, grinning, and several sniper looks hit me for insulting their precious. I closed the door and went back. I needed a few more readings if I wanted to know some of the sleeve notes by heart.

Fifteen minutes later, Zok and Lola came out of the room. "Frankie Teardrop" was over, so Zok just put the needle back into the first groove, while Lola went to the washroom. I caught a glimpse of dark circles around her eyes. Some guys stood up and left the party. I wished I had some of Miki's powder in my pocket, but I hadn't had a chance to meet with him after the march. "Frankie, Frankie . . . Aaaaahhh!" wailed the voice from the vinyl. It was past midnight, and I decided to leave.

The door to the washroom wasn't locked, but something was blocking it from the inside. I pushed a bit harder, and the door opened. Lola was lying down, on the black ceramic floor, by the tub. Her stunning blonde hair was spread like a golden halo around her pale face, and her knees were neatly bent to one side. The drops of blood, bigger around her wrists, formed a beautiful irregular flag of black and gold and red. The flag of despair.

OF ORGIES AND DREAMS

The summer made everything stink. The plain around Sombor was cut with irrigation channels, and the still water in them would become dark and heavy in the heat, smelling of decay and oblivion. The new soldiers who had just arrived in July, with access to the showers only once a week, wore their heavy odor of oil and sweat like ID–by their stench one could recognize where they came from. The sour reek of milk marked the mountaineers, the stern smell of walnut oil mixed with cheap deodorant came from the suburbanites, and the city guys wore a multiple-layered sandwich of tobacco, blue cheese and truck exhaust. There was a little less stench in town than in the garrison, so I used every opportunity to stay in my rented room.

Maci and Moša, my friends from Kragujevac, arrived with the new conscripts in July, and kept coming to shower in my warehouse. We'd sit with a bottle of wine planning elaborate anonymous orgies for our return to civilian life: where to do it, how to invite others so they wouldn't know who invited them, how to bring the girls, what to drink. We got stuck on getting everyone home, and postponed further planning for fall. The summer made us all stupid.

One weekend–around another national holiday–I felt safe enough to sleep overnight in my room. Around eight on Sunday morning, my landlady knocked politely at the door. "The coffee is waiting," she said. For a moment, I felt truly at home, with birdsong coming through the open window from the tree outside, the gentle morning light shyly crawling across the carpet, and my mother waiting for me to have our first coffee together.

Mrs. Makarik was dressed better than usual, and when I complimented her, she explained that she went to church early.

"I had a dream," she said while bringing a plate of hot cookies. "It was a very strange dream, indeed. Don't be afraid, and tell me what you think it means."

"Why would I be afraid of your dream, Mrs. Makarik?"

"Because you were in it, dear. I dreamt I was sleeping on my couch, just like in reality, and a sound woke me up. I turned around and I saw you standing in the middle of the room, looking at me. You were naked and, well, you were very big, very powerful. And you didn't say or do anything; you just stood there, looking at me. Very strange indeed."

"It must be the summer, Mrs. Makarik. Summer does such things."

NINA

"She wanted to fuck you!" said Nina. "I can't believe, she is what–over seventy?"

"She is," I said. "That's because soldiers are dicks on duty. We have no names, no faces, no past, no future. Wherever they push us–we shall go, stiff and strong."

Somebody pushed me trying to get past. The small café called Bodyosh was full again, with many people standing outside, on the pavement. Nina and I were at the bar. There was nobody else I knew. She just felt like having a beer and came expecting to find me, since she knew this was a place I'd started frequenting. Which was no small feat, considering she lived far from the café and didn't drive.

"School is over?"

"Forever," she said.

"What do you mean, forever? What are you going to study?"

"I don't have a clue. My parents are pushing me into economy, which is boring as hell. I wanted to study literature, but there's no chance I'd get a job in a million years. I'd probably have to marry, but then what's the use of studying? Are you interested in marrying me?" She looked straight into my eyes without blinking, and for a moment I wasn't sure how to answer.

"I'm interested in pretty much everything about you," I said, "except marriage. Mrs. Makarik asked me first."

"But you're in love with Lola."

This wasn't a question. Nevertheless, I searched for an answer.

"Does it show?"

"Not really, but I think she knows."

"Do I have a chance?"

"That I don't know, you'd have to ask her. Come to think of it, you probably do have a chance. She owes you her life, kind of, so she could decide to pay you back."

"Did she ever tell you why she did it that night?"

"She didn't have to. Only you don't understand it. You have plans, you're leaving in a few months, you don't know what this is like. I can see right now at least three people I've heard have tried the same. Pills, most of them."

We fell silent. Some German disco was blaring from the speakers.

"I am still a virgin, and I hate it," she said into my ear. "Let's go. Nobody must ever know, you hear me?"

Later, much later that night, a block away from the house of her parents, she stood on the tips of her toes to give me a kiss on the cheek, and then she gave me a small piece of paper, folded several times. "Read it when I'm gone," she said, and disappeared around the corner.

Under the light of the street lamp I unfolded her letter. It was short:

"Thank you. And if you're planning on talking with Lola, hurry up. The two of us are leaving for the coast in ten days, and we're not coming back."

SUICIDE BY MARRIAGE

I wasn't able to find Lola in the days before she and Nina left for the Adriatic Sea. I kept going either too late or to the wrong place. We'd never had a chance to talk alone after that night in Zok's house. She wore long sleeves for some time, then wide bracelets. I met her two or three times in town, but she was always in the company of others, and would just say, "Hello, soldier," avoiding my eyes.

And then they were gone, and Zok confirmed that they weren't planning on coming back. They took a tent with them and said they'd camp until they found husbands. "Suicide by marriage," they called it.

The weeks passed and there was no news from them. The time for my return to civilian life was approaching fast, and I had to train the new soldier at the warehouse and write some reports, so I saw Zok less often. Once I tried discreetly to ask him for Lola's address. I wanted to send the last, painful letter, as lovers do, but he elegantly changed the subject. I persuaded myself that Lola was one of those women who were much better as objects of desire than as memories, but I still didn't know what to do with the desire. Soon the summer was over, and I slipped into fall slowly rocking between love and a void, like a birch leaf falling off the branch.

Three weeks before leaving Sombor, I met Zok on the street. He grinned widely and said, "Have you heard the news?"

"What news?" I knew where he was aiming, but in my head it seemed all over, all just a strange memory. My valves were slowly shutting down.

"They found husbands. Nina fell in love with some German guy, he's a guitarist with a German band, and she's really not coming back. They are already in Munich, and they will come here just for their wedding later in the fall. Lola is in love with some chap who works at Belgrade television. They haven't set a wedding date yet, but it's serious."

"How do you know all this?"

"Lola told me this morning on the phone. I'm seeing her tonight."

"She's here?"

"Yes, she came last evening. They sold the tent in the end so she could return. She asked about you."

"Say hi for me, will you?"

I'd still had some chance while she was avoiding me; the fact that she asked about me meant that she'd outgrown me.

A few days later, Miki and Čeda found me in my warehouse sorting through some new training mines and said they were taking me out that evening. They had a special treat for me, they said, on account of my departure.

On the bus to town that night, Miki couldn't suppress his excitement. "This one is my masterpiece!" he said and pushed one of his white paper pouches into my hand.

"What does it do?"

"Indescribable. Pity I perfected it only now, when you're leaving. But Čeda and I still have three great months ahead, my man. Sorry!"

In town, we had a quick dinner, and then went in search of a poorly lit place with girls around. We stumbled upon a restaurant with a darkish back patio we'd never visited before, and only when we sat in the corner and our eyes grew accustomed to the darkness did I see that across from us Zok and Lola and two other girls were sitting, obviously enjoying their drinks after dinner. Just when I was thinking that this was awkward, Zok saw me and invited us to join them. I sat as far as possible from Lola and pretended to be extremely busy praising the beauty and elegance of the surroundings, which was someone's backyard full of cheap wooden picnic tables.

Miki and Čeda were delighted to be in the company of utterly beautiful beings from the parallel world. Miki took out several more pouches and distributed them to everyone around the table, offering short instructions. We obediently poured the contents into our drinks: even the wine foamed. "Not to worry, it's only natural," said Miki, "it will go away in a few seconds." And it did, leaving half of our glasses empty.

"Perfect way to waste our drinks," said one of the girls. "You owe us all another round."

"You just drink what's left, I don't think you'll need another round," said Miki confidently.

We sat and sipped our drinks. The conversation was tense between the soldiers and the two other girls, and Zok, Lola and I were silent.

"This isn't doing anything for me," said Lola. "Can I have another shot?"

"Me too, please," said Zok, and I joined. So the three of us got more pouches. I caught Miki's worried look aimed at me when the powder dissolved in my glass and I started drinking. "Easy, man," he said beneath his voice.

Soon we finished our drinks and one of the girls suggested we all move to a disco around the corner. We stood up and left. The last thing I remember was going down the street towards a building from which loud music spilled into the warm summer night. Lola was beside me, silent.

BLANKS

Miki and Čeda met me two days later in the canteen.

"Man, you scared me the other night," said Miki.

"I told you he's tough," said Čeda. "Nothing to worry about with the Old Man."

"What are you talking about, punks?" I said.

"A double dose of my masterpiece. What happened to that girl and the guy who also took a double, did you talk to them?"

"I don't know, I haven't seen them yet. But I didn't like that stuff, Miki. There was no high . . . Okay, there was no low either, but I felt almost nothing. What is the normal reaction? What happened to you?"

Miki and Čeda exchanged looks. Miki seemed worried again.

"You didn't get into a fight or anything like that? You didn't do something stupid?"

"The strange thing is I can't remember anything. I know I didn't pass out, because I remember getting out of a cab at four in the morning, but I can't remember anything else."

Čeda said, "Oh-oh!"

Miki gave him a look, and then turned to me again. "Listen, man, try to remember, it's important. What do you remember? What was before the cab? Where did you go?"

"What do you mean, where did I go? We all went to the disco. I suppose we had more drinks there, and I got too drunk."

"No. We went to the disco, but you did not. You went with that girl."

"I did what?"

"Listen, here's the thing: even with a single dose, that mix sometimes causes blanks in your memory, depending on your general condition and what you drink. White moments. They're usually short, a minute or two, and that's the good part about it, because you go blank, and you say funny things, true things, stuff that you think but dare not say, and then you come back again, and everyone is laughing their heads off at something you don't even know you've said. With your double dose you have more blanks than fills. So try to remember. Are you missing money, or a watch, or anything?"

"No. Wait, what was that about me going with the girl?"

"Yup," said Čeda. "We all went to the building where the disco is, and the two of you stayed a little behind, and then you said you were going for a walk."

"And the two other girls started making fun of your girl, don't you remember that?"

"No. So, did I come to the disco at all?"

"No. That guy who left with the two of you, he said he was going home."

"Fuck. I thought I got drunk at the disco . . . but there was no headache in the morning."

"Exactly. That's the beauty of my mix," said Miki. "Listen, talk to the two of them. Fill in the blanks. Compare stories. See if someone is missing something."

PROS

Other soldiers from my class were already leaving our garrison. Every morning someone would just disappear.

Nedim, a quiet Bosnian Muslim, came one evening into my office to say good-bye. He asked me to play one of my songs that he remembered and loved, the one about a blonde girl with almond eyes, on whose back I see the map of Siberia in the morning, but I was too gloomy to do that, so we just sat and drank. The yellow light in the warehouse cast deep shadows.

"What will you do now, Nedim?"

"I don't know, Old Man. I live in a small town, you've probably never heard the name, and there's only this one factory there. They make screws. I'll probably look for a job there. My father knows some people in the factory."

"Do you have a girlfriend?"

"I used to, but she moved to Sarajevo while I was here and stopped writing, so I guess we're not together anymore."

"Why don't you move to Sarajevo? It's big; there must be something for you there."

"I know–the whole city is only waiting for my arrival." He laughed. "Leave it, Old Man. There's no shelter from destiny . . . and destiny was always an enemy for me and mine."

The wind from the Hungarian plains struck below the roof, producing a long wail. The cornfields on the other side of railroad tracks responded with a frightened murmur.

"What about you?"

"I'm not sure," I said. "There are so many things, but they all hang in the air. I had a job in Belgrade, but it ended with my coming here. My parents are not in good health; it gets better and it gets worse, so I never know. I had these stupid hopes that at least some of the troubles would just not be bothered to wait for my return, but they didn't cooperate."

"Were you afraid of the army?" he said.

"Who wasn't?"

"And this could turn out to be the best part of our lives. There was nothing to worry about, because there was nothing you could do. Nothing to decide, nothing to choose. Like in a womb."

"Yeah. I remember how my father, and all my male cousins, and all their male friends, would occasionally slip into talking about their army days, and I always thought one must be dim-witted to love the army. Now I understand them."

"Well," said Nedim, standing up, "they kept saying how our task here was to protect our homeland. Nothing happened while we were here. I guess we did a good job."

"We're pros, man."

"We're pros."

SO LONG, SOLDIER

Three days before leaving Sombor, I went to town. I canceled my rental agreement, picked up my clothes and said good-bye to Mrs. Makarik. Then I went to find Zok and have a drink with him. I found him in a café, sitting with Lola and two unknown girls. He didn't seem happy to see me, and Lola stood up as I approached and went to stand at the bar.

"What's wrong?" I said.

"I don't know, she seems odd lately," he said.

"But why is she boycotting me?"

"How would I know? She is boycotting pretty much everyone."

"Zok, the other night . . ."

"Oh, yes." He wiped his forehead. "That was some bad shit, man. I don't remember anything. I got lost and only found my house at three in the morning."

"What do you remember after we left that patio? Because I have so many blanks, it's scary."

"Well, I remember we left for the disco, and then it hit me like a hammer, and I said I wanted to go home. Lola and you kept me company for a few blocks."

"And?"

"And then the two of you said that it hit you, too, and you said we'd better take a good walk. I headed for home, and you two turned towards the center of town. The next thing I remember was finally finding my house."

"I have to talk to her," I said and went to the bar.

Lola just stood there, a bottle of beer in her hand, staring at the half-empty whiskey bottles on the shelf above the large mirror. Chet Baker was spilling longing through the speakers hidden somewhere above our heads. Her eyes looked tired, and there was a thin new shadow on her face, but she looked more beautiful than ever, tanned, and her hair paler than usual, a new gold for new fall. We stood in silence for a while, and then she said, without looking in my direction, "Hello, soldier."

"Hello, Lola."

She looked into my eyes in the mirror, quickly, then took a lock of her hair and started twisting it.

"Give me a cigarette." I pulled one with my lips from the pack, lit it up and handed it to her. Our little game.

"I hear we took a walk the other night," I said. "Did you hear about it?"

"Aha," she said.

"I didn't tell you anything that would make me blush now, did I? You aren't missing anything?"

"No," she said. "Are you missing anything?"

"Ah, the list is long, but seriously–I don't remember anything, not even when we walked Zok home. The last thing I can recall is all of us going out of that dark place, and you were beside me. Nothing else, till morning. Miki told me it was his mix. Since we hit double right away, it just wiped me out. How about you?"

She carefully looked at me and opened her mouth to say something, then stopped.

"What?"

"I have blanks, too, but much less than you."

"When did you return home?"

"A little bit before four in the morning."

"Whew! We spent, what, four, five hours together? Where did we go? What did I say?"

She looked at me again, and said, "You are serious."

"I am. Why?"

She pulled a smoke, and said, "So you're leaving, soldier."

"I guess."

"I don't want to see you ever again. I mean it."

"You will miss me when I'm gone."

"I will remember you, but I will not miss you."

"Well, that one was from the hip, but not too bad."

"There's nothing you can say about pain that you would understand."

We fell silent again. This was our first conversation alone. Or maybe second. I wished I could remember.

"There are many kinds–"

"There are all kinds of pain," she interrupted. "You just don't know."

I had nothing to lose anymore. I just had the last letter to deliver. As lovers do.

"When I first met you, Lola," I started, and suddenly didn't know where to go from there. I felt the eyes of others on us, and I was afraid that Baker was singing too softly to cover us. I turned around. Nobody was watching. They all stared intensely at the table before them. There was no excuse. So I continued.

"I always thought you were beautiful, but you seemed to be hysterical, laughing without reason, crying without reason, hating the wrong people, loving them the next day. I thought you were spoiled. Then I started paying attention, I don't know when and why, and I caught something in you, something dark, something that almost scared me away. And I thought it was crazy, these things in somebody not yet eighteen. Then I realized you were much older than eighteen, you were older even than me sometimes."

She kept playing with her hair, and I couldn't see her eyes anymore.

"I started catching myself thinking about you. More and more. My world: soldiers, stench, dirt, sweat, commands, discipline, idiocy. Your world . . . I don't know anymore what your world is. Anything that mine isn't. You were my exit from this shithole. You think I didn't want to be able to spend all my time with you? You think I never dreamt of running away with you? That I was never ashamed of the ugly uniform, stinking of oil and who knows what, and I was never grateful for you just being around, just agreeing to sit at the same table, and just spill whatever it is you spill around?"

Her head was bent a little, her face hidden. I was glad it was so. I was glad she wasn't looking at me.

"The only reason I never wanted to tell you about anything I felt was that I wanted to protect you. Maybe it was stupid. Surely it was stupid, but, hey, I read all those comics about gallant heroes when I was a child . . . Then Nina and you went to the coast, and I heard from Zok you fell in love, and you're getting married, and I wanted to explode, and I was happy for you, happy–like hell, and I just had to tell you this. So at least now I know why you'll never want to see me again."

As soon as I finished, Chet Baker started singing, "Every Time We Say Good-bye I Die a Little . . ." Fortunately, she didn't speak English.

Lola finally left her hair alone and turned to me.

"My father's a drunkard. A bad one. When he comes home, and he gets angry with me, he doesn't hit me. Instead, he beats my younger brother. Why? Because I am a girl and girls need to stay beautiful to get married. He doesn't want to ruin his investment. He hopes I'll marry rich, and he'll scoop up some of that money. You don't have any idea how it hurts watching my brother being hit instead of me. I thought I'd love to leave, to just go away, find some stranger and hide my address forever. But pain ties you to the place. You can't leave. It is your pain and you belong to it. That's why I can't love you. You have to leave me here. And I'm not getting married. Ever."

She hugged me. She squeezed me hard. "So long, soldier."

I turned to go.

"And I hope you retrieve your memories. You might like them."

She turned her back on me.

MEETING MY LOST MOMENTS

I took my uniform off after breakfast. I spent another couple of hours in the garrison, signing documents and saying good-bye to people. It was strange to walk around in civilian dress. The Iron Man didn't come to shake hands, but Ensign Tintor dropped by the canteen. Seeing me in civilian clothes, he said, "Ah, I remember you from somewhere." I bought a round of drinks, and then it was over. I took the bus to town and caught a connection to Belgrade almost right away. I didn't have time to buy anything to read, so I stared out the window into the fields covered with gold and black and red.

Memories are strange. Memories are brutal. They don't pick the time or place, they don't ask if it's okay to just spill over your day. We'd been driving for at least an hour when a sudden flash broke into my mind: Zok is walking down the poorly lit street. Lola and I are watching him, then we turn the corner. We walk towards the center, towards Hotel Freedom. Blank.

The room at Mrs. Makarik's. It's dark. The light coming from the street lamp leaves shadows of branches outside. We kiss. I pull back to see her face, to make sure it's her. Blank.

Lola and I are making love on the couch. It's immensely gentle, and slow, our bodies on a big, peaceful wave that won't wash any shore, that will just roll forever. Blank.

Kissing, kissing, kissing. Blank.

Her head on my shoulder. The shiny tip of her cigarette drawing a heart in the air, then she makes two fast moves, crossing it. Blank.

We make love again. Hungry this time, attacking each other, retreating briefly, attacking again. Blank.

I'm returning from the bathroom, naked, passing by Mrs. Makarik who sleeps tight and hears nothing, and, opening the door, I almost fall over the telephone cable. Lola must have brought the telephone into the room. Then I hear her talking to someone: "You understand we can't get married now. I've just fucked a soldier here. He's just coming into the room. Yes, I'm a whore." I throw myself on the fork of the old black telephone, cutting her off. Blank.

She is crying on my shoulder. Blank.

We are in the cab. The dark blue of dawn turns everything to steel. She gets out a block away from her house. Blank.

6

GAME: THE PUSSYCAT GOES AROUND YOU

The rules

The participants squat in a circle. One of them—the Pussycat—has a handkerchief in her hand and slowly circles the others. At one point, she drops it under one of the participants and continues to walk or run around them all. The chosen one has to catch the Pussycat before she finishes a full circle. If she does, she becomes the Pussycat; if not, she stays crouching on the ground.

The reality

The first few Pussycats are excited—they giggle when they drop the handkerchief, they start running too soon—and it's easy to catch them fast. After a while, one of the players learns how to be deceitful enough to keep fooling the rest. The smart Pussycat does everything very inconspicuously and never runs after she drops her handkerchief.

The game eventually has to end, because everyone is bored—the players in the circle because they can't change the situation, and the sly Pussycat because she has no real partners among the crouching fools.

TANGOING DILEMMAS

You can't like military boots when you put them on for the first time: they are stiff and heavy, they hurt you, and at the end of the day–when you finally remove them–the stench of your own feet makes your head want to walk away from the rest of your body. But after a while you start getting accustomed to them. They protect you, keep you warm, make you feel masculine. And keep you stable, keep you upright.

In November 1982 I put my regular brown shoes back on. Suddenly, instead of being comfortable, I felt naked, wobbly, and prone to falling. My step was too light. And so, stepping lightly, I returned to the fields I left behind, only to discover that plowing was needed.

While I was in the army, I had numerous plans for what I was going to do after taking my uniform off. Visit friends, buy the records I'd missed when they'd come out, sleep every day till noon. Go where there's no uniform in sight.

When I came home, I did none of it. My friends were busy or in the army, my money was all spent on the room in Sombor, and after waking up every morning before dawn it wasn't possible to just decide to oversleep. Besides, I should have known there was no place without uniforms in Yugoslavia.

My father's Parkinson's was worse, and my mother's health was not good, either. I traveled to Belgrade to see if I could find some job, and there was nothing in sight. Ratomir wasn't the boss anymore at *Omladinske*–he'd left for another magazine–but they had no openings any time soon.

There was nothing I could stick to, not much I could hope for, and that was good. I always felt that in times of falling through it was best to touch the bottom. When you do, there's that hard plane under your feet that you can use to spring back to the surface. So I stretched my legs, waiting to feel the rocks beneath my feet, but nothing came.

My hometown needs the mercy of spring to show some beauty. At all other times of year it is gray, dilapidated and depressing. The winter months are the hardest–there's not much to do in the evenings except hit some joint and wait for a familiar face. But after I got back from the army, the only familiar faces that appeared were my old friends Paun and Zora. Zora, an ex-girlfriend of mine, just came back from the United States for Christmas break and didn't know what to do with herself. Small-town friendships are like marriage: you see one another daily and you know everything about one another. If you go away for a year, as Zora and I had, or if you spend more time with your records than with people, like Paun had, you're out, and quickly. It takes some time to unplug the sink full of dirty water and unshared memories.

New Year's Eve in our part of the country usually feels like a festive Apocalypse, with those who don't have anything organized facing depression. This year nobody invited Paun, Zora or me to any party, so I told them to come to my place. My parents were in the other room, watching TV, and the three of us stayed in my half of the apartment, chatting and soaking ourselves with wine and beer. After midnight we shared a joint that turned out to be a downer, and we sat on my bed, panting, watching our dilemmas tangoing merrily in the middle of the room, waving back at us and saying, "You are so indecisive! Can't you pick one of us?"

Zora went back to the States, and Paun chose to spend more time with his records at home, so I started going out alone. Belgrade spit me out, Sombor was a painful spot, and Kragujevac felt like the train station in a Leonard Cohen song: I went to wait every night, coming home without Lili Marlene.

And I knew: I had to leave Kragujevac, and soon.

A SWITCHBLADE IS GOOD

In April 1983 they called me from *Omladinske* and offered me the job of junior editor in the political section. The new editor-in-chief, Milo, told me over the phone that another guy would be brought in with me: Mirko Mlakar, a journalist from Split, Croatia. "He's a little strange, you'll see, but he can write," said Milo with a chuckle. He also said that the SYS people would find some place to sleep for the two of us, just until we settled down and found something on our own.

The mention of SYS made me react like a lab rat that took the wrong turn in his labyrinth and now expected an electric shock. While I'd dreamt of finding a job with *Omladinske,* I'd conveniently failed to remember that SYS was their publisher. Irena still had her job–now being someone else's secretary–and when we spoke after I came home from the army she confirmed that only several positions were filled by new names. It was almost the same team as when I was expelled. Would it be wise to go back and expose myself? If the year and a half didn't erase any of my bitterness, how could I expect them to be changed?

I needed a job. I didn't believe anymore in advisers, and I had nothing to ask this time. I called Milo two days later to tell him I was coming. I was looking forward to another few months in Hotel Jugoslavija.

When I arrived in Belgrade in May to start working with *Omladinske,* the representative from SYS told us that our temporary residence had been arranged with the City Parks, who had their own hotel, serving to accommodate their workers from outside Belgrade. The name of the hotel was the Collection Center. The greatest living Serbian playwright, Dušan Kovačević, had a new play of the same name, and it was very popular. It was a story about afterlife, and "the Collection Center" was Kovačević's name for Purgatory.

After the short improvised party was over, and Mlakar and I tasted our new jobs a little, Sima, the driver assigned to *Omladinske,* gave us a ride to the Collection Center. The trip lasted almost an hour, and we were by the road to Zagreb–the Highway of Brotherhood and Unity–when Sima finally said, "We're almost there, guys." There were no buildings around, just a hidden road taking us into a dark, bushy forest. After a couple of minutes, the wood suddenly opened to reveal a set of barracks interlinked with makeshift corridors.

"Sima," I said, "there is something familiar about the name of our hotel. Does it ring a bell?"

"Oh, yes," he said. "In the last three months they've discovered several corpses in this wood. There were a few reports in the newspapers on that."

"Did they find out who did it?" said Mlakar.

"No," said Sima.

A tired, uninterested man at reception put down his crossword, lowered the volume on his transistor radio playing folk music and asked us with which section of City Parks we worked.

"We're not with City Parks, we're journalists," said Mlakar.

"About the murders again?" he said, rolling his eyes. "Ask the manager."

"No, we were sent by SYS to stay here. At least we think so," I said. "But if you don't have our names on the list, that's fine, we'll tell them that they screwed up–"

"You're staying *here?*" he asked and gave us a long look.

"Or maybe not," I said.

"Let me see . . . here's some letter," and he pulled out a sealed envelope from under the drawer. I recognized the SYS logo. He opened it, read it slowly–moving his lips–and gave us a key to a room, saying he would send the hotel manager to talk to us.

"What about?" I said.

"Special instructions. You'll see," he snapped.

Our room was the last in the building on the left, at the end of a corridor lined with cheap plastic tiles, the type used for temporary buildings. The white walls were bare, the doors on both sides unpainted, and the ceiling had a row of neon fixtures full of flies. The door before ours was open. A girl of about twenty was sitting on the bed, reading comics. She lifted her head to check us out from head to toe. Then she slapped herself on the face. "Mosquito," she said, and went back to her reading.

The inside of our room looked exactly like the corridor. Two hospital beds with iron frames across from one another, horse blankets on them, a table with three chairs in the middle, and a tiny shower cabin with a sink in the corner. The window that looked out on a giant wild bush was closed and the room smelled of disinfectant. Mlakar put his bag down and opened the window, and a small cloud of mosquitoes flew in.

"We ended up in jail sooner than we thought, eh, colleague?" he said. I put my bag down, sat on a bed, lit a cigarette and watched him unpack. Mlakar was a slender guy, taller than I, with short black hair and the dark tan of someone from Dalmatia. He seemed intelligent, but he would always shrink your space, talking loudly, taking more room than he needed, throwing his feet on the table–any table, anywhere–as if his life depended on raising his legs. A long, ugly scar burned down the side of his throat.

"I'll take this bed," he said, and stared at me, expecting a challenge. I was tired. He started placing his clothes neatly on the improvised shelves in the corner, taking almost all of them.

Several minutes later, there was knocking at the door. "Come in!" yelled Mlakar from the shower, and a man came into our room. He was stocky, with fat, short fingers and a net of thin red lines on the front of his nose.

"Hi, guys," he said, pulling up a chair and slamming a bottle with amber liquid on the table. He lit a cigarette. "I forgot the glasses," he said. "Doesn't matter, we'll drink from the bottle. Even if you have syphilis, this brandy is strong enough to save me."

"Who are you?" Mlakar said.

"I'm God here," he said. It wasn't a joke. "I'm the manager. I came to welcome you, and give you a couple of instructions."

He took a long swig from the bottle and handed it to me. I took a short sip; it was sweet and warm. Mlakar passed.

"We don't have many rules here, but what we have is written in stone. First, handguns are prohibited. If you want them, they have to be left at the reception desk when you enter the building, and you can pick them up when leaving. Knives are tolerated. In this situation, with murders and everything, I'd even recommend a knife in your pocket. A switchblade is good. Handy." He narrowed his eyes, as if contemplating other weapons.

"You'll see: we have people from all over Yugoslavia living here. This is a hotel for singles, so no children, which is good. Pay attention to what you say: these are hardworking people, not much educated, and get insulted easily. We had a couple of bloody fights here last year."

He and I swigged again from the bottle. He tried to scratch a red stain off his pants. Then he looked at us.

"We have single women here. Fuck them if they let you, but be careful. Any one of them says you've raped her—you're out. I'd be careful whom I fuck. Some of them are already taken, usually by the cooks, and some of the cooks take penicillin. I don't know why they put out for cooks. They don't have to give pussy for food; there's plenty of food here. Who knows?"

He looked at Mlakar, who made a face to show he didn't understand it, either.

"Officially, bedtime is ten o'clock, but we don't care. We change the sheets once a week, and you take care of the trash in your room. Any questions?"

We didn't have any, so he sat a little longer, drank alone, and when he stood up to go he grabbed the bottle. At the door, he turned and said, "So, welcome to the Collection Center."

Mlakar and I lay down, dressed, on our beds. We were silent for some time, and then Mlakar said, "I don't have a knife."

"I have brass knuckles," I said. "What should we do about the mosquitoes?"

"How would I know? These are Serbian mosquitoes."

I stood up and switched the lights off, then opened the window wide, hoping that there would be some light outside to attract them. Or some living soul. Corpses don't work for mosquitoes.

We lay silent in the dark. The sounds of folk music came from another room. The joyous, muffled screams of a woman. The smell of cabbage. Some cook was at it. A whole squadron of mosquitoes was buzzing around my head, with some of them diving like bombers by my ears.

"Arbeit macht frei," said Mlakar, and let out a long fart that sounded like the howl of a lone wolf.

JOURNALISTS WITHOUT JOURNALS

Next morning Mlakar and I looked like we had measles. We ate some scrambled eggs in the restaurant that smelled of plastic dishes and grease, and had some watery tea. There was one bus going to town. To get to the station we had to run across the Highway of Brotherhood and Unity and Murderous Drivers. It took us an hour and a half to get to work.

After work, in the late afternoon, I spent several hours walking around, watching movies and visiting bookstores. I was trying to postpone going back to the hotel, until I got so tired that I could lie down and fall asleep right there on the street. It was almost eleven when the last bus dropped me off on the wrong side of the highway. There was no light, and the bush was close to the hotel road. I took the brass knuckles out of my bag and put them on.

Mlakar was reading something. Bloodthirsty bugs flew in fighting formation around the neon fixture, so I closed the window. Then Mlakar farted loudly, and I decided the bugs were better. I took a shower and was getting ready for bed when someone knocked quietly at the door. Thinking that it was the Hotel God again, I answered in my underwear. The girl from the room next to ours stood there, in see-through baby-dolls, holding some comics in her arms.

"Can I come in?"

"Sure. Let me put something on," I said.

"Don't bother," she said. "I've seen better, I've fucked worse." Mlakar pulled the sheets over his stomach and continued to read. She sat on the edge of my bed, still clutching her comics.

"I have nothing to offer you except some Nescafé."

"That's okay, I just came to see if you guys have anything to read. I'm done with these, so we can exchange." She put the comics between us.

"I don't think we have anything, yet. We've just moved in . . ."

"I know. I saw you last evening. You're journalists, so I thought . . ."

"How do you know we're journalists?"

"Everybody knows that two journalists have come to live with us. It's big news around here," she said, toying with her light brown hair.

"How long have you been living in this hotel?"

"About a year now. I come from a village near Leskovac. My older brother stayed to work with Father in the fields, and there was nothing for me to do, so I wanted to make some money, to help my father. I send them cash every month. But I'm leaving soon."

"You found a better job?"

"No, I'm going to join the army in July."

"Why would you join the army?"

"Because of my father. See, they just discovered a few months ago that my brother had a heart condition, and so he's incapable of serving. My father was devastated. Down there it's a great pride to send your son to serve in the army. They have huge celebrations, there's music, tons of food, it looks like a wedding when a recruit leaves the village. Only our house will not be having any such thing. My brother can't do anything about it. He demanded to be taken, but they wouldn't let him. So I decided to serve. My dad is very happy about it."

While she was talking, I noticed her right arm was red on the inside. At first it looked like a burn, but thin parallel lines stretched from her armpit all the way down to her wrists.

"What's with your hand?" I said.

She looked at it as if she'd never seen it before. "Oh, that. Nothing. Scratched."

"A wound like that? How?"

"Well, yesterday we had to unload some hundred-pound sacks, and one of them was falling onto this guy's leg. So I jumped in and caught the sack. I didn't have a good grip, and it slid down my hand and the burlap scratched me."

"A hundred pounds? From the height of a truck? It could've broken your spine," I said.

She laughed. "My spine? Hundred-pound sacks are the smallest we get, man. Don't you worry about my spine, it's hard."

"Listen, if you're finished comparing your muscles, I'd like to sleep now," said Mlakar.

"A bad dick hates even the pubic hair," she told him, and left.

Later, lying in the dark, I kept wondering what was going on. Was this thing with the Collection Center a joke somebody was playing on us? I'd noticed that Belgrade looked different from before I went to the army. Now it was a grayish, dirty old town, with traces of decay showing up here and there, with people who were less well dressed than two years ago. Three years after Tito's death the economic crisis was visible–there were shortages in many areas, and in some cases whole categories of merchandise were impossible to find in the markets. Women's stockings, tampons, sunflower oil and coffee were just some of the items one could now find only on the black market.

It was only now that I could see how strange was the twist my life had taken in the past two years: on the one hand, I was submerged into depths where strange fish were swimming, getting to know my Yugoslavia better; on the other hand, I couldn't see the things happening on the surface. Someone had had a big shift in identity, but was it me, or everything around me?

I kept wondering what happened to that guy who was pronounced Student of the Generation, who won all those awards for his writing, music and acting. What happened to the secretary of the Communist Party cell at the Faculty of Law? Where was the guy from Hotel Jugoslavija?

Whatever happened to him, it was in some other, happier country. This was something new. I was experiencing the speed of free fall.

THE MAKING OF BABY SOAP

A month after I started to work with *Omladinske,* we changed the name to *NON*–short for *New Omladinske Novine*–but this Latin negation was also a good metaphor for our general stand: "no" to status quo, "no" to mediocrity, and a sound "no" to the mild, non-critical approach the majority of the Yugoslav media had. At least that's what we hoped.

We changed the format from newspaper size to magazine layout, and our designers changed the whole look. It got noticed and mostly well received, and we were eager to do some serious journalism, too. Someone at the editorial board meeting suggested we do something to mark the fifteenth anniversary of the student protests of 1968. This topic was still taboo in Yugoslavia, for several reasons.

In June 1968 mass protests erupted in Student City, the part of Belgrade where the majority of student residences were located. Several hundred protesters marched to the National Assembly in the center of Belgrade, but the police intervened using force, wounding an unknown number of people. This all happened in just one day; the rest of that week passed in numerous student gatherings to protest the police brutality, with artists offering their support and the disturbed public following the events in the media, but not joining in. This was something new for

Tito's time, the first mutiny in the land of plenty. The whole thing ended with Tito addressing the nation on TV and–to everyone's surprise–giving his formal support to the protesters and criticizing violence on both sides.

Those Party leaders who, in the week preceding Tito's speech, had suggested a state of emergency and harsh measures to be introduced were in power now. They didn't want any reminders of 1968 because these might include memories of their erroneous ways. The student leaders of the protest had been assimilated into the system. Those who profited this way also didn't want too many reminders of 1968.

As well, that year brought the first intense confrontation in Kosovo, the army intervening with the police, with an unknown number of casualties. The end of the year also marked the expansion of the Croat nationalist movement that would continue for the next three years. So, even those politicians who had clean hands regarding the June events considered 1968 a bad year for Yugoslav society in general. That was the year that officially didn't exist.

But we wanted to open the dossier on these events, bring them into focus and open the discussion on what they meant and how they affected Yugoslav society. The question we wanted to raise was simple: Did we all learn something, and do we have a more democratic society today?

We anticipated reactions from many sides, and decided to keep the plan under cover. We wanted to dedicate the whole political section of one issue of *NON* to 1968, cover included, with all other sections reflecting the central topic.

The first step was to gather pictures and to find some participants who would be willing to talk publicly. The official state news agency, Tanjug, claimed they didn't have any photos in their archives, although that was simply impossible, while the majority of the professional photographers whose pictures were published at the time said they had destroyed their negatives because they thought it was a thing of the past. When I went to the public library in Kragujevac to do my research, I had to sign several documents before I was given access to the collection of newspapers from 1968, and even then there were two or three "intellectuals in civilian clothes"–as a friend of mine used to call the secret police–always sitting at the next table, taking notes and pretending to read some magazines.

Finally, in June 1983, we had decent material ready, and all of us editors read it several times to make sure everything was in place, with no clumsy factual mistake that could offer the police an excuse to censor the paper.

Our printer was located in a dirty building a few hundred yards behind the National Assembly and only a few steps from the police station. The process of printing was such that there were several phases where we needed to proof the prepress material. So, every Thursday, on our printing days, one editor was on duty in the printer's offices with one of our two designers. It happened that it was my turn the week our 1968 issue was ready.

In the morning, when Miroslav–our art director and my closest friend at *NON*–and I went to our printer's offices, everything seemed normal: standard mistakes, regular questions, old jokes with the women in the typesetting department. Miroslav and I liked hanging out there. The girls were fun and well read, and a few of them kept trying to draw his attention–he had the long messy hair of an artist and the good-looking face of a movie star. Besides, it was the last clean department at the printer's. The rest of the facility was smeared with the ubiquitous black paint and chunks of lead type, with pieces of paper around the floor and the acidic smell of glue.

Around noon, Danko, the main editor of the political section, dropped by to see how things were going, but soon left, since everything looked in order. When the printed strips were ready and we moved into the layout department, the first signs of trouble started.

It was always unbelievable to me how the printer–and every other printer in Yugoslavia–had amazingly well politically educated workers in layout. This department was the last defense of the system, since once the pages were put together the plates would be made for high-speed printing. If something needed to be stopped, this was the last stage where it was still cheap and silent.

"Oh, hot stuff in this issue," said one of the workers, gluing together one of the pages. "I guess you guys really desire a long vacation."

He was pretty loud when saying this, so one of his colleagues came over.

"It's about time someone tackled 1968," he said. Mention of this magic number brought several other workers around our desk. A few minutes later the shift foreman came into the room and approached our desk.

"Hi, guys," he said cheerfully. "I hear we have hot stuff. Mind if I make a photocopy of these few pages, to read over lunch? Speaking of which–we'll take a break now, and continue in an hour."

Miroslav and I went back to the magazine offices. Everyone was excited about the issue, and our colleagues were all there. That was unusual: everyone took Thursdays off, after the hectic pace of Wednesdays spent rewriting articles and putting together the final touches on the new issue.

"Everything okay there?" said Milo.

"They're asking questions, but so far so good," said Miroslav. Milo returned to his office.

Less than half an hour later, our secretary transferred an urgent call to Milo, after which he came out, pale. "They're stopping the issue," he said. "I have to go to the printer at once." Miroslav went with him, as I wasn't needed anymore. The self-protection apparatus of the system had started and there was little any of us could do now. Milo called a little later from the printer: "Everyone stay in the office," he told me. "I'm coming."

Some time later, he told us what he thought had happened: someone from the printer's office must have taken copies to State Security, and they alarmed our publisher, the folks at SYS. The SYS people were pissed off we had done this behind their backs, and called Milo to order him to "adjust" the issue if we wanted it printed. What this meant was: we took out almost everything about 1968, except an introductory article, which was watered down into a simple memento of some interesting events that were–thanks to the wisdom of our Party leadership and its flexibility–a thing of the past. All pictures showing conflict between students and police were removed, and the pages were filled with articles we'd prepared for our next issue.

It was a perfect action of the state. They stopped the issue on time; there were no printed samples; they did it through an advisory action, avoiding police, court and publicity; and they made us print the changed issue on time, keeping the illusion that everything was normal. Surely we could have said no to their demand for changes, but that would only mean they'd have to change the whole editorial board, and no media were ready to give us publicity that would protect us. How do I know? Nobody else published anything on 1968.

We stayed long hours in the office that day, and on Friday morning our new issue was on the newsstands, mild as baby soap, guaranteed to cause no tears.

MIDNIGHT AVENGER

Beuk had been drunk since early morning. His walk was only slightly insecure, nothing that would betray him, but his words kept rolling on top of each other like pebbles in a mountain river. Our secretary, Lula, brought coffees for Milena and me, and she rolled her eyes as she was putting the cups down. "I think he slept in the office again," she said. "I found a bunch of empty beer bottles in the photo lab this morning."

Beuk was our photo editor and one of the best life photographers around. But his alcoholism brought him to the point where you just never knew: if he was sober when you took him on a job you would get some amazing pictures; but if it was another of his wet days, he would do lousy stuff and constantly interfere with your conversation. He claimed he was a Jew, and that his real name was Baruh, and he claimed he had five extramarital children, all with different women, but he never showed us any pictures of any of them. And he might not have been a Jew at all—there was a Bosnian name Beuk.

Milena was expected to leave soon for national TV, and I was being trained to replace her as editor of culture. We were both very busy that day—she was writing her editorial and I was trying to make some sense of a piece one of the new contributors had brought in earlier that morning, a piece with an important story but lousily written.

Around noon, Milo came in and announced that a truck with some new equipment had arrived. "Since we have no money to pay the movers, we have to carry it in on our own. Now, I know that everyone is crazy busy, but I'm going to start bringing it in myself, and if you're not shameless, you will help." He went downstairs alone, and Beuk said, "I knew we were all idiots, I didn't know we were shameless, too." I thought it was funny, but deadlines make me too nervous to laugh, so I was the only one who remained silent. Alcoholics want people to laugh at their jokes, and I felt Beuk's look on me.

Milo brought in a heavy package, puffing and panting loudly enough to make sure everyone got the message. Indeed, all the men left the office with him to help. Except me–I was already on my fifth coffee and twentieth cigarette, loudly cursing high-school teachers of Serbian for letting someone as illiterate as our contributor slide through.

When they returned with more packages, Beuk–after dropping his–came to my desk and leaned over so I could smell his sour breath. "So you are the only smart one around here. These physical jobs are too low for you?"

Continuing to type, I just said, "Beuk, would you get off it, please?"

Without another word he tried to punch me on the side of the head, but, being drunk, he missed and just scratched me. My chair was too close to the desk for me to stand up, so I just covered my head and tried to avoid further blows as he kept trying to hit me. Milena yelled at him to leave me alone, and a few seconds later someone held him back. I got off relatively cheaply, with no major cuts or bruises except one under my left eye.

My adrenaline was so high that my ears were ringing, and I stood up, looked at him–they were still holding him, and he was cursing badly–and left the office.

I tried to read in the afternoon–ice over my left eye–but the adrenaline made every hour drag unbearably slowly. And ice doesn't cool off anything except meat. I took a sedative, but it didn't work. It was not the physical pain that bothered me. There had been some younger contributors in the office when it happened, the stories would circulate, and as far as they were concerned, you could be Gandhi, but if someone hit you, you'd have to hit back, at least once, if you wanted to hold their respect. "Son, your pride is the most valuable possession you have," said my father. "Never let anyone step over you," said my mother.

At eleven that night, I changed into some black clothes and took my knife from the shelf. It was an Italian six-inch switchblade, thin and dangerous. Over the years I'd practiced with it and, although I wasn't quite ready for an action movie, I was comfortable. I put on some heavy shoes and my Russian fur-lined black leather gloves, locked the door behind me and snuck out onto the street. Beuk's drunken days were all the same: when he would reach the point where he couldn't find his way to the train to Novi Sad, where he lived, he would just sleep in the office. He was plastered again today, so he would be in the office again that night. I left the radio in my room playing quietly. I was living just around the corner from our office, in an apartment I shared with five other guys, and I wanted my roommates to think I'd never left the apartment. Yes, I was creating my alibi. I was twenty-five and I was smarter than the police. And if you don't hit back at twenty-five, when will you?

The streets were still rather crowded, so I moved carefully from shadow to shadow, standing in an entrance to a building, behind a tree or next to a truck whenever someone came towards me. The usual three-minute trip took fifteen. I crept up to the second floor in the dark. I knew every step. I stood before the door and pressed my ear against it. At first I could hear only the rush of my own blood, and then it subsided slowly, allowing a precise picture of what was going on inside: the radio was on, his steps were slow and insecure, and there was the clink of a bottle hitting another bottle. Was someone keeping Beuk company? Then I realized that the sound of glass came from straight ahead, where the balcony-turned-mini-kitchen was. He was taking another beer. The slow, stumbling steps were coming back, passing by the main door, entering the foyer, entering the photo lab in the corner. He was inside his darkroom now, the radio between him and me, and he wouldn't hear me entering. I pushed the key silently into the lock and raised the latch with my left hand. The only light was coming from his lab. I closed the door behind me and locked it. I took off my coat, pressed the small button on my knife to open it and hid it in my left sleeve. I was now in front of the main light switch. He was an experienced outdoorsman, and I was certain he had his usual hunting knife with him–I wanted to see his hands. I hit the switch.

"Good evening, Beuk."

There was no answer. I cleared my throat and repeated louder, "Beuk?" Still no answer. I stepped over to the radio and turned it down.

The change in volume told him someone was there and he came out. He had a half-empty bottle in his hands, his face was pale, hair greasy, and his eyes were blank. He stood there for a second or two, then put the bottle slowly down on my desk and said, "You came to kill me."

It was not a question, and there was no change in pitch in that short line. It was matter-of-fact, as if he'd said, "You've finished an article."

And that changed everything.

In that quiet, flat voice, I heard several things at once–that he was at peace with anything that might follow and that he realized what he'd done earlier was wrong, and I also recognized the voice of my colleague, the guy who was brilliantly witty at times, who could take pictures like Cartier-Bresson. That one simple line woke me up, and I was suddenly tired of everything: tired of that dirty office where we spent our lives, of the cheap, ugly furniture, of the crummy food we ate every day, of my tiny rented room, of the zillion buses I had to take to make peace between the two sides of my life, of my sneaking through life trying to cut out some space for my boring ass, of that yellow light that shines on all poor people of this world.

I took the knife out of my sleeve, closed it and put it on my desk, between us. I felt terribly ashamed. The avenger in a black robe. The smart-ass alibi maker. The shithead with a knife.

"We both look stupid now," I said, sitting on the edge of the desk.

"I was drunk. I don't know. It was bad. Kill me if you want, what can I do?"

"You know I can't do something like that. We're not made for it, Beuk."

"We are made for anything," he said.

"If we go there, we only make way for the dim-witted bastards of this world to jump into our shoes. That's how I see it: every time a smart person does something stupid and has to go away, a jerk will come into her place."

"That sounds fascist. Maybe we are the stupid jerks that should empty space for better people to come in."

There was the guy I liked. He'd taught me everything about photography. I'd bought my camera from him. He'd given me the keys of the photo lab. How did I come here, to this point? When did I take a wrong turn? Was it my insecurity? I wasn't sure I was insecure. Too many deadlines? Too much yellow light around us? How would Beuk and I look if Cartier-Bresson took a picture of us now: two areas of black against the background of threatening shadows?

"Listen, if that happens again, I'll be very pissed." I picked up my knife. "And we didn't see each other tonight."

"I don't know who you are," he said.

THE SECRET OF THE BLACK HAND

I had to stay late in the office that Friday in October 1983, trying to finish editing several pages of the culture section, so I could take a day off. My father needed to pass some medical tests on Monday, and I had to be in my hometown for him.

I narrowly missed the seven o'clock bus, so I purchased a ticket for the last ride to Kragujevac that evening. I had two hours to kill, and I decided to buy something to read and try to find a place next to the furnace in the only station restaurant still open. The air in the dirty joint was full of smoke and the smell of wet overcoats. The only seat available was at the table in the corner, where an old peasant in traditional Serbian clothes drank his beer alone. He let me sit with him, and I felt it would be rude to read my magazine, so I ordered a coffee and we started chatting. Weather, soccer, watery coffee, and then we got into personal details. Five grandchildren from his three sons were all good, as was his wife. One of the daughters-in-law wasn't to his taste–too quarrelsome. Me? Traveling to visit my parents, working class, both retired now. What do I do? I'm a journalist. With whom? With a youth magazine.

"So you work for them."

"You mean–the Communist Party? No, we're not theirs. Our publisher is a different organization."

"Don't fool yourself, son–we all work for them. I'm not complaining, I was a Chetnik, so it's good they left me alive. But my children all had to leave our village, to work in factories. Why did they have to go? Because communards take everything we peasants produce. I fill my storage with corn, they come the next week and take half away. Obligatory sell. My mice destroy less than communards. I'm telling you–whatever we do, we do it for them. Mark my words."

A month later I did remember the old peasant's words.

Ljubiša Ristić was the leading Yugoslav theater director of his time. In 1977 he founded, with several other prominent artists, the movement he named KPGT, an acronym from four different words the founding Yugoslav nations used for theater. KPGT promoted the melting together of the country's many nationalities, and practiced what it preached by gathering artists from all parts of the country to work together. Ristić was the absolute center of the universe he created, king raven in a field of small birds. Since he had been involved in the events of 1968, and a year later expelled from the Party, the liberal media–whose darling he was–considered him a dissident and glorified everything he did. Milena–who had just gone to work in TV–adored him, and had given him a lot of space in our magazine over the years she edited the culture section.

Towards the end of 1983 Ristić started working on his new project, *The Secret of the Black Hand*. The Black Hand was a secret Serbian terrorist society formed in 1911 with the goal of creating a Greater Serbia. Its other name was Union or Death, and it was directly involved in the assassination of Archduke Franz Ferdinand, the heir-apparent of Austria. A provocative topic from a provocative artist–everyone paid attention, and the media became frenetic about it.

Ristić's early interviews showed that he still didn't have a clear perception of Colonel Apis, the leader of the Black Hand. In some interviews he claimed that Apis wanted to unite the south Slavs into Yugoslavia, and in others that he was a symbol of mistaken nationalism. The only thing obvious from his remarks was that he perceived the *Black Hand* project as his crown jewel. The timing seemed right. Tito had died three years before; the

Communist Party didn't like Ristić much, but was losing its grip on the media.

Ristić mixed, for good measure, the fear of the coming 1984 into his interviews. Orwell's dystopia was always an important issue in Yugoslav cultural circles, because we always danced on the edge of it but never really fell into it. Some elements were pretty realistic, with one percent of the population being members of the inner circle (if not the Inner Party), 18 percent in the Outer Party (in Yugoslavia, involuntary and opportunistic Party members) and the rest of us being proles. But our Big Brother had always been an enlightened despot, and now he was dead. Our TV was also a bit better.

Finally, in December 1983 *The Secret of the Black Hand* had its premiere. I went to see the show, and I was stunned. The grand stage of Sava Center was full of performers at all times, there was a white horse on the stage, more than 140 extras, the seats were sold out (around four thousand people)–but there was no structure, the holes in the dramaturgy were large and obvious, there was almost no space for acting in his staging, and all I saw was the big bluff Ristić wanted to pull on us. Only then did it become clear why he gave so many advance interviews: the director probably needed to hear himself talk, hoping to crystallize his conflicting ideas into a consistent piece. But in my opinion, he still needed to give a few hundred interviews more.

I published my review in the next issue of *NON,* at the beginning of 1984, trying to debunk his manipulation.

Milena called me the day after it came out.

"I read your review," she said, leaving the end of the sentence in the air. It was always her method, something she developed when interviewing artists, something that would inevitably push them into saying things they maybe wouldn't normally. Silence is rarely bearable. But I knew that trick.

She waited in vain, then filled the silence herself. "I don't know if you had to publish that."

"Why not?"

"Because he doesn't deserve that. And that's your private opinion."

"Well, that's all we can write–our private opinions. I guess you saw that crap. Don't say you liked it."

She avoided answering.

"They will be using your article, that's what they've been waiting for."

"Who?"

"Them."

"What are you talking about? The whole media is on his side. He is a genius just because the Communists don't like him. Ours might be the only magazine that will publish anything against his show."

"Okay, wait and see."

I didn't have to wait long. A few days later, *Politika*–the leading Yugoslav newspaper, with strong connections to the ruling circles–published an article attacking Ristić. Somewhere at the beginning of *Politika*'s article was a quote from my own, and the sentence after that said, "As we can see, even the young intellectuals of this country can see through his tricks."

UNDERGROUND EXCHANGE

Sarah Lawson came to Belgrade in the mid-1980s to do research for her doctoral thesis on the Yugoslav political system, and we met through a mutual acquaintance.

Belgrade is a strange city for foreigners, a perfect place if you don't stay too long. In most cities anywhere in the world, when you move there, you probably feel lonely until you make some new friends. In Belgrade, you will be lonely later.

When you start meeting the local people, you're caught in a beam of warm and undivided attention: people fall over one another to meet you, and they want you as a friend. But after a while you begin to realize that the Belgraders love themselves in you more than they love you in themselves. You are their ideal beautifying mirror, because your fresh eyes see only the charming things in everything that daily routine otherwise turns into an ugly experience, or makes invisible. The Belgraders love it, of course–they live in a city of champions, where egos fly high and a whole cultural industry caters to the notion of their city as the center of the world. And everything is used for that purpose: a victory proves that we are the best, and a defeat happens because everyone hates us–but being hated by everyone still means the world revolves around us.

I watched Sarah's new friends showing her cozy boat-cafés on the river, elite restaurants where artists would meet, taking her around as their badge, their pet, polishing their own image with an American guest ("A genuine American," some of them would say, as if talking about a pair of Levi's). I waited. Sarah didn't seem to have problems with telling her opinions, and I was wondering what would happen when she lost her beginner's perspective and started seeing things the way they were.

And when she entered the second phase, her circle of friends diminished. It coincided with my feeling lonely–I was drifting through meaningless relationships, my job was leading me nowhere–and we became close. Sarah helped me see my own surroundings from a distance, and I helped her better understand Belgrade's complicated ways. We never fell in love, but we loved each other.

It started when I played a Tom Waits record for her, and she asked me who it was. Then I discovered she didn't know about Charles Bukowski, who was already selling hundreds of thousands of books in Europe and was making quite a splash in Yugoslavia, with more and more of my new contributors imitating his style. Bukowski and Waits were so important for me that I assumed they were household names in the U.S.A. On the other hand, Sarah knew and loved two Belgrade underground bands, Partibrejkers and Disciplina Kičme, who had a couple of records each, and were far from the charts; I didn't know much about them. It prompted me to think that "alternative culture" might be the wrong phrase, because it suggested content that served as an alternative to the mainstream. Alternative, therefore, does not exist without mainstream; it is a distorted mirror, but still a mirror. Underground, on the other hand, is a big, unstoppable river finding its own strange ways under the cultural establishment, below governmental control, meandering without media interest and institutional support. It was fascinating that Sarah knew the Belgrade underground, and I knew the West Coast's.

She reacted peculiarly to some of the mainstream Yugoslav rock I played for her, applying pure American standards and surprising me with her logic, so I asked her to start writing music reviews for *NON*. After a couple of her reviews were published I noticed that some of the artists who came to our offices started asking about her. Since they were all trying to be beyond cool, the mere fact that they showed interest was a sign of success for Sarah.

At the end of 1987, Sarah returned to the United States. She had finished her thesis and there was no sense in her staying longer. I didn't expect to be so sad after she left.

HE THOUGHT IT STARTED

I wasn't the only one who returned home with Europe in his backpack that past summer when we traveled by InterRail. Although Nagip never found his cone-making machine, he discovered the flower market in Amsterdam. When he arrived home, several big packages were waiting for him at the post office, all full of strange dried flowers and leaves. Although he worked at the arms factory, he started doing ikebana.

His arrangements were large, and he distorted–on purpose–the traditional ideals of this Japanese art, but there was pure energy and beauty in his works. Like the rest of his friends I was surprised, and so I started thinking that there must have been something in his cultural background–we didn't know much about him–that preceded the ikebana part. I asked him to tell me more about his tribe.

Nagip's clan, Goranci, lived on a Kosovo mountain named Gora. They were an ethnic group of Serbian descent surrounded by Albanians in the region of Kosovo. During the mid- to late seventeenth century they adopted Albanian language, costumes and customs as well as first and last names, and converted to Islam. Yet they insisted on their Serbian origins. There wasn't much in written history about them, and the surrounding Albanians almost swallowed them, so they fought like lions to differentiate. Some of them tried to save their identity by moving out of Kosovo, and Nagip told me there were a few families of Goranci in Kragujevac, one of them owning a popular pastry shop across the street from his father's.

Prior to this sudden flowering of creativity Nagip and I almost never talked about anything but music–we shared a passion for CTI jazz and some obscure Spanish songwriters. Suddenly, all we talked about was art. Although I didn't have much spare time when visiting my parents in Kragujevac, Nagip and I stayed in touch.

When I arrived that morning in our office in Belgrade, and went to sift through the newspapers on Lula's desk, I saw a large headline on the front pages of all of them: "A MASSACRE IN KRAGUJEVAC." The report said that in the afternoon of the previous day a man drove on a motorbike to the famous pastry shop in the center of town, pulled out a double-barreled shotgun from beneath his coat and shot all members of the family who owned the shop.

Nagip was at work, so I called my friend Olivera in Kragujevac. Small towns have their own gray markets of information, and I wanted more details.

"The name of the murderer sounds familiar–Tomislav something–and he is our age," I said.

"You do know him," she said. "Remember Toma, our classmate from elementary school, the one whose parents lived in Germany, and who loved guns and motorcycles?"

When I stayed silent, she added, "Marina was his sister."

"Oh, that one. Did he have some problem with the victims?"

"No," said Olivera, "he didn't even know them. The rumor is he heard on the news that afternoon about some murder in Kosovo, about some Serb killing his Albanian neighbor when he caught him stealing stuff from his backyard, so Toma–stupid as he was and uninformed about anything that wasn't related to bikes and guns–thought that it had started."

"What started?"

"The final showdown. You know, from that joke everyone's telling these days."

"What joke?"

"Well, you know: Four guys are playing cards–an Albanian, a Serb, a Croat and a Montenegrin. The Serb sees the Croat hiding an ace under the table, so he jumps up and hits him in the face, and the Montenegrin almost immediately hits the Albanian on the head, and they leave. Outside, the Serb asks the Montenegrin, 'Why did you hit the Albanian?' and the guy says, 'I saw you hitting the Croat, so I thought it had started.'"

"But they were not even Albanians, you know that? What bloody irony."

"Toma was stupid in murder, like in everything else."

SPLIT

Peace, too, has an expiry date. In the first months of 1987, after a few even years of one step forward, two steps back, I started feeling the pressure rise again. There was nothing I could point my finger at, at least nothing in our offices at *NON*, so I realized that the pressure came from outside. The economic situation wasn't getting better, in spite of mild reforms, or maybe because of them. Power restrictions were commonplace, with more and more ridiculous interventions trying to quell the crisis. First it was no electrical power for two hours every other day, then it was four hours at a time, then cities were divided into areas and a few areas in each city would stay in the dark for eight hours, then they lost track and started blackouts in an unpredictable way. Everyone was getting nervous. We all still hoped for our country to recover, but somehow with less enthusiasm, less belief.

The pressure, in our offices, increased tension. Deadlines became deadlier, opinions opinionated, photographs became graphic.

When Palma proposed writing an article on the sex life of modern socialist kids, I didn't think it would go unnoticed, but I thought it to be exactly what our magazine was made for: stir up the boring surface of the official socialist picture, make that milk show the coffee beneath. Palma wasn't the most talented of the contributors I had, but he was young and in sync with the scene, and when he told me that an increasing number of primary-school students had their first sexual experience before age twelve, I believed him. After all, some of my former classmates were now high-school professors and they'd told me the new generations rarely used a compass in their sexual escapades.

When Palma's article was published I was suspended for three months with no pay. The officials didn't dispute the facts, but they were furious about the part in which a twelve-year-old girl said she had sex with two of her classmates in her bedroom, while her parents watched *Dynasty* on TV in the living room. It wasn't teenagers having group sex, it was the capitalist soap opera that enraged them. I didn't even know which circles wanted me out–it could have been some hardcore Party official, or an editor of the state television who felt endangered for putting the American soap on, or simply a group of parents whose pleasure in watching *Dynasty* had been permanently spoiled–but a meeting was called, and there was a poorly staged debate, and I was out for three months.

I went to the Adriatic coast, to soothe my nerves. And suddenly I found myself in Split, the big Croatian port, in Tarle's house, for the summer.

Tarle was a journalist, writer and theater director I'd met when I'd come to Split two months earlier to see his show. The show had been done as street theater, a procession depicting the many centuries of Split, and included fire-eaters, jugglers, naked women and men, and some violence. It was passionate and very good, and Tarle and I became friends through art. We sat for long hours in dark Split bars and discussed theater and writing.

Tarle's apartment was in the core of Diocletian's palace in Split, maybe fifty yards from the sea. The narrow streets and the walls of the palace were built by the Romans when this city was Spalatum. The house I was staying in was six centuries old, a historical monument.

Tarle's wife, Zdenka, a poet with several published books, was a slow dancer, the magician of her own stage. Tarle had one kind of charisma, something about him that was piercing and almost diabolical. Zdenka was the feminine side of the same principle, soft and magnetic. I was in the middle, hanging out with Tarle when I needed action, sitting long hours with Zdenka puffing strong Dalmatian marijuana and sipping wine when I needed peace. And running away from both to a distant beach when I felt like thinking.

I lost my sense of time in Split. The slow movement of the ancient city in the summer heat, and the even slower moves of the amazingly beautiful women, put me into a state between reality and dreams. The first couple of weeks flew by, and then more, and more, and I started thinking about moving to Split. But reveries don't last long. A telegram came with the news that my mother wasn't feeling well and my father's health had deteriorated to the point that he had to stay at the hospital, so I finally had to go back to Belgrade. My Split friends threw a party for me, and that was that–reality would wait for me the next morning at the train station.

I went to bed at one but couldn't get to sleep. The heat in those last days of August was unbearable. I felt removed, disjointed, levitating in a strange space between diabolical and angelical, between centuries, between hectic Belgrade and slow Split, wondering where to go from there.

At three in the morning I could have sworn I'd just heard the sandals of the Roman patrol around the corner and the rattling of their swords. I still couldn't sleep.

I lit a cigarette and stood naked at the window overlooking the small square. The air was saturated with salt and iodine coming from the sea. I felt like a fish swimming thorough centuries, a colorful fish from one of Emir Kusturica's movies; the one that saw it all but felt too tired to communicate it. How do fish communicate? What are the consequences of their existence? To become the chorus dressed in olive oil in a tin can on a breakfast table? It's easy with revolutionaries: they melt their flame into ideas, spill the ideas to their revolutionary cell, and the cell turns the ideas into actions. I am a writer. I pour my acid into bitterness, my bitterness into irony, my irony into observations. Then I leave them to dry on paper. And submit them. Submit them to my editor; he would submit some of them to the State Security Service and the majority to the readers. Some of the readers would read it, some wouldn't. Some of them who did so would get pissed off. Was I communicating at all after passing through that process?

And that might have been one of the things keeping me awake that night: submitting. I felt my life had become shaped like a funnel. In the beginning there was that large empty space around me, and I could choose my direction, I could select the part I wanted to fill. Then the space narrowed, slowly in the beginning, later faster and faster. I was caught by the swirl. The choices became rare or disappeared altogether. Suddenly, one day, I felt I was in the tube leading only down, pushed by others behind me. A grille waited below the funnel, the border between day and night, and once I'd passed that border it would be the shit creek all the way to the sea. But who made the funnel for us all? I felt the presence of an invisible structure around me.

Was that invisible structure always present?

The question that bothered me that night was not whether the omnipotent, invisible structure was in place when it needed to stop you–it always was–the issue was whether that machine was there for the passage, too? That was the scary thought: would it push you forward without you knowing about it, and if it did, as I suspected, why and when? What were the motives of our invisible puppeteers? Achieving total control over our lives, the kind of control that would trigger victories as well as falls, according to the unpredictable needs of shadowy masters?

The Roman patrol came again. Or was it just a pair of local cops? Palace stones have the same sound under any kind of military boots.

Take Danko, for example. Danko was a member of the Party, the editor of the political section in the magazine and Milo's deputy. He wasn't really a communist. Leninism calls for communists to adhere to the principles of revolution at all times, in all situations, and to plan all their actions so they benefit the general cause. Danko was primarily concerned with how to get promoted, how to get an apartment from our publishers, stuff like that. Petty things, same as everywhere in the world, same as with the rest of us. The Yugoslav Communist Party was a rigid and boring organization and the revolution was a tamed animal, a beast you had to feed but you could live with. Danko was in the Party because a member was more trusted, had a better chance for promotion. Even if he went wrong somewhere, even if he committed a crime–unless the crime was very serious–his punishment would be a well-meant critique or maybe an expulsion from the Party. The confusing part was, I couldn't just write him off–several of his articles had been refused in the past and he was frequently vocal in criticizing the moves of the central Party leadership.

Yet he had been promoted to deputy editor-in-chief even though he wasn't the best journalist in the political section. And he had been given a large apartment recently. Why? Did he accept a certain offer from the Old Husky somewhere along the road? I doubted it. Was he a promising Party member? Not at all. Why, then? Was he pushed forward to fill in the space someone more dangerous to the Party might have taken?

Another patrol down there. Romans, or cops, or both. I could hear their talk and that would be Latin, but again, the words *codex* and *lex* and *militia* all belong to the state vocabulary, independent of time or social system.

Several more hours passed. Bluish light filled my room, the color of the sea, the color of dawn, the announcement of reality.

I put on my shorts and started packing. A little later Zdenka came into my room. The house was still silent.

"You're leaving?"

I nodded. Silence. Packing. Zdenka was smoking. A word from some early passerby flew in through the window. An insignificant, empty word, one of those too hollow to pick up off the floor.

I shut my bag. Zdenka was on the bed, in lotus position.

"Tarle is still sleeping?" I asked just to break the silence.

She nodded in her usual slow and serious way. I sat next to her for a moment. We sighed in unison. The Choir of Worried Individuals.

"I have nothing handy to give you for the road."

"I travel light."

"I have only this: Think of the breathing."

RELAXED, PEACEFUL, MEET YOURSELF

The underground of the City Hospital in Kragujevac. My father and I walk down the empty corridors, towards the blue door. He has his walking cane with him, and leans on my left arm, but we still move slowly. He had lost several pounds during his last stay in the hospital. His suit now hangs on his shoulders and his French cap is two sizes larger than it should be. I am traveling to Kragujevac twice a week, to take him to the oncology department for radiotherapy. They removed a tumor from his bladder, and his surgeon gave a good prognosis. The radiation is just for security, so he doesn't have to take chemotherapy.

I open the door at the end of the corridor, and there are only two women inside the small waiting room, one of them with a large hat that covers her forehead. They are just resting, their session is over, and they get up to leave. We knock on another door, and a young nurse opens it, stepping aside. We enter a tiny room with only two chairs and one desk before the wall of tinted glass that separates it from the radiotherapy chamber. Another nurse, who operates the machine, comes back from cleaning the table where the patients lie. They are both chatty, and smiling, and they jokingly flirt with Dad. Our little tarts, our angels of life. They take him inside, help him remove his clothes, wrap him in white sheets and gently help him climb up on the table. They return, shut the lead door behind, and they turn the switch on. The heavy door is a stop to everything: X-rays, sound, happiness. When my father can't hear us they flirt with me, too, only more dangerously. I'd already had a dream of fucking them beneath the huge white machine with the lower end shaped like a funnel.

One of the nurses has to fill the usual report in Dad's file. She opens the folder, takes a sheet of paper from within and writes on it. Then she puts the pen down, sighs and says, "I can't understand why they're torturing him."

"What do you mean?"

"Well, it says here that his cancer has spread on his vital organs. Why don't they leave him in peace?"

"It cannot be . . . His doctor told me that Dušan will be fine–"

"Dušan?" She looks at me, confused, then at the folder on the desk. "Oh, sorry. I took the wrong folder. This is someone else."

Miroslav stood up and closed the window next to my desk. "I can't work with all that noise," he said.

Someone was protesting again on the Boulevard of Revolution. First there were students fighting to lower the fees, then metalworkers who complained about their low salaries, then farmers, then the Kosovo Serbs asking for protection from Albanian separatists. We didn't know who it was this time. When I looked out I saw a crowd of about a thousand, marching towards the Yugoslav Assembly, a few hundred yards from the offices of *NON.* I read "Belgrade is working, Priština is being built" on one of the posters they carried, and then the crowd passed by.

We continued to work. The protests in the past months became so frequent that we didn't even bother sending someone out to cover them. A little later one of our photographers came in from the street and told us the demonstrations were against the Slovenian leadership, for giving full support to the Albanian miners on strike in the biggest Kosovo mine, Trepča.

"Slobo encouraged them," said Gavrilo, our new editor-in-chief. "We'll see much more of this."

I remembered seeing the report on the evening news on Belgrade TV. Slobodan Milošević, the leader of the Serbian Communists, visited Kosovo Polje, a small town in Kosovo. During his meeting with the local cadre the Kosovo Serbs gathered to protest. The Albanians were pressuring them into exodus by burning their homes, raping the women, attacking the schoolchildren. The police started beating the Serbs. Milošević came out, saw the beating, and the police–otherwise comfortable with beating people, but not in front of politicians–stopped their action abruptly. Milošević, his face pale, addressed the gathered Serbs impromptu, without any sound equipment. His first sentence secured his place in history, and our place in the hell to come: "Nobody will dare beat you!" A short silence of total surprise, followed by an uproar.

In the following days this well-staged sequence was shown many times, and even a few roundtables were organized to celebrate this fresh approach of the Serbian politician. In Tito's time the accepted position was that a weak Serbia meant a strong Yugoslavia. The people of Serbia were thirsty for a charismatic leader, and they'd seemingly found him. In less than two months Milošević's posters were hanging on the walls behind middle-aged office workers everywhere I went.

My generation was much less amused. No one at *NON* thought much about the new leader, and none of the Belgrade magazines with younger editors supported him. Our generation had been brought up in the spirit of Yugoslavia, in the true spirit of brotherhood and unity, but Milošević appeared in the nick of time to awaken the old phobias in people born before or during World War II. It was literally the last moment for someone like Milošević to seize power, and he did–only a few years later the generation with bad memories and old passions would have been retired and powerless.

"You should go see Buca. He is your cousin, after all. He is Aunt Ranka's son."

I shouldn't have mentioned Buca. He was the leader of the Belgrade Communists, and he had just published a letter attacking Milošević's approach to Kosovo problems as rushed and irresponsible. I said I admired him for doing that, and now Mom was using it as a pretext for her own agenda.

"Mother, we are such distant cousins, there is not even a name for it."

"Still, blood is blood."

"But I don't need Buca, Mother. I did something with my life, without anyone's help. If I go meet with him now, and people hear about it, everyone will say that he was the key to everything I ever did."

Mom continues to pour milk into the bottle she just rinsed with hot water. The funnel is too narrow, so I stand next to her to hold it.

"Nobody has to know, son. You'll see–Buca is a good man. I knew him since he was a kid. He's just a little older than you, just a few years. I know he holds a high position in the Party, but his nose is not in the clouds for it. He's a people's man, son."

"Everything is fine with my job, Mom. Why go see him now? And what would I say–why haven't I visited him all these years while I was in Belgrade?"

"Son," and she puts the bottle away, "we don't know how your father will be a year from now. We don't know what will happen to *NON*. You told me they are thinking of shutting down your magazine–"

"It's just my thought, Mom. Nobody said anything like that."

"You should believe your instincts, son. But you know what I mean–nothing is for sure. Why not have someone powerful on your side? You don't have to ask anything from Buca. Just go and say hi. Just tell him that his Aunt Ana sends her regards. Please?"

In September an Albanian recruit shot and killed four of his comrades in a garrison in central Serbia. Although only one of the victims was a Serb, the Belgrade media screamed that the tragedy was more proof of Albanian hatred for Serbs. Several days after that, Milošević staged the overthrow of Ivan Stambolić, his mentor and friend of twenty-five years, as well as the removal of Dragiša Pavlović, the leader of the Belgrade Communists. This event, widely known as the Eighth Session (it was the eighth meeting of the Central Committee of the League of Communists of Serbia), instilled great alarm in me, and this time I was ahead of my friends. Although they didn't like Milošević, they considered him just another apparatchik in a time when the grip of the Communists was weakening every day. They simply didn't pay much attention to this new development.

Dragiša Pavlović was the same Buca my mother urged me to visit. After our last conversation I gathered courage and made that call. Mother was right: he was a humble man who was almost ashamed of his own power. The way he was not only dismissed but also humiliated during the Eighth Session, the way the whole thing was orchestrated, the way Belgrade TV presented the whole lynch and the way ordinary people were ready to swallow anything Milošević put before them reminded me very much of Hitler's coming to power, and suddenly I didn't have only distaste for Slobodan Milošević, I started perceiving him as an enemy.

Vesna is a doctor, and a friend of mine. She is interested in liminal techniques of healing, and a few months before, she attended a course in hypnosis. We are drinking a late-afternoon coffee in her luxurious downtown apartment across from the St. Marcus Church, and she is explaining how she will cure the twitch in my left eye that appeared suddenly and wouldn't go away.

"The twitch is probably caused by some neurosis. There are two ways for healing it: either we go into psychoanalysis to try and dig out something suppressed that's causing it, or we first try hypnotizing you. Hypnosis is faster, if it works. This technique doesn't delve for causes. It serves to make you aware of your own problem, so your body can start healing it. You do know that you have a problem, but you need to *see* your eye twitching. We are taking it from cerebral to experiential level. Are you with me so far?"

I nod. "You won't use me while I'm under your command?"

"You wish. Seriously–here's how it will look: I will bring you into a state of semiconsciousness and then lead you to face your own problem. It won't take long, maybe a half hour."

I lie on her couch and make myself comfortable, if it's possible at all–Vesna is a good-looking woman. We've tried to fall in love, and it didn't work. I close my eyes, and she starts with her suggestions, in a low voice. Her low voice is sensual, so we both giggle. After a while, I take it seriously, and allow her to guide me into that strange state. It's not a hypnotic trance–I am too aware of everything–but it feels nice.

"Now, imagine yourself in a place where you always feel good."

I do–it's a secluded beach on the Adriatic coast. The beach is triangular: to my left and right the rocks are opening wider towards the sea, and behind me a narrow passage between two boulders allows only one visitor at a time.

"You are relaxed and feeling great. You see yourself standing, and you are slowly approaching yourself from behind."

The second me is entering the beach through the spout.

"Now you are coming closer. Closer. Closer still. You are relaxed, everything is fine. Now you are really close to yourself. Everything is peaceful, you are enjoying this meeting. Slowly, you are going to the right of yourself. You want to walk around and see your face. Go now. Relaxed, peaceful, meet yourself. Now you are standing right before yourself. Look yourself in the face. Pay attention to your left eye."

I come around myself. I can't see my twitching eye. My eyes are covered with big impenetrable sunglasses.

Throughout Serbia, Milošević's brownshirts were staging protests under the pretext of keeping Yugoslavia together–they claimed that Albanian separatism threatened not only Serbia but also Yugoslavia as a whole. I agreed with them, but I disagreed with their methods. Watching those ugly, hysterical faces of Milošević's phalanxes, listening to their illiterate quasi-political babbling, their odes to their leader, I remembered the title of Edgar Winter's album in my collection, *They Only Come Out at Night,* and I felt as if a long, bad night had fallen over Serbia. I felt as if Milošević had overturned a big stone lying in the shade, in the back of our garden, and that indescribable horrors crawled out from under it. It was obvious to me that this man and his nationalist bugs would attack everything I loved about my country. Besides, I was absolutely positive he was a Politician with a Vision, and I always believed that Politicians with Vision should be immediately lined up against the closest wall and shot, because they never fail to inflict great suffering while packing people into their dream.

Someone told me once, "The only way to kill a locomotive is while it's still a kettle." Believing that satire can erode politicians, and thinking that Milošević was still laughable,

I wrote a satire that summer and published it in *NON,* under a pseudonym I used only rarely, and only for satire. But the piece, except for some quiet jokes at the office regarding the end of my career, went unnoticed. It didn't discourage me, as I'd already decided that I would use any opportunity, any media outlet attainable, any occasion that would arise to warn people against him and his troopers.

The choices were disappearing fast. The Belgrade media were falling like dominoes into Milošević's hands, turning overnight into loudspeakers of his campaign.

It's two in the morning and I'm walking home through some poorly lit back streets. Every few yards I see a cat, and suddenly I realize that Belgrade is full of stray cats. Some of them are quiet and look content, and some are bristling and seem dangerous, perhaps even rabid–but they are all well fed.

Nobody has ever seen a chubby stray dog. This city must be full of mice.

Some cities have dragons sleeping under them. Their fiery breath inspires citizens to do great deeds, to perform heroic acts; it warms up the city and protects it. Belgrade, it seems, has a rat sleeping under it. Like its colleague, the dragon, this rat is colossal. Its gigantic ears are recording our whispers. Its gargantuan eyes are the funnels we all fall into. Its vast gray fur is the asphalt we are walking on. Its enormous snout sprouts thin antennae that examine us all–these we see as lampposts.

The giant rat feeds on giant fear. That is our fear.

SLAUGHTER TIME

It is late evening in the late fall of 1991. The fog is slowly setting in. The light is the color of bad steel and the air is cold.

There is no sound–the editor has wisely decided that the images speak for themselves. The camera pans slowly across the corpses in the yard of a country home somewhere in Croatia. I am sitting in a rented apartment beside the Temple of Saint Sava, in Belgrade, watching the evening news. I have a dinner tray on my knees, so I have to be careful when I tilt my head, trying to see the faces on the screen better, trying to understand how they were killed. Their throats were cut. A whole family of Serbs, maybe even two families, seven or eight corpses in that video. Only one man, it seems, tried to escape. He was killed with a single bullet, from behind, one of his arms still on the wooden fence around the upper yard.

They showed that on purpose, to harden me up. What I just saw was a draft notice, an invitation to the bloody party.

It's fall again, slaughter time.

7

GAME: THE STING

The rules

One person stands in the middle, with everyone else behind him in a semicircle. He covers his eyes with his right hand and sticks out his left palm behind him, his left arm below his right armpit. Then someone from the gang hits him on the palm. When he turns around to try to figure out who hit him, everyone buzzes, saying "Zzzzzz" and raising their hands. They all pretend to be the bee that stung him. He has only one guess after each blow.

When he finally finds the person who hit him, they exchange places.

The reality

This game usually starts with the weakest or the clumsiest person as "it." The blows are frequently merciless. Contestants cannot arrange the order of hitting, because their voices would betray them, so sometimes several people hit the person in the middle at once. When "it" uncovers his eyes after suffering the storm of blows, all he sees are the smiling faces of his friends.

The game usually ends with crying.

A PLACE FOR HER TO START

One day, sitting at my desk at *NON*, I overheard some unknown female voices, but I was busy and didn't pay attention. When I finished editing the short piece I was working on, I raised my head and saw a young woman talking to Gavrilo, and him smiling. Next to her was a beautiful girl, probably a high-school student, and I simply had to see her face up close. I approached and Gavrilo introduced us: the woman talking was his old classmate, and the girl next to her was her younger cousin, who wanted to write for *NON*. Her name was Silvija.

My instincts don't work all the time; they warn me only sometimes, of some things, and maybe that's why they work for me. They don't bore me, and I tend to pay more attention when they speak, and tend to listen and do the things they suggest. This time, my instincts winked at me.

Half an hour later, when the two of them were gone, I went into Gavrilo's office and asked about Silvija.

"I was thinking of assigning her to our political section," he said.

"You're sick. Throwing a seventeen-year-old into politics? Culture section would be a natural place for her to start."

The next day Silvija and I met, and one coffee led to another, and soon there was no fear of my thirtieth anymore, and the phalanxes passing under our offices almost daily became invisible, and when my term at *NON* ended two months later it meant a new beginning for me and nothing to be scared of.

Petar Popović, founder and editor-in-chief of the magazine *Rock*, called me one day and asked me if I wanted to take over the magazine from him. I got the job I didn't even dare dream of, I was in love after a long drought, and the heavy clouds gathering on the political horizon didn't scare me, since I finally had a roof over my head.

SPECIAL PHOTO-FILTER

It is the summer of 1988, and three of us are standing on the promenade in Split. My friend Zvone, editor-in-chief of *Iskra* and first-class rock photographer, has invited us to stay as long as we wish at his magazine offices in the penthouse of an old building. In return, Mića the Turk and I are to do an article on Split for his magazine, the way the two inland guys see the city. The way we saw it was–we loved it, but thought that Split needed more laughter, more subversion. The city was too staid. So we decided to pose nude in the heart of the city's tourist area, not fifteen feet from some expensive restaurants and a few steps from the sea.

Right now while we smoke, Zvone is doing something like push-ups on the pavement. Stefan Lupino is a big European photographic name of the time and he always does push-ups before he starts a session. The parody is obvious: Lupino is a body builder, Zvone is tall and thin. Lupino has the dark look of a Balkan man, Zvone is blond. Lupino's models are gorgeous Parisian women, Mića the Turk and I are two skinny Serbian guys.

"Look, Zvopino," says Turk, "I want my thing to look awesome in the picture. My grandchildren will see it one day and I don't want them to think that I was a schmuck. No, my shmok has to look like a shmok, but not me. Got it?"

"Don't even think of taking the business into your hands here," says Zvone, "they will arrest us. What am I saying–they will arrest us anyway."

"Correction: they will arrest you–we have train tickets for tonight, remember?" says Turk.

It's not so easy to be a nude model, especially on the street. Attracted by Zvone's athletics, kids start gathering around.

"This is not good," says Turk. "You better call some of your girlfriends, Zvopino, and get rid of these children."

The children leave, but the parents gather, dangerously close. Zvone says, "It's now or never," we take our trunks off and he clicks several times. While getting dressed again, we can hear the mumble of disapproval from the crowd around us.

Later that evening we leave Split. I have a week of holiday left, so I don't go back to Belgrade to my job as an editor of *Rock* magazine until later, but when I go back to work, the editorial secretary has already hung my nude posters all over the place. Colleagues cheer loudly when I appear and gather around one of the posters, pretending to analyze the art.

"You look, well, not quite respectable, if you know what I mean," says one.

"That's because the Croats have these special photo-filters to make us Serbs look smaller, I've heard about it," says another.

"But you showed your dick to the Croats, and that's what counts," somebody commends me.

I join the cheerful laughter, but I can't get rid of this feeling in my stomach that something is wrong. I've had it for more than a week now. Because two days before we left Split, Turk and I met an incredibly sexy girl on a lonely stretch of path by the coast and Turk invited her for a drink. She turned around and looked carefully to make sure no one was watching before she said: "Guys, I'd gladly go, but I must not be seen with you, understand?"

"Why?" I was confused. "Because we're tourists?"

"No, because you are Serbs."

ALMOST LOGICAL

When the big tectonic plates of politics start crashing against one another, nobody is protected. Even if there was a person who didn't follow the news, she would probably still notice that something strange was going on–by the shifts in her friendships, if nothing else. A strange nervousness set in, a bad wind started blowing, some night when we were all sleeping.

Living between two cities–Belgrade and Kragujevac–and being a journalist, chasing public stories that made for good media material, made me miss the small or not-so-small things happening to my friends. Some of them thought I had better things to do and stopped telling me the new anecdotes. Others probably assumed I was not interested anymore, a high-flying media personality who didn't care.

One way or another, only Olivera would still fill me in on people she thought I still cared about. Gaga was leaving Kragujevac, having found a man who lived in Sweden and who became the father of her child. I started seeing my old classmate Make more often. He was teaching math in our old high school and had fallen in love with one of his students, Sanja, while she was still in eleventh grade. Since she lived close to my parents, he started using me as a shield. The three of us pretended I was going out with her and he was just hanging out with us by pure coincidence. That was it from my old friends–three people, one of whom was getting ready to leave.

One weekend, while I was visiting my parents, Olivera called.

"Did you hear the news?"

"Probably not," I said, "I'm a journalist, remember? I hear only what's published."

"It's serious," she said. And, after a long pause, "Moša is dead."

"Dead? How?"

"Russian roulette."

"You must be joking. That happens only in movies."

"No. Really. For the last couple of years he's been living in Belgrade. You saw him once there, I think?"

"Yes, I did. But I don't have a clue what he was doing there."

"Well, he had his own small business. Importing stuff. Nothing too big, but it was going well enough. And you know how times are–whoever starts earning some money, gangsters want their cut. So he got a gun. One evening he and a friend sat in an apartment, drank a little–but they were not drunk–and just chatted, you know. Moša pulled out his revolver and started playing with it. His friend says that Moša pulled out all the ammo, leaving only one bullet inside. They were talking about *The Deer Hunter.* Remember the famous scene? Well, Moša wanted to replay that one, he rolled the barrel and put the gun against his head, and pulled the trigger. Just once. That was that."

For some time I'd been hearing many people talk about how cheap life had become in Serbia. The feeling of imminent war was removing the joy from us, leaving our hopes reduced to only one: survival. In such a frame, the picture of Moša laughing and pulling the trigger, no matter how absurd, looked almost logical. But still. But still.

THE ROSE OF WANDERING

My friend, a journalist, mentioned Miroslav Mandić while we were sitting in his apartment, waiting for the evening movie to start on TV. Hearing his name mentioned, my friend's partner reacted right away.

"Amazing guy," she said, a twinkle in her eyes. "A-mazing!"

"Shut up," said my friend mildly, "he's an artist, not a stud."

"*An Artist and a Stud*–that's what that stupid movie should've been called, not *An Officer and a Gentleman.*"

"That's his biggest problem, right there," said my friend, lighting a cigarette.

"What, that he's too hot?" she said.

"No. That most people don't understand what he's doing and then try to hang out with him for their own reasons."

"What's there to understand?" she said. "He's a rambler, and he's so romantic."

"See," he said. "Exactly what I told you. A rambler? He calls it *walking for art.*"

"Walking for art?"

"Yes. He has this theory that energy is a form of art, because there is no art without energy–at least, no good art. So he walks, because walking is a slow dissipation of energy, and thus he increases the level of art in the world, or creates conditions for better art–I'm not sure. As he walks he makes small mementos, sketches, poetry, and then he has an exhibition of these to document his walks. Sometimes it's not walking, it's some other activity–it's activity that's important."

"What's his source of income, if he's moving all the time?"

"Whatever he gets from his supporters. Someone gives him a room to stay, someone money, someone their old camera, whatever they can. He doesn't ask."

"Women take good care of him," his partner interrupted.

"Enough already," he said.

"He looks like a boxer." She really wanted us to understand. "Has this square face and broken nose, but I think women subconsciously take him as an ideal lover–someone who accepts whatever he's given, keeps the distance in his eyes, and inevitably leaves in the end."

"Why don't you get a dog?" my friend said to her, then turned to me. "Miroslav was in jail, too."

"For what?"

"Some article he published. I think he was one of the last people jailed for their art in this country."

"When was that?"

"Around 1980, 1981, I'm not sure. Eight months."

"Hmm. That was the time I came to Belgrade to work as a politician. The system was falling apart already."

"Well, you know how it is–a groggy boxer is the most dangerous boxer."

My friend gave me Miroslav Mandić's number. He was staying in Zemun, in an apartment his friend was leaving to him for the time being. I called him the next day and we set a time for our meeting. I wanted to interview him for *NON,* where I now freelanced occasionally.

Miroslav indeed looked like a boxer, with broad shoulders, big hands and square jaw, but there was something soft in his eyes. He wanted to serve something, as I was his guest, but there was absolutely nothing in the kitchen, so we drank tap water. Slowly, in small sips, as if it were cognac. He would listen carefully to my every question, think about it for a second, and then give me an answer, always looking me straight in the eyes. I understood my friend's partner: Miroslav had charisma to burn.

"A couple of years back I did this project I called 'A Road to America, or, the New Life of the Indians.' I walked eight hours on a twenty-five-foot path, accompanied by selections from eight centuries of music history. After I did it I continued thinking about it, and realized that there was a deeper meaning to our walking, that it was an art form per se. And that's how I started my walks."

"It's difficult to defend that," I said.

"What do you mean?" he asked, genuinely puzzled.

"Walking as art. Then any physical activity can be proclaimed for art, can it not? Can I, for example, drive for poetry? Those same roads, just sit in my car?"

"You probably could, if you had your reasons to do it, and if you perceived it as creating art. See, I am interested in creating in the field of the invisible. We are jailed inside the visible; we think that everything we do, or create, has to be visible, to leave some trace. But walking is releasing energy and creating energy at the same time. Our whole life is based on moments," he exclaimed, his eyes burning. "Our conception is a moment. Life after that is just going on. Ideas come in a moment, they happen."

"But art has to leave traces behind, if it's of any worth. If it's good it will change people in a very material way . . ."

"If Michelangelo were alive today, he would sculpt in invisible energies, not in stone. Walking creates invisible energies, but they are very real. I believe that the eros of living is in carrying some suffering and difficulties on our shoulders, so we can become worthy of those others who suffer. Pain is sifting through us: behind us are negative thoughts, energies, and we are becoming finer, better."

There was something very innocent about him, something almost saintly. You didn't have to agree with him. He was the captain of his own life, and he never intended to commandeer anyone else's.

I took several photos with my old camera, and left his shelter two hours later. Our interview came out in *NON* the following week. It was the first interview with him after jail.

Time passed and I would only occasionally hear some snippets about him. He copied twelve novels in handwriting to produce the energy of admiration. Then he sat on display in the Museum of Contemporary Art in Belgrade, for months, publicly writing a novel.

And then I heard that he was trying to find some money for his next project, which would last for ten years and take him away from Belgrade. After chasing his latest telephone number for a month, I got a good lead in the winter of 1988. I called one evening, as I was told to ("Only in the evening, the later the better. He can't be there during the day."), and reached him. He gave me a complicated set of instructions on how to find the place where he stayed, and I drove there. Seeing the building, I had to check the address again, as it was a barrack, in the middle of a field, amidst the desolate concrete blocks of New Belgrade. There was only a variety store in the barrack, closed and poorly lit with a yellowish security light. I knocked at the glass door, and he appeared from between the shelves and waved at me to go behind the store. He let me in through the back door, and we sat on some sacks of flour. It felt as if we were about to start a revolution.

"You're on night watch here?" I said.

"No." He smiled. "The store belongs to a friend of mine and he lets me sleep here."

"There's no heat."

"The heat would spoil the food."

"How long have you been here?"

"Two months. I hope to gather some money for my new trip and leave soon."

"That's what I've heard. And that's why I came to see you. What is it this time? I hear it's a long one . . ."

"Ten years," he said, smiling happily.

"Where to?"

"Europe. I decided to call it 'The Rose of Wandering.'"

"Poetic. Why the rose?"

"Many reasons. I liked Gertrude Stein's 'A rose is a rose is a rose,' but that's only part of it. There was this German mystic Angelus Silesius, who lived in the sixteenth century and who said, 'A rose is flowering without a Why. It is flowering because it is flowering.' I also don't have a Why. Simply, I want to create a blue rose with my walking, an invisible but beautiful flower that will be drawn in energy across this planet. I want to make it in energy only, so we can imagine it. You see, suddenly the earth will not be a geo-political phenomenon anymore, it won't be definable through a new world order, as Left or Right, this or that—we shall define it as a rose. Because I will trace the rose on Earth, the invisible blue rose. In ten years of walking I plan to walk 25,000 miles, and that's the length of the equator. So it will be one great rose around us."

"Sounds . . ." I struggled to find a word, and gave up. "Can you get support from some institution?"

He laughed. "They think it's a tourist project. Who would give me money to wander through Europe for ten years?"

"But it will be expensive."

"Not necessarily. If I can get enough to start the project, then it will unfold on its own. I meet many good people out there."

"I'm afraid I don't have much money. Until recently I had my dream job, with *Rock* magazine, but I was fired. They found out I wrote some satire against Milošević, although I published it under a pseudonym. I'm freelancing now, it's an article here and an article there, small change."

"That's fine," he said, "your friendship counts, too."

"Friendship? You'll need more than invisible energy if you want to eat on the road. I brought you a little something." And I took a blue fifty-mark bill out of my back pocket. "Here. Have a beer in Munich on me."

"Thank you, man," he said, and became a little confused. Then, as if remembering where he put his lifejacket, he said, "Do you have my book of poetry?"

"No."

He reached behind one of the sacks and pulled a thin book out of a canvas bag. It was beautiful, printed in the old way, with lead letters put together by hand, with a blue cloth spine and a heavy cardboard cover. The title was *I am you are me.*

"Thank you, sir," I said. "Sign it now."

He signed it for me, we shook hands, and I left the barrack.

I, too, wanted to be his friend, although I wasn't sure it was possible at all to be his friend. He was a genuine loner, and his way of life made it impossible for us–the stationary, the rooted people–to cope with him. All we could do, it seemed, was to help in any way we could and keep our fingers crossed while he was on one of his many trips, walking for art, walking for us, washing our sins away–our lonely Jesus with the broken nose.

Our Jesus who was leaving.

THE RELEASE DEPARTMENT

Adrenaline from being fired from *Rock* pushed me into a feverish state of mind. I remembered that my former employer, SYS, had a publishing house, and I knew the guys who worked there–they disliked SYS as much as I did. That was always the case in Yugoslavia: on every ocean of your enemies you'd find an island of your friends; on every friendly island, you'd meet a sheriff who would like to hang you. Every institution of the system had at least a few people who fought against it from the inside.

Fifteen minutes after I learned I was fired, I called Dragan Simić, who was editor-in-chief of the publishing wing of SYS, and told him I had written a book about Bruce Springsteen. A lunch later he accepted my proposal, and I just needed to write that book. I only partially lied to him that the manuscript was ready–I had, over the years, written a few articles about Springsteen, and I had a lot of research material. Before I sat down to write, I canceled my old apartment and rented another one, a secluded one-bedroom in an old house on Boulevard of Revolution. Adrenaline makes you destructive: my new apartment was a hellhole compared to the old one, but I needed a change. I moved fast, and for the next month I was spending twenty hours every day listening to Bruce Springsteen and banging my small Olympia with fire. I played "No Surrender" so loud that my shelf with a few hundred records–mounted dangerously close to the speakers–one day fell on my desk, and I avoided death by rock and roll only because I was dancing in the middle of the room. Once a week I'd go out for food and to meet with Silvija–my only link with reality, and the only reality I wanted.

My book about Springsteen came out early in 1989. The critics gave it a warm welcome and I started traveling around to promote it, and I felt like a star for a month or so.

Then, one early morning in March, the sharp ringing of the old green phone in my damp rented apartment made me jump from bed. It was my mother, crying and trying to say something, blurting out short pieces of words through her sobs. As her syllables started falling into place, I realized I was about to hear the message whose approach had been scaring me for the past twelve years.

"The telegram, the telegram . . . arrived," she said.

"Calm down, Mom, calm down. When did it arrive?"

"This morning . . . now . . . it just arrived now–"

"What . . . Who brought it?"

"The postman–"

"Our postman?"

"Our postman."

"Who sent it?"

"They . . . the hospital sent it."

"The hospital? Are you sitting down, Mom? Sit down, please. Have some water. Calm down."

She started sobbing again. My room was cold. My teeth started clattering and the only way I could stop it was if I clenched my jaw, but I had to talk to her because now the words were the only straw we had on this threatening ocean of the day that was dawning.

"What are you saying, son," she went on, "what are you saying? My comrade has gone, how can I calm down?"

"Please calm down. I'll find a car, or I'll take a cab, I don't know, but I'll be there in two hours."

I didn't know who to call, so I called my publisher at home, and he promised to find a driver to take me to Kragujevac. Indeed, soon an SYS driver called and said he was coming to pick me up. I took a look in the mirror and realized the clothes I'd thrown on were mostly red and green, the colors of *The Scream,* all of them screaming back at me. I changed into black.

By the time I got to my mother's apartment, it was already full of neighbors. I didn't ask anyone how they'd heard about my father's death–I didn't want to hear that Mother had gone crying from door to door. I was the man of the house now. I had to organize things, make sure my father left this world in the way he would have wanted. I went across the street to the cemetery office to arrange for funeral services, and when I returned, my cousins Zoran, Bojan and Boban arrived. We were all fatherless now: Zoran and Bojan's father–my uncle Mita–had died just three months earlier.

—

I drove to the hospital with Zoran to pick up my father's things. There were four beds in his room, and the three survivors looked somber when they saw me. I opened the drawer of the nightstand beside my father's bed and started taking things out. His old gray transistor radio (news and sports), his Swiss pocket knife (I'd bought it in Amsterdam for him to peel his daily apples; Mom had asked him a long time ago to always offer her a slice because she never remembered to eat fruit, and he always did), a bottle and a glass (Parkinson's made walking difficult and he couldn't get up often to get water), his cane (I'd found him a good one, dark and elegant, made of very light wood), his blank lotto tickets (he played every week after he fell ill; he dreamt of winning big, providing security for Mom and me forever), his slippers and his bathrobe (brown, with a hood; Mom asked me to find the best one for her man to look good even in his illness). The room was silent, except for the hushed sounds of traffic outside. The air smelled faintly of Lysol and urine. I hated the three other men. If Death had visited this room last night, wasn't my father's bed farthest from the window? Does Death come through the window?

"When did he die?" I asked.

"We don't know," said one of the men. "We had dinner, and he ate normally. It was a fine dinner, they brought us mashed potatoes with schnitzel, and there was salad on the side–"

"We watched television," said another. "There was a soccer match, and I remember that he watched the whole thing, as we kept cursing the referee."

"Yes, and afterwards there was this movie with Clint Eastwood. A good one, where he plays the detective, and he is eating when someone robs a bank, and he comes to the robber and pulls his gun–"

The details. I watched it happen to my father after he got seriously ill, when they diagnosed a tumor in his bladder, on top of the diabetes, on top of the Parkinson's, on top of the two heart attacks he never reported and they discovered only by chance. When things get grim with one's health, one clings to life, even to details that would otherwise be instantly forgotten.

"When did they discover his death?"

"Early this morning." This man I knew–he was the father of a high-school friend. Always weak, always in poor health. How come he's still alive? "Yellows go on yellowing; the rosy cheeks leave"–an old Serbian saying.

"He watched the movie with us, and then just turned to the wall to sleep. God bless his soul. I wish I would die like that."

"He was a good man," said another. "Are you the only child?"

"Yes, I am."

"You are a good son. You shaved your father. And you live in Belgrade?"

"I do." Father's stuff was in my bag, and I was ready to go.

"Your mother will be all alone now. Poor woman."

Sickening sick bastards. I left the room. A nurse was waiting outside for me.

"You need to identify your father in the morgue. Can you do it now?"

I felt Zoran look at me. But if this was part of the ritual, then there was nothing one could do. And nothing that one should do.

"I think I can," I said.

—

The corridor was in black and white tiles, and on one side, near the bottom of the wall, someone had written small numbers from 1 to 8. Did they play chess on the floor waiting for corpses and their live relatives?

The doctor on duty was in a room close to the entrance. "I'm sorry for your loss," he said. "Whom did you come to identify?"

I gave him the name, and he opened a notebook and moved his finger slowly down the page. He found my father's name, and said, "That's 3C. Let me take you there."

At the end of a long corridor he unlocked the door and stepped aside. "This is where the body is. Please visit the Release Department when you're finished, to sign the documents."

The body? What happened to father, brother, husband, lover? What happened to man? What happened to sir, mister, comrade, patient?

We watched as the doctor turned the corner, and then I opened the door. It was a small room, poorly lit and cold. There were two tables inside, and on one of them I saw my father. I stepped closer, Zoran behind me. Father was in his white undershirt and looked the same as when I'd left him two days before, when I visited to shave him and bring him some food that Mother had cooked. He must have died in his sleep, really, since his eyes were peacefully closed and his whole face looked relaxed. What was the last dream unfolding before his inner eye when his heart stopped and that precise stillness set in? Were mother and I in it? Was he rich? Was he healthy and strong again?

I reached out and gently touched his cheek. I felt the white hairs of his beard protruding a little.

"Always shave against the grain, son. It cuts deeper, under the skin, and it makes for the closest shave one can get," he said when I was four and watched him shave with a small mirror in his hand at our faucet in the yard.

"Does it hurt, Dad?"

"What hurts, son? What can hurt us, the real men?"

I never had the heart to go against the grain when I shaved him.

The Release Department was in a small room down the corridor. I knocked on the door, and a mumbling female voice told me to come inside. Zoran stayed in the hall.

A gorgeous woman with short black hair sat at the long desk by the window, and before her were a cup of coffee and a box of cookies. She was having her breakfast and reading the newspaper. Glass jars covered most of the desk, except for the small area where she sat. All of them had yellow stickers on them and were full of pale liquid and floating stuff. I recognized hearts, kidneys, brains and some other organs I'd never seen in our biology textbook in high school. She swallowed the last bit of cookie and stood up to greet me. She wore her breasts like microphones, her lips were the color of cherries, and her white coat was only partially buttoned, letting me see a pair of perfect legs in stockings. She had blue eyes, and a discreet gray eye shadow.

With the tip of her tongue she removed a cookie crumb that stuck to her upper lip. She said, "Don't I know you?"

"I don't think we've met. I would remember."

She treated me with a smile. "What was your relation to the deceased?"

"I'm his son. The patient's name is Dušan Todorović."

"Oh, now I know: I saw you playing once, a few years ago. It was very fine music. Romantic. But I outgrew that, romanticism, I mean. This is not a job for such things. You're Dragan, right? I'm Jela."

She sat, flipped through a box full of folders, found some forms and started filling them out.

"I'm sorry I can't offer you a seat. They are painting my office. I'm here just temporarily."

Standing above her, waiting to sign the form, I could see her breasts now. The summer tan had almost faded away, but the line of whiteness was still there, very low. If she were my lover, would this all hurt less?

"Sign here," she said, pointing to a spot on the page. I signed.

"I'm sorry about your father, Dragan. When it's all over, drop by sometime for coffee. I promise my own office looks better than this."

She handed me the form and another smile.

Mother and I spent the afternoon surrounded by a never-ending procession of people. Our cousins, our neighbors, Dad's colleagues, my friends, Mother's colleagues and friends . . . they each sat for a while with us, drinking a shot of rakija for my father's soul and repeating the phrases that were supposed to ease our pain: how it was better for Father to finally die and get some rest after his long illness, how it was all fate and there was nothing anyone could have done about it, and how we had to carry on because that was what he would have wanted. That slow drizzle of formulated consolations couldn't even touch our grief, but had a hypnotic effect, turning after a while into a distant murmur of quiet rain sedating us as pure sound, rather than as content. Some of the cousins decided to stay overnight, and both Mother and I were grateful for it. I couldn't face the idea of her and me lying in our separate rooms, remembering Dušan. The two of us were dangerous for each other now. We had no instant comforts, and each line one of us would say could cut the other badly.

When the lights went out, I spent some time staring at the ceiling. By then I had many sedatives in my veins, and my thoughts were slow and insecure, and every now and then the gorgeous nurse from the hospital would come and show me another part of her perfect body. She wasn't making love to me in those final moments before I entered the world of dreams; she just came, took all her clothes off and sat on the edge of my bed.

"Think of the women like me who are still to come," she said. "Think of us and all will be good."

Then there was that next day. The only thing I remember was the dull sound of soil hitting the lid on my father's casket as Mother and I threw the ritual handfuls, drawing the final border separating the living from the dead.

SEEING NAKED WOMEN

"She just stood there, in front of the big mirror in the corridor, combing her pubic hair. The craziest story ever, I'm telling you," says Dule. "Listen: Kos and I were sitting in the office, right across the corridor from the studio. The last news was already done, and the evening movie was on, and we were just waiting for Dragan's show to start and then go home. We were the editors on duty, but it was hot, early June, so Kos and I started drinking beer around six, when everyone was pretty much gone."

Dule pulls another swig of beer from the bottle and wipes his mouth with his hand. A few of us have joined him in the back of Sava Center, in one of the bars that serves mostly businessmen and us, the crew from Channel 3 of Belgrade's national television. We've just moved into this big convention center in Novi Beograd. Dule is one of the head producers and he is entertaining us with the story that took place in our old building, right next to the central studios of the national TV, two years before. The Dragan that he is mentioning is me.

"I'd heard about this show that was run last that night, but I'd never seen it. I mean, in those days we were still producing an experimental program, and they kept our signal really low, so there was no chance for me to receive it across the river where I live. They told me the show was about eroticism, and was wild, but I had no clue. What was the name?"

"*You've Got Friday.* I didn't name it. One of the editors did," I said.

"What a stupid name," said Dule. "Nevertheless, Kos and I were sitting there, just talking. The TV was on, but the movie was really boring, so we were just drinking beer and trying to cool off. Beer after beer–we had quite a few. I mean, you drank it, it just evaporated from you–it was that hot. Dragan's show was about to start, and Kos stood up to go to the washroom before it began, so we could watch in peace. He came to the door, opened it and then froze. He stood there for some time, then carefully closed it, came back and–without saying a word–took our beers and poured them out the window. His face was white as paper. He sat down, lit a cigarette and started smoking. Still not a word from him. After a while, when I thought he'd calmed down, I asked what happened. Kos just said, 'Dule, you have no idea how drunk we must be. I started hallucinating. I just saw a naked woman out there, powdering her tits.' And so I stood up to show him I wasn't drunk. I walked over and opened the door and I saw a totally naked woman, standing in front of a large mirror in the corridor, combing her pubic hair. I closed the door and said to Kos, 'You are fucking right. We are hallucinating.'

"And so we sat there in silence. The window was too high to jump out, and you can't go where you see your hallucination, so we just hoped that if we sat long enough, we'd sober up and then we could go home. After some time, Dragan came in, and we asked him to call us a cab. The next day we met Dragan at the office, and we told him we'd been so drunk we started seeing naked women. 'But there *was* a naked woman there,' he said, 'a stripper, and she was here to do a live striptease on my show. She needed to put on some body makeup, and the only large mirror is in the corridor.'"

Everyone bursts into laughter, but his story brings back mixed memories for me. The early days of my TV career were interesting and ugly at the same time. In 1989 an independent TV station was founded in Belgrade's Home of Youth, called the OK Channel. I'd gone there to be interviewed about my Springsteen book, and they must have liked something about my appearance, because a week later they called me back to offer me a talk show. I accepted, and it was fun to do it, but soon the station was shut down by the government, and it was over. It was too liberal for their taste. To quell the accusations that it was pure censorship, the national TV had to pretend that the OK Channel had taken, illegally, the frequencies reserved for the third channel of the national TV that they were just preparing to launch. Overnight, they had to start the new channel, and they gathered a team of mostly young people to begin an experimental run. Their boss had seen me on the OK Channel, liked my work and called me to offer me a contract for a show dedicated to eroticism. I knew it would serve politicians as sensationalist fun for the masses, to distract them from noticing our crumbling economy, but I also knew it would be beneficial in liberating the citizens of a country where prejudices about sex were persistent. And, as it was also a huge challenge and I could never say no to a challenge, I accepted.

The first few months were immensely fun, and my show was the hottest topic in Belgrade. I kept bringing in writers, sociologists, even politicians to talk live about their sex life. But–as the authorities started revealing their true intentions by introducing more and more politics into our programming–its popularity was precisely the reason why my show had to be shut down. They got the attention they wanted, and now they didn't want to share it with anyone. To avoid a scandal, they decided to kill my show with pressure: from being a live show it became a pre-recorded thing, then I was denied equipment, then they would give me only three hours to edit an hour-long show, and finally I gave up.

I withdrew and decided to start working on my new book, an anthology of Tom Waits's poetry.

MARCH 9, 1991

Saturday morning, March 9, 1991, was sunny. The Serbian Renewal Movement and its leader, Vuk Drašković, had called their supporters to gather in Belgrade for mass protests against Slobodan Milošević, but I wasn't interested in any party in Serbia, and I didn't plan to attend. A year before I'd done a large article for *Start,* the leading Croatian magazine, about the newly formed Serbian opposition parties, popping up like mushrooms. I interviewed all the leaders, and liked none of them. Not one of the opposition parties offered any coherent platform, political or economic, and they just kept barking against Milošević. Drašković claimed that Milošević stole the first multiparty elections in December, and I agreed–there was no way he could have won 65 percent of the votes, which was the official result–but I thought that the other parties had failed to offer their strongest candidates, and so they shared the responsibility for his becoming the president of Serbia.

I went for a walk instead of joining the protests that day. A friend of mine had a paper shop on the corner of the street where I lived, close to where the meeting was scheduled, and I wanted to visit him, maybe buy some aquarelle paper. I found him in his shop on the third floor of the shiny new shopping mall, and he offered me a coffee. We stayed there for an hour, people coming into his store, a normal atmosphere.

Then we heard a huge commotion on the street below. I leaned out and saw the crowd moving away from the square where the meeting was being held, some of them trying to run through the masses, tripping and falling. "Something is going on," I said, "I have to go."

I ran down the stairs to the street and started making my way against the stream of people. I saw panic on their faces. Some women were crying hysterically. I tried to stop a man to ask him what was going on, and he said, "It's a slaughter up there, don't go that way, you'll run straight into them," and continued to run. Someone was calling for a doctor, someone else warning people to make way for the wounded. I stood with my back to the façade of the mall, and I saw two men carrying a third between them. His shirt was bloody, but I couldn't see where the blood was coming from. Then I saw it: his jaw was hanging loosely from pieces of his cheeks. His face had been torn apart by a forceful blow. After they passed, I asked one of the guys following them what happened. He told me that the wounded man had been struck in the teeth with a police baton, losing almost all of them and fighting not to choke on his blood and tongue. It was impossible to continue against what was now a stampede. I turned around, went to the back of the mall and ran towards a passage that would take me to the square through the back streets and some old buildings. As I was coming out of the passage, a cloud of tear gas hit my nostrils. Since I was running and breathing deeply, I got a huge dose and I started coughing and crying. I felt a sudden rush of blind anger.

I remembered learning in the army that the worst thing to do in such situations was to wipe your eyes, as it only makes the chemicals sink deeper, so I let the tears flow and grabbed a tablecloth from a restaurant patio to protect my face as best as I could. I saw a water cannon spray the crowd, masses of protesters throwing bottles and rocks at the police, several gas canisters shot from handguns flying upward, bringing more tears and choking, and in the distance heavy fighting, batons and wooden bats flying both ways between cops and protesters, screams, horror. Some people were withdrawing my way, some would just stop around the corner to catch their breath and find an improvised weapon, anything, and then return to the battle. Three teenagers, kneeling a few steps away from me, were trying to remove paving stones from the street with their bare hands, their nails bloodied.

I decided to go home, get some better protection and return to the streets. I lived a hundred yards from the combat zone, so it all could be done fast.

Silvija told me on the phone that there was a live broadcast on Studio B, the opposition TV, so I switched on my TV. By the time I'd washed my face and flushed the tear gas from my system, the fight had come to a halt. A large crowd of people was still standing on the square in front of the National Theater, Vuk Drašković was on the balcony of the building, and squadrons of police surrounded the whole area. Silvija called me again and asked me to come pick her up so we could join the protests together. When I got to her apartment, the reporters on the radio and TV were calling in to describe the smaller conflicts now flaring up in other downtown areas. Public transportation was shut down, except on the outskirts, and reporters said it was difficult to move around at all, since protesters had set up barricades on many streets. They read the list of the protesters' demands, one of which was to fire the editor-in-chief of Channel 3, Ivan Krivec, for breaking the pre-electoral silence on the weekend when Serbia voted for its president. By early afternoon there were reports of two casualties: a high-school student shot by the police and one policeman whom the angry mob threw from a high stairwell down to the street.

Until now this whole situation with Milošević's rule had seemed relevant only on the cerebral level, it was only a mind game. Although I had already tasted the iron fist of his dictatorship, I knew that many other people hadn't; to them he was just another politician to support or to spit on. But now his true intentions became transparent, and all my darkest suspicions of his regime were confirmed–it was totalitarianism of the worst kind–he would have some determined enemies. There was something good in all this.

When Silvija and I finally got out on the streets, Belgrade looked like a war zone. There was no traffic, heavy concrete planters had been dragged into the middle of the crossroads, people with scarves on their faces stood guard, the sulfuric smell of rotten eggs from tear gas still hung in the air. On the barricades, people would flash three fingers at us–the traditional Serbian sign that was forbidden during the communist regime and the Serbian Renewal Movement reintroduced–to check if we were with them or not. We felt proud. We felt hopeful: when the world hears about this, when they see how the Serbs stand up against Milošević, he will be stopped. We walked through the downtown streets for a few hours and then I followed Silvija home. I had to prepare for my resignation that evening.

When I got to my apartment around six, the state TV

was reporting that tanks had been ordered to take positions on the major intersections to preserve order, as the official stance was that the protests were aiming to overthrow the government. Our show on Channel 3 was supposed to start at nine. The demands of the protesters opened an ethical issue for me, and I was sure I couldn't work with Krivec anymore. But I needed to make it official, so I sat in my car to drive across the bridge to Sava Center and inform him of my resignation. Turning right at the traffic light I almost hit a tank, hidden close to a building. The streets were empty, and the city looked as it had fifty years earlier during the German occupation.

The two women who co-hosted the show with me were very different from one another. Snežana, a chubby blonde who used to be a movie critic for some magazines before discovering the magic of TV, was close to Krivec. Many people on Channel 3 avoided having conversations in front of her, as they knew she would report it all to our boss. Biljana Vilimon was a painter who made a career of her erotic art and liked to play the object of desire. She wore her opinions on her lapel, a daring and creative woman, and, although she was sometimes difficult in her demands, I loved working with her.

The two of them were already at the studio when I arrived. Snežana looked frightened, while Biljana was in a fighting mood. Krivec's secretary told us he'd been on the phone for the better part of the day, probably consulting with his superiors about what to do. As we talked, Krivec came out of his office. He looked a little pale and nervous, but, as if nothing had happened, asked us who our guests were for that evening. Biljana and I informed him that we'd called our guests to cancel.

"What do you mean, cancel? The show must go on, don't we all know that?"

"Krivec, there is no show anymore," said Biljana. "I'm out."

"Me too," I said. "We can't pretend nothing happened. This changes everything."

He looked surprised for a second, and then said, "Okay, then there is no show. You don't need to bother coming here anymore. Snežana, step into my office–I need to talk to you."

Once I got into trouble with Milošević's circle, there was no steady job for me. The masks had indeed fallen off, and there were no smiling faces behind them.

The voice on the radio, an excited, breathless male voice, kept repeating: "If you hear this, please come and join us. There are only two hundred of us and strong police forces have been seen in the surrounding streets. I repeat: we are students who are conducting a peaceful protest against police brutality. Please join us. They won't attack if there are enough of us."

It is two thirty in the morning, that same night. I can't sleep, and keep both my radio and TV on in a schizophrenic attempt to hear every detail of every new development around town. My friends confirm my worst fears over the phone: it seems that thousands are being arrested under the mantle of darkness and the threat of tanks. There's been some shooting and many contradictory reports of casualties. Listening to the independent Radio B92 and comparing its reports to those of the state TV, I get the impression that they are talking about events on opposite sides of the globe, only incidentally happening at the same time.

The place where the students are gathered is just around the corner from where I live. I take my balaclava, an old scarf, a bottle of water and the thickest jacket I have. That day I'd just learned my first lesson about confronting the police: they are trained to hit either on the head or in the kidney area. A thick balaclava and a good jacket can prolong your life on the streets. A soaked scarf offers some protection against tear gas, enough to get you to the closest building entrance.

I tiptoe down to the sidewalk from my sixth-floor apartment and stick to the shadows of my narrow street, waiting for my eyes to get accustomed to the darkness. Through the open window of an apartment on the first floor, I hear the same radio station and I see the silhouette of a man nervously walking in circles. I move slowly, from shadow to shadow. Fifty yards behind me, around the other corner, is a tank.

I am a journalist, but not tonight. I don't carry any of the tools of my profession. No camera, no recorder in my pockets. This is not about glory, not about publicity, not about recording facts; this is the game of numbers, and I want to be another number where it counts.

Finally, I'm there. I see a group of about a hundred young people, sitting on the cold asphalt of a March night around the fountain on the square. Somebody is up there, speaking to them, and although I can't see him, I recognize his voice: Leka, my old friend from my army service, now a leading Yugoslav actor. I can also see other shapes slipping from passages and side streets and joining the crowd.

I come out into the light.

That was the day I declared my war.

EXPIRY DATE

When I was working at *Rock* I discovered that somehow my money was disappearing really fast, and I didn't know where. I lived modestly, and, except for books and records, I didn't buy much else.

One morning I was walking down my street thinking of how to solve a situation that had come up at work, not paying attention to those around me, when I suddenly heard several voices saying "Good morning, Mr. Dragan!" from across the street. I looked up and saw a group of taxi drivers, standing on the corner, at the cab stop, having their first coffee. So, that was the answer. If they all knew my name and saluted me with such broad smiles, I probably fed their families well.

The next day I found an ad in the newspaper, and went and bought a car. It was an old yellow Zastava 101. In the months after I bought it, not only did the price of gas keep going up, but fewer and fewer gas stations had any to sell at all. My car was parked on the street in front of the apartment I rented, and I drove it only a couple times a week. Soon, I was using it only to go to Kragujevac for the weekend, when I couldn't stand another two hours of torture in the bus full of people who stank because they had no money for deodorant.

In 1991 the war in Slovenia had started, and gas prices skyrocketed as fuel was redirected to military depots. Rationing began. The distribution became organized as a lottery: two or three gas stations would get fuel every day, but nobody knew which ones. Even they would get only enough to last a few hours. Long lines of desperate drivers were an ordinary picture, and fights would frequently erupt after the last drops of gas were squeezed out.

One evening that summer, a friend gave me an urgent call. "I just drove by the gas station close to my house," she said, "and I couldn't believe my luck–they were just opening. I have a full tank now, but hurry up, the line is already forming."

I didn't hesitate; I made some coffee and poured it into a thermos, fixed a couple of sandwiches, and I was on my way. I arrived there half an hour after she hung up, but the line already stretched more than half a mile. So I parked at the end, found a station on the radio and poured myself coffee into a plastic cup. It was eight thirty in the evening.

Around midnight, there was only one car before me, and I was already counting the money, when the guy in the blue overalls knocked at my window and said, "No need to wait any longer. This is the last car. We're out of gas." I went out to check, and the driver before me said his tank was only half filled when the pump stopped working. "But better something than nothing," he said. I kicked my car and drove home. The red lamp had been on for some time already, and the last drops of gas went into the engine just around the corner from where I lived. I pushed the car for the last few yards, took out the cassettes and the tool bag from the trunk, and locked it. To me, a big, firm "nothing" was always much more dignified than "something."

The punks from the street noticed that the car just stayed there, in the same spot, and after several weeks they started plucking it: first the radio, then the windshield, then the seats. I tried not to notice when I'd pass by, but I couldn't help thinking what a perfect metaphor it was: a car that wasn't going to take me anywhere.

Soon I moved, again, and I left the wreck there. When some policeman phoned me, I told him that the man with my name–the one he was looking for–had moved to Zambia.

My driver's license was up for renewal around that time, and I decided to let it expire. Going to the police department, I'd heard, had become costly. Stories were circulating that some of those who renewed their licenses would soon afterwards be drafted: the police had their current address and would forward it to the army.

I gathered all my documents one day and realized that everything had expired: my library card, my journalist card, my reservist ID, even my pension booklet. I moved again, for the second time in seven months, and I practically went underground. I did not exist anymore in the official records. My passport was okay, and that was all I cared about. That was my ticket to freedom, in case I decided to use it.

PRAYER

It was the beginning of the summer, three months after the big demonstration. Silvija's parents had left for the coast and we stayed at their apartment. One day we rented a video to watch in the afternoon, waiting for Dejan and Milica. It turned out to be an extremely depressing film, *Awakenings,* I think. Our friends came in the evening and asked why we were so somber. We told them and they asked to borrow the cassette for the night. Our warnings didn't stop them.

The next day, around three in the afternoon, Dejan brought the cassette back. He told me he was in a hurry, so I went downstairs, in front of the building, to wait for him. When he opened the window of his Opel, I saw that he was gloomy, too. "It is terrible," he said.

"The film? I told you," I said.

"The news," he said, "haven't you heard the news? It started."

"What started?"

"The war," he said, and left.

And I remember standing there, on the hot asphalt, in front of building number 6 in Milorada Šapčanina Street in Belgrade, anno Domini 1991, and I remember that it was somehow solemn, and the music that I always hear in my head was suddenly strong and God-like, the Bach of my inner cathedral, and I remember that only one thought kept repeating itself, no matter how hard I tried to chase it away, and the thought that kept coming was:

"This is my war. It is my turn."

And everybody in my family, for centuries, had had at least one war. And everybody learned how to kill, and how to live, and I saw that it was good. And all my life had been hedonistic until now, since that is the way that our men live, and it was so. And I fucked left and right, and I thought up and down, and I lived, and I saw that it was good. And the big cloud was coming on the horizon, and I had a dream, and no children stayed alive in my dream. And I saw two dark pillars coming towards me, and I thought, Oh, these must be my tornadoes, and it was so. And I looked to the left, and I looked to the right, and I was calm because behind me, to my right, there stood a temple of no particular god, and I knew that that temple, without walls, without anything but ionic pillars and the roof, was my shelter, and I saw that it was good. And I am opening the umbrella of my skin over the people I love, because the rain has already started and the first bullets are knocking on our windows. And, O Zeus, give the thunder to my hands, and Sofia, give the wisdom to my heart, and Perun, you long-forgotten God of Slavs, let your lightning strike them in the eye, and Vesna, Goddess of Spring, let thy love be my ruler forever. Because my time has come, and I'm scared shitless, and I don't want to die, and I don't have kids, and I didn't publish enough books, and I haven't told the best stories of my guts, and many good women would like to fuck me, and there's no point in disappointing them, because we are all your seed, Vesna, Goddess of Spring, Goddess of Love, my Goddess. Amen.

JOHNNY GOES TO WAR

In 1991, after the war had started and the border between Serbia and Croatia had already closed, Branimir Johnny

Štulić came to Belgrade. His parents still lived in Zagreb, but he wanted to tell his Belgrade friends that they were not isolated.

At that time, my friends had already started leaving the country. Nobody talked about it, neither the ones who traveled nor the ones who stayed. Gangsters of all kinds were out on the streets of Serbia, with two tasks: to scare the opponents of the regime, and to organize paramilitary forces (since Serbia was never officially at war with Croatia). Also, the right-wing political parties started demanding that all those who left should be treated as traitors and their possessions nationalized.

It was no wonder that the friends who were leaving would call me only one or two nights before the trip. I didn't have the chance to say good-bye to some of them at all. Three days or a week later, someone would say, "Oh, they called from London." The tone would always be offhand, as if saying, "Oh, it's so humid today."

Johnny Štulić was born in Croatia, of a mixed Serbian-Croatian marriage. In 1981 he brought out the first album with his band, Azra, and, releasing a new record every six months on average, quickly became a leading name on the Yugoslavian rock scene. His strongly politicized songs got an unprecedented response from several generations at once and became a kind of underground code. He was the first musician to abandon the golden rule of uninformed silence ("I don't know, therefore I exist"). At a time when the Yugoslav Communist Party still had a strong hold on the media and culture, he wrote in support of the anti-Communist Solidarnošć movement in Poland, he ridiculed communist hard-liners, the working class, the failed revolution of 1968, and yes, he wrote some of the most amazing songs about love. Johnny left Yugoslavia in 1985 and went to live in Holland, and–

absurdly as it happens–it was after he left that we became friends.

When he reappeared in Belgrade in 1991, he had just finished making a superb record in Sarajevo and was looking for a label, as his original company was Croatian. We were both slightly crazy at the time, for different reasons. His fans, who belonged to both the nations at war, had been cut in two. I still hoped that understanding could halt the war, and that the understanding could be achieved by talk. He told me how he wanted to found this party he intended to name the Party of Work (Naked Dick), and insisted that this was the full name, including brackets and what was between them. "If you believe that the working class really rules in this country, all you will have in the end is a naked dick," he said. I thought that this went well with my old idea to do live interviews, in front of an audience, but not for any recording or broadcasting media. So we traveled through the Serbian province for two weeks, to the places where God had said good-bye a long time ago, and we did our little show. He would sing a little with his acoustic guitar, then I would come out and we'd talk about the Naked Dick Party, then he'd sing again, and we'd go. He didn't want any money for this, and I took in only enough to cover the expenses. Pure fiction, or pure absurd, whatever you want: we were promoting two things that didn't exist. His party didn't have its headquarters, or money, or even membership cards, and his Sarajevan album wasn't released until five years later. A madly beautiful woman was our driver, a painter, and her drunken boyfriend was always with us. Johnny would tell funny stories from his past, and we would laugh, and there was something desperate in all that.

"When I was in the Yugoslav Army," he said while we

were driving along the Ibar River, "I did this impression of a Nazi officer who is incredibly stupid and ugly. Someone had tipped off the security officer, and he calls me one day, and says, 'Štulić, do your impression for me.' So I did–I thought they wanted it for some army show or something. And then he says, 'Štulić, this is the People's Army, with a great tradition of fighting the Nazis, and we won't allow anything like that here. If you want to do an impression, do an impression of an officer of the Yugoslav Army!'"

One night, in between our hopeless travels, we sat in my apartment in Belgrade and drank. "Why did you leave?" I asked him.

"Because they would have killed me if I hadn't," he said. "Lennon, Marley, Hendrix, Che, all people of the Revolution are dead. I am one of them, it would be the same."

"You can't be serious."

"I am. I know, it sounds like paranoia, but I guess that all those dead heroes just didn't want to sound paranoid."

We fell silent for some time. Then I said, "Why are we doing this?"

"Our tour?" he asked. "We have to do something, I guess."

Around that time several hundred young mothers organized a demonstration called All the President's Babies, and carried their numbered babies to the front porch of Milošević's villa, symbolically giving them to him, since they were not able to take care of them anymore. "Babies of the nation to the Father of the nation" was one of the slogans. Someone else had collected all the court songs, odes written for the rulers of Serbia by leading Serbian poets through the ages, and published *The Anthology of Boot-licking Serbian Poetry.* It sold out in less than a month.

ZVONE, JUST A BULLET AWAY

During the war, all connections between Croatia and Serbia were cut off, including mail and telephone, and the rare foreign correspondents I met in Belgrade were unable to tell me anything about my friend Zvone.

In 1991, Mića the Turk went to the front, to write a story about the battle for Vukovar.

There he heard Zvone's name for the first time since the war started. He had boarded a bus full of Croatian POWs who were waiting to be exchanged for Serbian prisoners and he met a Croat who told him that he had run into Zvone right there in Vukovar, where he was taking pictures for some Croatian magazine.

It turned out that, one night, Turk and Zvone must have been no more than a few hundred yards away from each other. Both Serbian and Croatian governments were forcibly mobilizing their citizens at that time, so it was just a touch of luck that neither had to shoot at the other.

"I can't sleep anymore," said Turk when we talked about this.

"Yes, I understand," I said, thinking he meant the horrors of war.

"No, you don't," said Turk. "They are shelling the city as if they want to destroy it totally. You can't believe the level of destruction there. I can't sleep because of silence. In the night there, you hear grenades, bullets, explosions, screams, and you get used to it. Here, I hear only this unbearable silence."

JERINA

In the late fall of 1991, my cousin and I were driving along the Ibar River, where I had driven only a few months before with Johnny Štulić. My cousin had just come out of hospital, with a shell fragment in his neck and two fingers missing on his right hand. He had been in the battle of Vukovar.

Close to the Valley of Lilacs, but across the river, the ruins of a medieval fortress stand on the top of a steep hill. Among the blocks of local Kopaonik stone, piled ten centuries ago into an estate for some Serbian feudal lord, among those rocks shaped into metaphors of power, today only the crickets, snakes and long lizards live.

I have never learned for certain to whom that once powerful castle belonged. Once I saw a TV documentary about some ruins on the Ibar, but it was filmed from a helicopter, so I was not sure that it was this fortress. Power seen from above does not look like power seen from below. When I was a boy, my father told me it was Jerina's castle. She was the wife of a very powerful medieval Serbian lord, and she was famous for building many, many castles. People at that time hated her, since they had to work so hard on those buildings. They gave her the name the Damned Jerina, and over time she became the Dark Shadow of Doom.

Serbian peasants, even today, as soon as they see ominous traces of power, tend to blame Jerina. Wherever there is a stone on top of a stone, and below there's a snake, "That belonged to Jerina."

We stopped the car in front of a motel in the Valley of Lilacs. A mountain creek could be heard somewhere in the bushes around. It was a sunny day. My cousin and I got out and looked up, towards "Jerina's" castle. These rotten, broken teeth of a once powerful jaw woke my appetite for dinner. My cousin saw something else.

He was at Vukovar. He had met Jerina.

RECIPES FOR MEMORIES

HOMEMADE BITTER LEMON

Peel 1 pound of lemons and 2 grapefruits and grind them in a meat grinder. Add 2 pounds of sugar, 6 bags of lemon acid powder, and 9 quarts of water, and let it stand for 24 hours. Mix occasionally. Sift through gauze. Makes approx. 10 quarts.

Sometime towards the end of 1992, the year when international sanctions against Serbia were imposed, the first of these recipes appeared. Some of them were really old, clearly written during previous wars and now rediscovered in some attic. Others appeared out of necessity, as a defense against poverty, made with just basic ingredients normally found at home.

HOW TO PRESERVE MEAT WITHOUT A REFRIGERATOR

Bake a large piece of fat pork in the oven. When done, cut the meat into small pieces and put it all in a deep and narrow pot, and pour the lard on top of it so it covers all the meat. Not a single piece should protrude through the surface. Cover it with a cloth to protect it from flies. Leave it for the lard to thicken. Meat can stay fresh for a week like this, even in summer.

Some of these recipes fascinated me. They were obviously the result of much experimenting and a great instinct for putting the right ingredients together. They aimed at replacing commercially made desserts and drinks, or even complex ingredients used for making other food. There was one for making two pounds of chocolate with only a few spoonfuls of cocoa, and another for making an exact replica of the delicious Raffaello, the crispy, creamy balls rolled in coconut.

CHOCOLATE

Cook ⅓ cup of milk with 1 pound of sugar, half a pack of margarine and one pouch of vanilla sugar. In another pot mix ½ pound of flour and 3 tablespoons of cocoa, then add the milk mix, stirring fast. While stirring, keep it on a stove, but remove as soon as it is united. Add coconut flour, almonds or pieces of dry fruit if you wish. Oil the pan slightly, spill the mass onto it and leave in a freezer half an hour to an hour. Cut into squares and keep in a cold place.

These recipes were a beautiful display of the resourcefulness of Serbian women, of their long experience with wars and poverty, and of their resolve to give some joy to their families whenever possible. They showed the stubbornness, the defiant approach to undeserved punishment. Sanctions were in place to force the regime to succumb to the requests of international politics–in reality, the regime thrived and ordinary people suffered, as always. The irony was that all these recipes actually resulted in better, healthier versions of the originals. They turned our homes from ordinary habitats into palaces of hedonistic kings, but still–they all sounded sad. They were not instructions; they were pages torn from a diary of better days.

After a while, watching in awe as these recipes mushroomed and started being published first in women's magazines, then in newspapers, and then changing hands over a cup of coffee, I started realizing that they were immensely dangerous. It seemed that literally everything could be replaced, every food item we used to buy in supermarkets, each drink we enjoyed in summer, all those expensive trifles we purchased in duty-free shops when returning from abroad. I expected some day to see a recipe for making gasoline from water, cornflour from sand, or another one for putting together a jet from old shoes. There were substitutes for everything.

If we grow accustomed to substitutes, I thought, the memories of better times would slowly fade, and we would settle for whatever life handed us instead. That was the final, and the worst, recipe, the one that would keep the lunatics in power for a thousand years.

The more I thought about it, the more I suspected that the first of these recipes had come from the secret vaults of some shady ministry, creating an avalanche behind it, and the more I vowed never to try any of them. I thought it better to remember originals than choke on substitutes.

HOMEMADE SMART BOMB

Mix together: humiliation at being ostracized from the world community, anger at not being able to find gasoline anywhere but from black marketeers at prices you can't afford, nervousness over freezing in your cold apartment, hunger after not seeing tropical fruit for months, fear of sickness before the empty drugstores, apathy at being unable to plan anything, depression of dark streets in times of saving energy for hospitals, lethargy caused by no embassy willing to give you a visa, and shake well. Cook it, no–simmer it–for months. Don't mix it. Don't even open the lid. From time to time throw in other ingredients

> at will: job loss, shoes falling apart, coat torn on shoulders, broken car, wounds from clashes with police when demonstrating against the regime. Spit in it, piss in it, shit in it; that's your life, your bomb, your days on Earth. Then, one day, when you hear the distant thunder from under the lid, write the name of a country on a piece of paper and throw that in, too. Close the lid quickly and sit on it. In the morning you will be in that country. (Cut your previous life into small pieces and keep it in a dark and warm place.)

IN THE HOUSE OF ILL REPUTE

A month after I left TV, someone told me that a new radio station in Belgrade was looking for journalists. Politika had just added a TV channel and a radio station to its roster of print media.

Nobody believed that this and the other new media popping up was the sign of democracy blooming in Serbia. Milošević played the same game from the beginning. When he came to power Serbia was still officially a one-party state. He introduced the multiparty system, but only because he knew that the credibility of the Communist Party was spent. He immediately founded his own Socialist Party of Serbia; his wife did the same with her own Yugoslav United Left. Both their parties consisted mainly of Communists searching for a new lease on political life, including some surprises, such as Ljubiša Ristić, the theater director whose show about the Black Hand I'd criticized a few years before. Then the secret police founded some twenty other satellite parties, confusing people, including the true opposition, into thinking that it was all a big joke, and that the only proper political party was Milošević's SPS. He was now playing the same game with the media: what use was it to have another outlet if it was in his hands from the very beginning?

After I had been fired from *Rock* by Politika's (they were the publisher) president, I didn't feel like going back to the same building–by this time, their leading newspaper, *Politika,* was a caricature of its former self, having turned into a pure propaganda mouthpiece–but I didn't have much choice if I wanted to stay in journalism.

The head of the radio station was Nada Mišić, a blonde, elegant woman, calm and self-assured. She told me she knew who I was, and that she would like to have me on her team. I proposed two shows and she accepted both of them.

My Monday show, *McLuhan's Café,* was a cultural magazine, reporting on events from all over Yugoslavia and airing interviews with artists. On Saturday afternoons I had the *Dignified Radio Show,* live satirical theater. Its name (although I didn't tell Nada this) was a take on Milošević's frequent use of this word. When promoting Serbian nationalism in his speeches, *dignified* was his favorite modifier. Everything he would mention was dignified–approach, stance, attitude and manner. To the uneducated masses it gave the impression that he cared about their dignity and honor.

At first I didn't realize how enormous a task I'd undertaken in starting a live drama show. And I insisted on live, not only because I was a big admirer of Orson Welles and other pioneers of the live radio play but also because the political events at that time were spinning out of control, the news worsening at a shocking speed, and I wanted to respond to that pace in real time.

"Ecological uniforms: a new product from the renowned arms factory Zastava puts you in tune with nature. Our uniforms double as body bags, hermetically sealing your body and protecting the environment from the odors you would normally discharge as a corpse. Be a responsible citizen. If you want to die, protect your family and the whole population from your stench. Come home in one piece–ecological uniforms from Zastava."

But soon the war had started. News from the Croatian front was getting worse every day and we were all affected by it. In my case it meant effectively having to kill one show and significantly change the other. The pan-Yugoslav cultural magazine lost its purpose simply because there was no country to cover anymore, and my theater show had to lose its anti-war-anti-commercials because they weren't funny anymore. I started a new show, a six-hour talk-radio spot called *On the Border.* We were all on the borderline between sanity and madness.

I'd met Aleksandar Tijanić when I was still with *NON.* He edited *Intervju,* the magazine of Politika, and I occasionally published articles there. As the secretary-general of the in-house Party organization, he was a rising star. The *Intervju* magazine bloomed for some time, but it suddenly became apparent that it was creating huge losses. Tijanić had to go, while the magazine stayed somewhere between life and death. Communist apparatchiks are protected from fiscal responsibilities, and so one day it was announced that Tijanić was back, this time as the chief of Politika's radio and TV. Many of us thought this move had been the result of his publishing a flattering article about Milošević's wife, Mirjana Marković, two years before.

Things changed with his coming. Nada called me into her office one day and, closing the door behind her, said, "It's getting more and more difficult to defend you."

"Defend me–from whom?"

"From Tijanić. Did you ever come into conflict with him?"

"No. I worked for him once and we were on semi-friendly terms. What's his problem?"

"Almost everything you do. He calls me twice every week, after each of your shows. Cool it off for a while. Make it milder, let him fall asleep."

"Him? Asleep?"

"I run this station, and I think you're doing a good job. But you know how powerful he is in this house."

"It must be dangerous for you, too. Do you want me to leave?"

"No. But keep this information in mind. It might help."

The information, of course, didn't help. Neither he nor she were naive in this matter; they both knew very well that the principle of self-censorship had ruled Yugoslav journalism for decades. Instead of placing an official ban on the media, the Communist censors always insisted on higher interests, state secrets and the danger from foreign enemies, persuading journalists that patriotism meant self-control.

Why had she decided to defend me? Was I a pawn in a game of interests? Was she buying her conscience through me, working for the system, but using me as her personal dissident to bring some balance? There it was again: the indecipherable machine of the system buzzing threateningly close.

I was even more confused when, two months later, she called me again into her office to tell me she wanted me to report on the protests scheduled on the anniversary of the bloody March clashes of the previous year.

"Be careful," she said, again behind closed doors. "Just do straight reporting from the street. Do not get into anything that might provoke a reaction. Do not call people to join, don't mention the numbers, and don't talk about what Vuk Drašković and others said."

"What will I say, then?"

"You'll find something. Find a couple of middle-aged protesters, someone who is not too overheated, and interview them. Say that nobody wants to repeat the bloody events of last year, and that we all wish for a peaceful ending."

March 9, 1992, was again a beautiful day, perfect weather for demonstrations: sunny (bad for police as it encourages people to go out), breezy (tear gas cannot work well) and cool (demonstrators are prompted to get more fiery to warm themselves up). I took my Walkman with me and listened to other stations' reporting while I was finding my way through the crowd. The speakers on Radio Politika made efforts to avoid taking sides, but some other stations were broadcasting direct lies. The state-run Radio Belgrade reported that fewer than three thousand people were at the event, while others were more generous, with counts of five to seven thousand. There is a method sociologists use when counting crowds. A friend of mine showed me how to do it, and by his method I figured there had to be at least thirty thousand people in that huge space by the Saint Sava Temple, and the protests hadn't even officially started. The information about numbers was considered crucial, since it was believed that many potential participants felt frightened by the campaign of threats the authorities had doled out in the preceding weeks, and that if they heard that others were coming in large numbers anyway, they'd be brave enough to come too.

The first time I went live I did pretty much as Nada told me: the traffic and weather report, and the general atmosphere of benevolence among the protesters. But then the official part started, and the crowd, now numbering closer to forty thousand, grew heated, and the other stations shifted into pure propaganda mode, condemning protesters and speakers, even calling for police action and arrests. But I had seen the police action, I remembered the tanks and the tear gas and the wounded, and I firmly believed we had the right, the obligation, to protest against a regime capable of defending itself with pure, brutal force. The next time they got me on line I reported that there were forty thousand protesters. After I finished they played music for a full fifteen minutes. I knew they'd gone to consult Nada and that they wouldn't call me again. (I wasn't the only reporter on the spot for our station.) I switched off the equipment and went to enjoy the feeling of mass hysteria.

Nobody talked to me about it over the next few days, and that was a bad sign; it meant I'd gone too far. Nothing happened, not to me, but two months later we got the sudden news that Nada had been replaced by someone who used to be the secretary for Politika's CEO. Officially, Nada was promoted, but it was to one of those positions that do not carry real power.

Our first meeting with Nada's successor confirmed what I suspected: they had found someone to just sit there and fulfill the wishes of his political masters. Mirko Marić was a silver-haired man in his late fifties, immensely happy to get such a position after years of secretarial jobs. He promised not to make any changes in the first few months of his rule, and declared his door open at all times.

He adopted a kind of fatherly approach that I found annoying, even humiliating. Nobody likes being patronized; I had additional trouble with that when it came from someone whose professional experience was less than mine. Soon it became obvious that Mirko and I would not work smoothly together, and we started avoiding each other. When he was expected to chair our meetings I wouldn't go to the station, and I chose to do all the studio jobs in the evening. For several months it worked, but then came the Serbian presidential elections of December 1992.

It was the only chance we all had, I thought, to stop the war and get out of the collective madness before it was too late. The protests couldn't do anything, it was obvious. Milošević had created a strong, well-armed and cruel police apparatus, fully capable of fighting even the army in case someone planned a coup, and he also had the army on his side. But the elections were something else. The country was under sanctions. The store shelves were emptier every day. There was no gas, public transportation suffered, and there were even rumors that the ambulance service would soon be restricted. I was absolutely certain that even those who liked Milošević would be sobered by now, when their family members were being killed in Croatia in a war that had no promise of victory. What is a victory in a civil war? One nation occupying the other? One nation getting more rights than all others? It was unthinkable, and I expected the Serbian voters to change it all.

I felt the need to do something, but I was nobody, or almost nobody, on the public scene. My third book–a biography of Tom Waits–had been already published by then, my face had been seen on TV, and I had fifteen years in the media behind me, but my specialty was underground culture, rock and roll and modern sociological phenomena, and that hardly makes for a public name. The only tool I had now was my radio shows. I remembered the writer after whom my old school was named, Radoje Domanović, whose most famous work was *The Leader.* It was a brilliant satire about an unknown man who suddenly appears in desperate times and fascinates people with his audacity, his confidence and his Pythian oracles, so they choose him to be the leader who would take them to the Promised Land. They set off on their journey, and their leader always takes them straight, only straight. Fascinated, people take it as a sign of his courage and vision. But going straight sometimes means falling into an abyss, or drowning in a river, and they start dying one by one. Only in the end, already decimated, do they realize he is blind.

I decided to do a dramatization of *The Leader* for my *Dignified Radio Show.* We had to record our play, since I wanted it precisely structured and tightly executed. I kept my idea under cover until I had to submit my monthly plan of themes, and I offered it only when I couldn't postpone it any longer. Mirko called me the next day to invite me that evening into his office, "for a coffee and a little chat."

With his door open as always, Mirko sat behind his desk, reading some newspapers. It was early evening, the time when nothing happens on news desks: newsmakers had gone home for the day, to their families, leaving us and our families to cope with whatever disgrace they'd come up with earlier that day. I took the chair Mirko offered, and I very slowly pulled a notebook out of my bag and placed a pen neatly on top of it. I wanted him to see that I would take notes of our meeting. This was the game I remembered from SYS, and later, from my army days: two partners; one has power, the other has nothing. His only protection is the eyes and ears of the others around them. The predator has to make sure everything is done in complete silence, if he wants to stay successful on the same turf. At the first sign of trouble it's better to run away and attack again later, when nobody is around. But I wasn't sure Mirko knew the rules, or if he wanted to play by them.

"I saw your plan for this month only today," he opened. When I didn't respond, he nudged me a little further: "It came in a little late. *The Leader,* huh?"

I stayed silent, looking him straight in the eyes. Accidentally or not, his desk was perfectly positioned for power games. I could see the roofs of the downtown buildings behind his back, and farther in the distance was Kalemegdan, the old fortress, the strength, the force. If he wanted a better metaphor, it would have had to be done in neon.

"You do know that I studied literature?" he said, and when I nodded, he added, "I loved Domanović, particularly that piece. Always. The best satire ever written, anywhere."

The coffee was strong and bitter, just the way I liked it.

"So, what I am about to say is not related to my taste, in any way."

Oh, good: we will adhere to the rules. He is trying to make this non-personal. There is no wolf, there is only the public good. I took my pen and started playing absentmindedly with it.

"I'm sure you realize in what times we live. People are agitated, edgy, and understandably so. There is no work, the country is under sanctions, and it will only get worse. Not to mention the war. And now we have the presidential elections coming. I don't think you should do *The Leader* now."

I put a puzzled look on my face. "What better time than now?"

"I understand why you say that, but let me tell you something: we have to keep our calm in these times. When everyone around us is hysterical, we, in the media, have to be composed. We can't afford to join the masses, because who will keep the distance then? Who will control the passions? Sure, it would be so easy, and so sweet, to take one side and push for it. And you know I would take the same side as you . . ."

"What side is that?"

His back straightened a little and the fatherly smile subdued. "The right side. But not now. Now we are taking no sides."

"How is my doing *The Leader* taking any side? That story doesn't contain any names, and I'm certainly not going to add any."

"Well, you don't have to. It's a satire, and satire is always aimed at someone. That one was written against the leader of that time, but when you broadcast it today the people will understand that it's aimed at the current leader. And we know who he is." He beamed.

I made a short note in my notebook.

"What are you writing?" His tone was severe.

"Oh, that? Nothing in particular. These days I simply take this notebook with me everywhere I go. I'm working on a dramatization, and ideas keep popping up."

"I hope you do understand this conversation is between the two of us. I know what you do, and I have a high opinion of your work. You are a smart and good journalist, and you've been around for . . . how long?"

"Let me see . . . Fifteen years, I think."

"Wow. See, I knew we would understand each other. After that long you surely know there are times when we need to use our self-control, when we have to restrain ourselves. And there are things that are more important than our quest for truth. Let me tell you–I have no doubts you would do a great radio play. In fact, why don't you do it, and keep it for after the elections? What do you say?"

"Mirko, the times are changing. Three years ago they officially allowed a multiparty system, and that is something new in our lives. Before that both of us kept hearing that self-control is the mother of proper communist journalism, but it's not anymore. When you have only one party, you have only one question: to publish, or not to publish? When you have more–and we have, what, twenty-six now?–"

"Twenty-nine," he said.

"–you don't have to keep your mouth shut, because you can't. And, like you said, not to mention the war and the poverty around us."

He took a sip of coffee and stood up. He stretched slowly, then put his hands deep into the pockets of his light gray dress pants and looked at the street below. The neon lights turned his profile into a mask. "You saw what Drašković did last year on the streets of our town, how they smashed the windows, and how they turned the protests into an orgy. It's a wild mob, not a group of politically minded people. You might be pouring gasoline on that fire, you know."

"I saw who started the conflict. And I saw the wounds, firsthand. The police weren't any better than the protesters."

I remembered the eyes of the Old Husky from a few years before and I had no patience for another Bogart. I lit a cigarette and stood next to him. I wanted to check his view. There was nothing to see down there. The streets in the center of Belgrade were shadowy and looked disoriented.

"What makes you believe so firmly that what I'm doing is dangerous?" I asked. "Nothing is dangerous in itself; it's only how one looks at it. You don't think I am so stupid as not to understand that at least fifty 'intellectuals in plain clothes' from this very house will listen to my show, hoping to find some reason to take me away? If I gave them one such thing, that would endanger you too, I agree, but I won't."

"You really don't understand," he said. "I know why they sent me here–because they thought it would be easier to control me, and those who work here through me. But they can't control you people, and that makes them angry, very angry. They can't allow themselves not to have total control over this radio, or every other media outlet. They will remove me, and they will put in someone much worse than me. And if he screws up, they will remove him, too, until they find someone to frighten everyone into leaving. They don't need you or me here. They don't need journalists. They only need speakers, to read whatever it is that they send to be read."

"They won't," I said. "They are too busy with their own fears now."

"These are the people who started this war," he said. "They won't stop at anything. They don't know what to do now, but it's too late to go back. These are the men at work, and it's our business to keep from falling under their bulldozer."

"See, the same way you say you know why they put you here, I also think I know why Nada kept me here. I mean, I'm an easy target. People are too scared to sweat over some journalist's fight for freedom of expression. But I suspected her reason for not firing me was that she wanted to have her own dissident. You remember those stories from the last war: you have two sons; you send one to fight with Tito, the other one against him. You can't lose."

He turned to me and looked me in the eyes. We stood there in silence, and then he said, "Okay, do what you want. But you will make a detailed script, you will bring it to me before you enter the studio, and you will not improvise."

"Deal."

Three days later I took my script and insisted on giving it directly to him instead of leaving it with his secretary. Then I went to see the girl who did the small introductions of the coming shows for the newspaper *Politika* and gave her my promotional material. I said that Mirko had approved the show, and she took the bait and wrote the introduction, which was printed that same evening. It was more risky to pull the plug on an already advertised show, and I wanted to have another ace up my sleeve.

Mirko, indeed, didn't have any comment, and the next evening we went into the recording studio and did the play. My editing slot was in the afternoon on the following day, in the three hours preceding our airtime, so I took the tape home with me. Three people protested against my doing it, one producer and two technicians, saying it was against the rules. "Fine, I'll take the consequences," I said, and left the building in a hurry. Taking the tapes outside was considered stealing, so I took the back exit.

I watched the news that evening, and the situation was overheated. Warnings flew from all sides: the opposition threatened street protests if the elections were rigged, and Milošević promised to send out his brutal police if anyone protested against anything. Accusations flooded the news: the opposition was a "servant of the West" and its leaders "foreign mercenaries." Milošević had five times more media space than any of his opponents.

I went out for a walk late in the evening. The streets were unusually empty. I went to the radio station, to hang out there with the night shift, and I came home late.

The editor who was scheduled to work with me on the final edit was not the fastest or the best at Radio Politika, so I just concentrated on cleaning the recording and picking the best takes. Finally, half an hour before airing, the edit was completed and we started rewinding the tape.

Mirko stuck his head through the door. He wasn't normally there on Saturday afternoons, but I thought he'd come to field the eventual phone calls after the show.

"Everything okay with the show?" he asked.

"Everything's just perfect," I said. "Is there an Oscar for radio plays?"

The editor stood up to reach for his cup of coffee, bent over the fast-spinning tape, touched it accidentally, and suddenly the whole wheel flew in the air, yards and yards of tape whirling all over the studio, like a thin brown snake that had just swallowed a flying saucer. The editor panicked and started pressing buttons, stepping on the tape and spilling his coffee all over it. When the wheel finally settled under a desk, I didn't have to look: the tape was destroyed. I looked at Mirko, and there was a huge smile on his face.

"If I ever saw a sign, this was one," he said.

I pulled a cassette tape from my bag.

"What's that?" said Mirko, his eyes narrowing.

"The final edit, version one," I said. "There wasn't an editor here last night, but the studio was empty and I couldn't sleep, so I thought I'd do some editing on my own. And, since there was no blank master tape, I put it all on this cassette. Dolby and everything. Good as gold, I promise."

Mirko turned and left. Half an hour later, our play went on the air. The next day Milošević won again. A month later I quit.

WARRIORS OF PEACE

I've known Mila for many years. She is a born activist, a natural guerrilla. In 1992, during the war in Croatia, she invited me to work with her at *Pacifik*, an anti-war magazine privately published several times a year under very difficult circumstances.

In January 1993, Mila tells me that she has been invited to join a small group of people in Austria who are working to found an AIM, an alternative information network, among the intellectuals of the former Yugoslavia. It would be a way of exchanging truth instead of all the varieties of government propaganda. The talks about this project had been initiated several months earlier, in the Ukraine, at a meeting of the Association of Free Radio Stations of Europe. Mila tells me that this meeting was sponsored by a strange group of people, a sort of free-love commune called Longo Mai, based in France. She has been told to go to Austria and to take one reliable coworker with her. Milica, who'd been in the Ukraine at that meeting, was not able to go just then, and Mila had suggested me. We are to travel at the end of January.

For the first time I could watch international diplomacy at work. At that time, it was impossible for a citizen of Serbia to get an Austrian visa, but with a fax from Longo Mai I just send my passport to the Austrian Embassy, and it comes back with a visa.

Everything is under a veil of secrecy. I don't talk too much about this trip. Instead of traveling through Croatia, which would shorten the trip to twelve hours maximum, we have to take the bus to Hungary, then to Slovenia, then the train to Austria. It will come to more than thirty-six hours altogether.

Bleiburg is a place on the Austrian-Slovenian border. Not even a village, just a group of houses in search of a post office. The local train carries noisy schoolchildren and tired, bored commuters. It stops at every other house and it takes us a couple of hours to travel the short distance from the border. It is almost dark when we arrive. There is nothing around, no cab, no public transportation, no driver we could ask for a ride. Mila asks a woman behind the station's counter about the *gasthaus* where we are supposed to wait. It turns out to be in the center of the village. We start walking and Mila tells me that we are supposed to wait in the guesthouse until someone comes to pick us up. I'm creeped out; I don't know why exactly. Bleiburg has no landmarks and no signs of life, except for an occasional car every five minutes or so. The air is fresh, subalpine; night is falling and that is never a traveler's friend; but there is something else. "There is something in history in regards to this place," Mila says, "though I can't remember what it was. Maybe some famous Nazi was born here, or something." Maybe. Not impossible for a village named Lead Town.

We arrive at the small guesthouse, with its gothic inscription in front. It turns out that we are the only customers. There is an older man with a young woman who looks like him behind the bar, and they don't answer our salutes. We sit in the corner; they stand behind the bar and watch us. After fifteen minutes or so, the woman comes and takes our order. We come from a country that at that moment is drowning in inflation, and we both have monthly income of about ten German marks, so we just order some coffee. And we wait. There is nothing to read, no TV around, some yodeling on the radio, and the owner and his daughter do not talk, not to us nor between themselves. After two hours, Mila makes a telephone call. At the other end, in the commune in the mountains, some woman instructs us to continue to wait.

Finally, after four hours during which nobody else comes into this place and we drink maybe seven or eight glasses of water each, two men appear at the door. We hadn't heard the sound of their engine; they had parked cautiously up the road. They wear dark coats and black hats with wide brims. They say something in German to the owner and the woman, and these two finally give us a friendly look. We go out and get into the van. There is an extra hour's drive up the mountains. As the vehicle slowly winds up the narrow mountain road and the lights in the small valley become dim, I finally remember what it was about Lead Town.

For a long time after World War II, it was a secret. Not until the eighties did the first articles about the massacre in this village in 1945 appear in Yugoslav print. When the Red Army started defeating Nazi troops in the last months of war, all who fought the communists–Chetniks from Serbia, along with the Croatian Ustashas–started withdrawing towards the northwest, towards the Austrian border. There they would meet British and American troops and surrender themselves happily. The Allies set up a concentration camp for these POWs and waited to see what to do with the people who all thought that they would end up in court and later continue to live in the West. We are talking about small fish here: a large majority of these "enemies" had been forcibly mobilized and had committed no war crime. The articles said that, according to the prisoners' lists found later, there were maybe fifteen thousand people in the Bleiburg concentration camp.

Then came the Russians and Tito's partisans, who asked to take over the prisoners. The Allies had difficulty finding food for all these POWs, so they agreed. Then the communists went through the lists of names, took off to prison a few score prisoners who were under suspicion for committing war crimes, to try them publicly in domestic courts, and closed the camp. Closed? In less than seventy-two hours, thousands of helpless prisoners were shot to death under the mantle of darkness in the woods surrounding Bleiburg. Mass graves in the woods still hide the bones.

When we searched for my lost uncle, the trail led to Bosnia, then somewhere towards the northwest, towards the Austrian border. Bleiburg?

The Longo Mai commune turns out to be a big ranch in the Austrian Alps. The place where our driver turns left doesn't have any sign and the road looks like the definition of a dead end. We pass two No Trespassing signs on the narrow stretch that leads us to the first curve behind the hill. Then, suddenly, the road is much wider as it sweeps through the woods. They are expecting us in the yard, several men and women, dogs, chickens, horses and some cattle, all freely wandering around at this late hour, and it looks very much like the Grateful Dead preparing for a world tour. They take us into the big four-story house and there we meet the delegation of journalists from the other republics of ex-Yugoslavia.

During dinner, in the warm and brotherly atmosphere, sitting on the benches around the long table, we learn more about our hosts. The original Longo Mai commune was founded in the sixties, in France, by an old millionaire. Later the commune established separate families in Austria and a few other European countries. The majority of the Austrian family is highly educated. Among them are two doctors, one lawyer and several professors. Two of the women and one man stay on the ranch all the time. One of the women is stunning, like a Swedish model. Children, about fifteen of them, are a collective responsibility, and the members of the commune teach the preschool kids. When they grow up, I am told, it will be up to them to decide if they will stay in the commune or leave. It is not laid out, but there is an obvious power structure: a man who looks like Klaus Kinski is silent and self-confident, and nothing starts without his being asked.

The next morning we start talking about the project. "Kinski" tells us the basic idea: Longo Mai is in a position to finance the purchase and installation of a network of computers in the capitals of all the former Yugoslav republics. This means the fastest available modems and PCs, and special software custom-designed by a German company. Each workstation is to be a local information-gathering center. In Belgrade I am to be the workstation operator. The raison d'être of the project is to create more understanding among the intelligentsia of different nationalities, but also to offer independent information to the world media, since the network that we create will be available to subscribers.

"Who is financing the whole thing?" I ask. The answer never comes.

"What do we publish, what kind of information?" someone else asks.

"It doesn't have to be an article ready for publishing. Almost anything will do: the price of bread, the percentage of inflation, public opinion on certain politicians, anything," explains a Longo Mai communist who is missing a finger.

"This news is for sale? Will we get paid for it?" asks the Montenegrin.

"Yes. We will serve as a reliable source for the world media."

"The original idea was different," protests Mila. "We wanted to communicate privately, and for humanitarian reasons, to keep the old connections alive, to build confidence between us, and thus help overcome our local nationalisms."

"For that idea we were not able to find the money," is No-Finger's answer. "But if we can sell the information, we can still keep everything else on the network.

"The software developed for us allows us to create separate channels, unavailable to the public," continues No-Finger. He turns out to be one of the engineers who are to install and maintain the network, but at the same time he is the man who stays on the ranch all the time. Interesting. I remember reading somewhere that the big-time intelligence services have research centers where they process exactly such information. These small details help make the bigger political pictures more precise.

So, is this whole thing to be considered a career move for me? A journalist who came in from the cold?

We spend the whole of that day discussing the project. At lunchtime, I sit next to Vesna Kesić, a well-known Croatian journalist and feminist. She starts discussing the hot issue of the day: a special commission led by the Polish politician Tadeusz Mazowiecki has just published the results of its inquiry into organized rape by Serbian troops in Bosnia. The number published was terrifying, says Vesna–more than fifty thousand women. All the world media reported on this. And this discussion leads us to our first international conflict that day.

Vesna argues that the fact that the number of raped women was so great proves that we have to talk about genocide against Muslims.

"Genocide is defined by extermination, not by rape," I say.

"So," says Vesna, "you are not disturbed by this number?"

"I would be if I trusted that report. But there are two big problems with it. One: you won't find the single name of a victim in the whole report, and two: take the numbers into account. The war in Bosnia has been going on for how long? Nine months? Ten? Make it ten. That is three hundred days. If you believe Mazowiecki, it turns out that every single day up to two hundred new women were raped. How did they find the time for battles?"

By this time, only Vesna and I can be heard around the table. Someone is translating to the Austrians. People are eating soup as if their lives depend on it.

Vesna sets her spoon down and turns to me. "As a man, I don't think you can understand how a woman who was raped feels about it. It is very probable that they wouldn't let their names be known because of shame."

I set my spoon down, too. "As an intellectual, you should know that Mazowiecki does not have a case here. No court in the world would take it seriously without at least one name. Except maybe in Croatia. Or Serbia."

The love of the others for the soup reaches unbelievable proportions.

"Mathematics does not help understand war. I still think it's possible, even probable, that this number is right," insists Vesna.

"Sure," I hear myself saying, "that's because it is well known that the Serbs are the best fuckers in the world."

I guess that Austrians don't have a word for "fucker," because the translator stopped translating.

"What did you say?" asked Vesna quietly.

"It was mythology. As is the stuff that you are saying."

I go out for a smoke. She goes upstairs. Inside, I think somebody has just drowned in the soup.

After lunch, the session continues. By sheer coincidence, some Longo Maians sit between Vesna and me. Narrow windows and the big fireplace of the old mountain house somehow take us all two centuries backwards. Exactly where we all belong.

There are more incidents, but this time between Montenegrin and Slovenian delegates, then between Croats and

Slovenians, then between Mila and the Austrians, then everyone starts arguing in their own languages and the Austrians stare at us, trying to decode something from our faces. Kinski begins to look shaken and wounded. He has turned into Fitzcarraldo, trying to take that ship across the mountain, even though the locals don't share his dream. "You see why war in the Balkans was inevitable?" I ask. He gives something that might be a smile. Or the result of a really fast early-morning shave.

Fortunately, the goodness of the World Community is unshakable, it seems. No-Finger, Kinski and the rest of them serve drinks and talk mild, and we slowly gather that in this fucked-up world it is wise to take glass beads while offered. So, deep in the night, when everyone is either drunk or broken, we eat domestic smoked ham and cheese, and someone brings out a guitar. Mila starts playing, and in self-defense we decide to sing together. Then we realize there is no song that everyone here knows. We don't yodel, Croatian songs demand several well-trained voices, Slovenian songs can't be sung without an accordion, Serbian songs are so sad that nobody dares to start one of them. It turns out that we all know international communist songs. We start with the "Internationale," then continue with the Italian "Bandiera Rossa," go for the Russian "Podmoskovnie Vecera" and end with a Yugoslav partisan's song, "Konjuh Planinom."

I think that in the meantime someone got sober and made all the plans, because the next morning I was given a modem and a bunch of floppy disks. Some other people got notebooks and stuff I didn't recognize. And in no time we were on the road home, whatever the home was. Warriors of peace–absolutely eager to fight between ourselves. Knights of benevolence–pissed off and in a bad mood. Undertakers of seclusion–all going in different directions.

On the way back, I stay with Silvija's distant cousins in Maribor, a Slovenian town close to the Austrian border. They drive me around on the weekend, but on Monday I am left alone and I go downtown. I enter a café and it's lunchtime and a line of people is already there. I understand Slovenian, and can speak some version of it, but I decide to go for the Serbian language and I ask someone loudly what time it is. That changes everything. The woman behind the counter turns to me, leaving all her customers in line, and asks if I come from Belgrade. When I confirm, her eyes become very shiny and she says, "Sir, tell your friends over there that we miss you so much. We miss our Yugoslavia."

I travel the night roads that lead me back to my country under heavy darkness. In the morning, I discover that the public transportation system in Belgrade is on strike, and I have to take a cab that charges thirty dollars for what normally would cost five. The driver has judged me by my heavy bag, and such a thing in Serbia at the time means that you come from or travel abroad, in both cases having hard currency with you. And my bag is heavy with the things bought in an Austrian supermarket–food, cosmetics and medicine, a survival kit for a country under sanctions.

A couple of months pass and I don't have any news from Longo Mai. When I developed the film I shot in Austria, a strange thing happened: the only faces I could see on the pictures were the faces of ex-Yugoslav delegates. Longo Maians were there, but each one had either turned his back on the camera or covered her face with a hand.

Mila calls in June, to say that the two engineers from the commune are already in Belgrade and waiting for me in her apartment. I take my secret weapons, the modem and the software, from the drawer, but I decide not to carry them with me. Again that feeling, or that logic: Why hadn't they called to say they were coming?

Mila lets me in and I see two familiar faces, No-Finger and another one, with dirty hair, the second engineer, waiting for me. After brief formalities, they get down to business: Did I bring the modem and the software with me?

"No," I say, "because I thought that you might want to install it in my apartment, since I am to be the operator in Belgrade."

They exchange looks. "Well, not really. We will install it in Milica's apartment, since it has been decided in the meantime that she will be the operator."

Milica was the original delegate in the Ukraine, at the first meeting.

"And what will be my role in the project?"

"None. It has been decided that you shouldn't be part of it."

"What do you mean by that? Who has decided so?"

"Well, it is not important. So, please tell us when you can bring the modem and the software. We would prefer it to be this afternoon, since we are in a hurry."

"Oh yes? Because there is a rumor that the Serbian borders will be closed, so you're in a hurry, eh? Too bad, because I suddenly remembered that I need to clean the modem. It's been dusty, you know, and it will probably take a couple of days, during which I would like Kinski to call me and explain the whole decision. Understood?"

Dirty Hair stood up threateningly. "What did you say?"

No-Finger gives a sign and Dirty Hair sits, very pale.

Mila turns to me. "I told them I am out of the whole project, too. Too much is muddy in this. Regarding the modem and the stuff, you decide."

"I have already decided–they won't get the things until Kinski gives me a satisfactory explanation."

No-Finger is the good cop today. "Listen, I know how you feel, but we need to finish this and go. Yes, it is about closing borders. My child is sick and is afraid to go to hospital without me. I just want to finish it and go. Please?"

I stare at him, then at Dirty Hair. I could swear that they shimmer one foot above the ground. They all must be part of a mirage on this desert horizon. "Come with me and I'll give you the stuff," I finally say to No-Finger.

The alternative informative network (AIM, for Alternativna Informativna Mreža) was in operation for some ten years after our meeting, though as a news agency rather than an anti-war hotline. Its customers were local media outlets. The centers were in Zagreb, Belgrade, Podgorica, Skopje, Sarajevo and Ljubljana. The original Slovenian team from Maribor fell out of the project immediately after the conference in Austria. The delegates claimed that on the way back the equipment (two laptops, one server and several modems) was confiscated by customs. Later I discovered that Radio Študent in Maribor, the station the Slovenian delegates came from, had surprisingly similar equipment. No-Finger and Dirty Hair, who traveled around setting up the network, charged sixty-five deutschmarks per hour, I heard later. At that time, their hour was worth six times more than an average monthly salary in Belgrade. In Zagreb alone, they charged a lot more than 180 working hours. The rumor goes that out of some 75,000 deutschmarks for the whole project, more than 50,000 stayed with the Longo Mai for the expenses of installation. Milica, who took over the Belgrade center, used the position to obtain a grant sufficient to emigrate to London. Vesna Kesić continued to travel to various peace conferences as an authentic victim from long-suffering Croatia. The report of Mazowiecki–when I finally got hold of a copy–mentioned 119 documented rapes, on all three sides of the Bosnian conflict, and deduced from that number that it probably represented some twelve thousand rape victims. Mazowiecki's numbers were never proved, but they were not forgotten, either. Mila emigrated to the United States. The big old mountain house of Longo Mai burned to the ground a year after our secret meeting. Or maybe it didn't.

THE GOLD I COULD AFFORD

It is June of 1993. Serbia is in its second year under sanctions. Life for everyone has become a humiliation. People are smuggling gasoline, food, medicine. But it's difficult to find cigarettes, and, even if you do, they are ridiculously expensive. So for weeks now I have been buying shag tobacco in the Zeleni Venac market, in the heart of Belgrade, from a man who had to run away from Zadar, on the Croatian coast. He had a café and his own business there, but was married to a Croat. One night his neighbor called him and said that he had seen a blacklist with this man's whole family on it. They had to leave everything behind and drive away that same night. Now the whole family, five of them, lives in a studio on the outskirts of Belgrade. He smuggles tobacco from Macedonia to feed his family. I buy his tobacco because it is the only gold I can afford.

One day, the police start checking the market. The state does not give up its monopoly that easily. I find my dealer in the crowd, and he thrusts at me a handful of his own tobacco and tells me to find him in the morning in a small café close to the market. Since then, we keep meeting secretly. I feed his kids, he services my nerves. Sometimes we roll that Macedonian tobacco together, pretending to try it. There's nothing to try, we both know how it is: it is bitter as poverty, strong as anger and yellow as the skin of a prisoner. It grows well where illusions don't.

RAMBO

A macho man from Montenegro who calls himself Rambo Amadeus sits across from me at the studio table. He is an eclectic musician who combines rock, rap, folk and jazz into an efficient, strong mixture that targets kitsch culture and strongly criticizes societal hypocrisy. Rambo is usually provocative and I'm looking forward to doing this talk show with him. A few weeks before, parliamentary elections were held in Serbia. In the last minutes before pre-electoral silence, Rambo appeared on TV and said, addressing voters in general, "Listen, you monkeys! In forty-eight hours you'll have the chance to change our lives, to get rid of this criminal, Milošević. Think carefully how you vote, otherwise I'll find out where you live!" Milošević's Socialist Party won a majority again.

We are in the studio of Art Channel, the alternative, private TV station in Belgrade where I now work. A transmitter of very limited power covers only parts of Belgrade, politics is taboo, and the salary is an insult. Nonetheless, it is one of the few remaining shelters for journalists who want to stay independent. Or, rather, this is one of the few remaining illusions of independent journalism.

When I come into the studio, two hours before the show, I find only one camera, and the cameraman is playing a shooting game on the editing computer. "We are taping some wedding ceremony," he tells me, "so you'll have only this camera. But don't worry, I'll change the shot every now and then."

So Macho Rambo and I start talking. We warm up with his career in general, then I go for his artistic standards, and then I steer him skillfully to his political beliefs. But something is wrong: this artist, this very engaged intellectual, is mild tonight. No matter how hard I try, he stays distanced.

During the second break, I ask him if he has problems with the interview and if, perhaps, that could be the reason why he is avoiding politics.

"No," he says laconically, "but is there any sense in talking to cattle?"

Then we start the third and last part of the show, and we are already into the sign-off courtesies, when I suddenly have this urge to do something absurd. In the middle of his sentence, I lift the microphone from the table between us, take the tablecloth and put it around my shoulders. Silence. We are on the air all the time.

After the show, Rambo the Cop-out asks, "What was it? You were trying to save the show?"

I respond truthfully, "No, I don't know what it was, I just had to do it."

THE SARAJEVO PARTY

Bosnia was the tampon zone–between the war and us, between madness and sanity, between the importance of life and absolute relativity of everything we knew and were.

When the first clashes in Slovenia started, there were only a few victims, the intervention of the Yugoslav Army seemed reluctant and mild, and it lasted for only several days, subsiding into bitterness and self-chosen ignorance. Most of my friends, including me, had already said goodbye to Slovenians. They had a different language, a culture that more resembled Austrian than any of the Yugoslav cultures; the republic was tiny, and there seemed to be nothing worth fighting for there.

We entered another level of denial when the war in

Croatia came, with very disturbing pictures and reports. Tanks driving over some small cars parked in the crossroads to stop the army. Corpses of older Serb civilians with their throats cut. Corpses of Croatian paramilitaries to boost morale. Belgrade TV insisted on a careful selection of Croatian iconography, showing only the images with people in black uniforms, with a letter U on their caps, to remind us of World War II and the pro-Nazi Croatian government, their forces called Ustashe, and the horrible crimes they'd committed against Serbs, Jews, Gypsies and Croatian communists. I was absolutely sure that in Zagreb the situation was more or less the same: they probably selected only those images containing people with beards, to remind them of the Chetniks, who had an equally bad reputation. Although the majority saw in this only a new chapter of a long story, to me it all looked very much like a broadcast of a bunch of madmen taking over a sanatorium. I hated the Croatian nationalists I saw on TV and in newspapers, but I absolutely abhorred their Serbian colleagues, and I wasn't isolated in this stance, knowing that many thousands of other Serbs and Croats felt the same way. Disgust made us immune to the virus of hatred.

To all of us, Bosnia was proof that we were right in our denial. Bosnia was the place where people of different nationalities, different religions and cultures, lived next door to one another. It was the republic with the largest number of mixed marriages, where even pop songs mixed the Oriental with the European, and one could have a Serbian appetizer, Croatian fish soup, a Muslim specialty of the day and an Austrian dessert without leaving the table. For months we dismissed the Slovenian and Croatian events as isolated madness. Every now and then I would hear myself saying, "If this broke out in Bosnia, I would run away from here."

And then a Serb was killed in a drive-by shooting at a wedding party. Then there were barricades on the hills around Sarajevo, then snipers killing people who gathered to protest against the war coming closer with each tragic event, then the Muslims massacred a military convoy pulling out of Sarajevo to ease the tension, then it all exploded. It all happened fast, too fast for us in Belgrade to do anything. Protests are slow; they include the process of informing people, scheduling, many talks and preparations, looking at the sky, negotiating with police. Murder is fast. It happens at the speed of a bullet, and that is the only speed known to people on adrenaline. By the time we understood that the same scenario was being played again, enough blood had been spilled to start crying for revenge.

The feeling I suddenly had was some form of true and irrepressible fear. It was fear without urgency, without the panic we experience when we see fire in our home. This was slow–more suspense than horror–a tenant that had come to stay rather than the secret police knocking hard at your door in the night. It wasn't even fear for my life. (Although I knew the chances of losing my life skyrocketed with the opening of this new slaughterhouse. There was a much bigger probability that Serbia would officially declare war and mobilize its reserve troops, and, at thirty-four, I would have been included. Going to war is a great lottery for the state and a miserable one for its citizens.)

A group of women, calling themselves the Women in Black, started daily protests, but I wasn't a woman. A group of intellectuals, mainly university professors, writers and philosophers, formed an organization called the Belgrade Circle of Intellectuals, holding frequent sessions and protesting the war in Bosnia, but when I inquired about becoming a member or giving support in some form, it turned out I wasn't an intellectual, either. All doors were closed, except for those leading to war: paramilitary organizations accepted new volunteers all the time. It was a fight for turf: some placed their bets on arms, some on the fight against them, but both sides were looking forward to the glory of their final victory.

Those of us who felt the need to do something were left the micro space (still narrowing; always shrinking) in the part of the media that resisted Milošević's phalanxes. And, yes, there were friends to talk to, but not quite. Everyone talked about the war, but in circles of friends everyone tends to agree. So we talked about it and we didn't talk about it.

Even after the war in Bosnia started, nobody anticipated what would happen to Sarajevo. Why would any modern military commander decide to keep a city under siege at the end of the twentieth century–not for a week, or a month, or a few months, but for years? This seemed so stupid that some of my friends had their doubts about the whole thing. It was already at the point when nobody in their right mind believed Milošević's media anymore. Some people suspected that, surely, something bad must have been going on down there, something bad for the Serbs, and then the siege had to be imposed to stop it, whatever that was. Others didn't believe that a total siege of a modern city was even possible. Or that the world community would allow something like that to keep dragging on for so long. The mere fact that nobody in the world intervened proved that the Serbian media were lying to us again.

My thirty-fifth birthday was that September, and I decided to dedicate my small celebration to Sarajevo. Nobody had any money, and I invited several friends to my rented apartment. I made traditional Bosnian food, the stuff we would normally order when visiting Sarajevo: a cheese pie (*burek*), yogurt or beer to go with it, and apples in sweet sauce stuffed with walnuts (*tufahije*). There wasn't anything public in my gesture; I just wanted us all to remember the people suffering only two hundred miles from us.

So Silvija and I welcomed our guests, only five people, and when everyone finally arrived and I told them the evening was titled "In Memoriam to Sarajevo," they all stared blankly at me. Nobody objected, and they loved the food, but nobody seemed to think it was a good idea, either.

When our friends left late that night, and Silvija and I were alone, the first explanation we came up with was that our guests hadn't liked the politicization of my birthday. But they were all politically minded people, discussing the issues of the day at every step, like the rest of us, like the whole country did at the time. How could one avoid politics when war is eating his country away? Then we thought perhaps they perceived my idea as directing the message to the wrong address: "Why are you telling it to us?" If that was true, they might have been offended, and I owed them some form of apology. That sounded plausible, so we left it at that and went to sleep.

That night I had one of those dreams in which nothing particular happens, from which you can't grab anything to carry with you to the light of day. There was no particular meaning, no specific conversation, no recognizable places or faces. Just the persistent feeling that something was very wrong, something I would understand much later, much, much later, when it was too late.

In the coming days I put the whole thing aside. Each tomorrow brought something more urgent than what was left undone from yesterday. Even if it didn't, we would find something–that was our defense. None of my friends present that night seemed to have any bad feelings, so I forgot about it.

Then, maybe a month later, maybe a little sooner, a person I trusted and frequently talked with, from our circle of friends, allowed that one of Milošević's goons was, maybe, partially, right about something he'd said. My friend said this with reservations, it was put in a conditional frame, it was structured very delicately, and I missed it at first. Or maybe I just wanted to agree, or needed to agree. Only at night, lying in bed, did I remember the line. But I dismissed it: the times were crazy, and people were tired.

Another month passed, or maybe a little less, maybe it was the following week, or the following day, but another person from our circle of friends said something else: although they didn't agree with what was done–maybe, partially, Milošević was right about some things. Nothing major. Small stuff. You know. No one can be all bad, right?

This time it disturbed me right away.

For me, there was a wall, an impenetrable wall between Milošević and his people on the one side and the good–in the ethical sense–on the other. One had to be stupid or immoral to trust Milošević–simple as that. Nothing in between. No buts or ifs, no perhapses, nothing conditional. Milošević awoke the murderous side of me: I believed he deserved to be shot without a trial, without reading him his rights, without even Harry Callaghan proposing to him to try his luck. Give me a gun and just one ride on the elevator with him, and I'll stop the war in Yugoslavia before the third floor, I kept saying to my circle of friends.

Now that I was alarmed I started seeing the pattern. We all talked about politics, but not really listening to one another. We all agreed the way friends agree, but small cracks started appearing here and there. Along with drops of gray water seeping through them. And I was probably getting wet from the same drizzle. How did we allow–and when did we allow–this regime to start changing us? Is it that simple: when you become tired and sleepy, the Goebbels' rule steps in and we all believe in lies repeated long enough? It meant that Sarajevo was not the only city under siege; so were Belgrade, and Kragujevac, and every town in Serbia. On the hills around Sarajevo were Serbs from Bosnia, hitting people with snipers and shells, turning them into memories; on the hills around our brains were Serbs from the media, hitting us with news and opinions, turning us into zombies. But wait–even this thought came through the crack in my reason. I can't compare Sarajevo and Belgrade. I can't balance pains. I shouldn't contrast mental to the actual death, or should I?

Then I remembered the evening of my birthday. The Sarajevo party. So that was that: the cracks were already there, but I hadn't been brave enough to see them.

THE LONG SILENT LINE

One early Sunday morning in 1993 I walked home through the center of Belgrade. I'd finished my all-night radio show, had the first morning coffee with the two friends who worked with me, and now was dragging my feet through the street of Knez Mihailo, longing for bed. Next to the American Cultural Center was a big white truck, one of those that deliver warm bread and pastry. The back of the truck was open, and three women stood on the platform, handing over loaves of bread to people who waited in line. I recognized one of the women on the truck. It was Danica Drašković, controversial wife of the Serbian opposition politician Vuk Drasković, and I remembered their party had announced they would be distributing bread to people in need that Sunday.

Obviously, it was a cheap political trick: the truck was parked next to an American institution so their employees and journalists could take note of this action and report it. They wanted to embarrass Milošević, which was okay with me, only I didn't like the idea of using hungry people for political reasons.

But what struck me was the length of the line behind the truck: it went on and on, almost to the end of the street, everyone in it staring at the tips of their shoes. The silence was deafening. Women, children and men would step forward when it was their turn, take a loaf, or two, three–whatever they'd be given–hide it under their coats, and leave, without a thank-you or even looking back.

I passed the line and, almost at the end, I stood on the side, pretending to be busy lighting my cigarette but looking at faces beneath my eyelashes. I was afraid. Afraid that I might see a familiar face.

A few years back, Make and his secret student girlfriend, Sanja, had wanted to go skiing together in Poland. Our old high school organized the trip, so Make begged me to go with them, as their cover. I went, although I didn't ski, and spent most of the time in the swimming pool of the grand hotel in a village in the Tatra Mountains. The weather was awful and there wasn't anything else to do. Once we tried to go in the evening to the only local disco, but there were only people sitting and drinking heavily, most of them in some kind of stupor. So after that we'd just sit after dinner at the same table and fill ourselves with cheap Polish thrills–good vodka and Russian caviar.

One evening, an odd couple sat at a table next to ours. He was fat, in his late thirties, his face red and ugly, and he was dressed to make anyone with even a trace of taste scream in pain. Across from him was an incredibly beautiful girl, probably around eighteen, dressed tastefully but in obviously cheap Polish clothes. He kept making rude moves, his fat fingers touching her, and he kept laughing loudly and pouring wine for the girl, who would blush with every rude gesture. She didn't dare look anywhere but at her plate, while he kept turning around, making sure that everyone saw him with her. At one point, hearing us speaking his language, he turned to Make and me and said, "What are you waiting for? Look at this pussy: she's gorgeous, but she'll fuck me for buying her dinner. They're incredibly poor. The whole place is full of them. Get something, guys!"

I looked briefly at the beauty, not wanting to deepen her shame, and felt incredibly sad. This was the most expensive hotel in all of Poland, for strangers only. She was probably working somewhere in the village below, and this man offered her a dinner she couldn't buy with her yearly salary. She wasn't a hooker, it was obvious, but there was no hope around, nowhere to be found, and all the guys of her age were drunk. So she accepted his invitation, just to run away for one night from the nightmare of her life.

And now, this Sunday morning in Belgrade, I was gripped with fear that some of the women I'd loved would be in this line, waiting for bread, braving their shame for a thin shelter from hunger.

I found none. But all those women who were in line—somebody must have loved them.

HALF MEN, HALF HORSES

In the midst of all the madness around us, my mother decided she couldn't bear to visit our country house anymore, now that my father was dead. Everything there reminded her of him. She gave me the green light to sell it, and I did, and immediately purchased a small apartment across from the old fortress of Kalemegdan, not far from the center of the city. Without a permanent job, writing articles here and there mostly for some new magazines that nobody read, I spent my time taking long walks in the pedestrian zone uphill from where I lived.

Momir is an artist. I run into him one day in the summer of 1994 during my walk. We know each other from our hometown, Kragujevac, and, although we don't meet often, we spend some time together whenever we bump into each other on the street. The day is from a brewer's dream, the girls are half naked and there's that vibration of insanity that comes with the summer into all the big cities of the world. We pick a small café on a shadowy sidewalk and take our beers outside to drink.

"So, how are things?" I ask.

"Good," he says, "I'm going to war."

"When?"

"Now," he says.

I drink my beer, light a cigarette and keep looking at him. He likes to joke and I expect a smile to loosen his face, the bearded face of a Serbian Che. But his eyes stay narrow and that smile doesn't come.

"You were drafted?" I ask.

"No, I'm going to volunteer. I was just on my way when I met you."

"Volunteer? With whom do you want to go to Bosnia?" At that time, even minor political parties in Serbia had their mini-armies there, not to mention major parties and the army of Bosnian Serbs.

"Doesn't matter," he responds. "There's no real life, everything is just waiting for the war to end. I did my part, now I'm going to fight."

The previous night, Belgrade TV had shown a story about some Bosnian Serbs being massacred by Muslims in some distant village. I thought that maybe he'd reacted to that.

"But that's exactly what they want," I say. "You watch too much television. Can't you see they're doing that on purpose: whenever they need new volunteers, they come up with some massacre that Muslims did. Remember how, at the beginning of Bosnia, Muslim TV showed some massacred bodies and accused Serbs, but two weeks later it was proved that those actually were the bodies of Serbs massacred by Muslims?"

Momir looks into my eyes carefully. "Corpses are corpses. Listen: there is no critical mass of soldiers in there to end the fighting one way or the other. What I mean is, it doesn't matter anymore, at least not to me, who will win this war. All that matters is for it to be over. Even when the war is ended it will take some time for this country to recover. So: the sooner, the better."

"Is that what you want–to be another corpse on the screen? If this is too slow for you, why not just go and live somewhere else?"

Momir has this laughter that cuts you in two. The Inquisition would have burned him for it. "Live where? Go to the States and do my macramé? They think it's for housewives, not for real artists. Italy? I wouldn't know how to order a beer. France? To wash dishes in a café on the Champs-Elysées? You know, if this was the 1930s, it would be much easier. You could go to Berlin to become a Nazi, or to Moscow to be a commie, or to America to join Capone. But now? I don't believe in capitalism, and I've seen what socialism does to you. Where do we go?"

I don't have a clue, but I don't want him to go to war. I look covertly at my watch. It is almost five. If we sit here long enough, and it's Friday, there is a good chance that the volunteers' offices will be closed for the weekend. So I order another round.

"Momir, we're all centaurs, half men, half horses. The

brains are up there, but sometimes we just don't think fast enough for these quick legs. They just take us somewhere and then the brain's no use to us. Brains do not work where grenades fly. That's what I'm saying: don't let your legs take you into the quagmire. Is this your war, is this my war? Did you make any, no matter how small, decision that led to this war? Did you vote for Milošević? Did we vote for the Muslim leaders? What's the biggest difference between before the war and now? We live much worse, the bastards in power live much better. Milošević has a son, so let him send his son to war. There, that's one volunteer that will make the critical mass, so you can stay here and drink with me."

"But I'm an anarchist. I have this woman, I have these hands, and I have this ugly head. There's nothing anywhere else in the world, no system, no power, no idea that I'm attracted to. I didn't even know I was an anarchist before this war. Now I do. And where do the anarchists fit? Nowhere. Even the idea of anarchy is dead. So, you know, at least I'm going to fight until I come up with something I can believe in."

It is difficult to beat him when you agree with him, and I go for the lowest level of persuasion. It's five twenty.

"When the war started, in Croatia, I said, okay, this is the same old thing. But the bad shit would be Bosnia. Jesus, people of different religions and nationalities are living side by side there. If that starts, I'm out, I'm definitely out of the country, the same day! But look, here I am. How's that happened? Because I looked around, like now: sexy women, good friends, nice cafés on the sidewalk . . . Sometimes one can live on air and whatever hangs in there. I think that's how prisoners in concentration camps survived. Read Salamov: you start enjoying the bread-crumbs when there's no more bread."

"That's for mice, not men."

"Possible. But mice live and tell about it. Heroes don't. I never thought you wanted to have a street named after you."

"Fuck you."

"No, fuck you. Besides, I really did. Look at your watch: it's 5:45, and it's Friday. You won't find any office open now."

So we sit and drink slowly. When I get home after ten, Silvija says, "You're drunk. What did you do?"

"I just saved my own life," I say.

Momir never went to war. But he never said thanks, either.

SARAH LAWSON, ON MY FLYING CARPET

I often think of Sarah Lawson.

I was never good with letters. Neither was Sarah Lawson, so we lost touch after a while. It was almost two years later–just before the war–when the telephone rang one morning in my Belgrade apartment and I heard Sarah's voice. She was calling from Slovenia, where a U.S. magazine had sent her to write an article about local politics. I was not fully awake and I don't even recall what we talked about, but that was my last conversation with her.

Then the wars in Yugoslavia started. Following the way the Western media reported on all that mess, I was somehow worried about whether Sarah knew that I hadn't changed, I hadn't become a nationalist, whether she dared say that she had a friend in Belgrade or whether she'd started hiding it. I struggled to write her a letter, but I wasn't able to stretch my hundred words of English enough to cover everything I felt, so I never finished it.

My dear Sarah,

It is beginning of March of 1993, and I don't know how much time has passed since we talked the last time you were in Slovenia . . . A year? Two? Everything happens so fast here that time is not understandable category anymore. In the past, sometimes I thought I had been old 40 instead of 30, or 30 instead of 18, but now I've gone further than ever before. Everybody here is very old.

This is probably the third or fourth time I am trying to write this letter. Sometimes it is too depressive, sometimes too much false happiness . . . So, I will just try to be cool and write.

This land is devastated.

My girlfriend is working on TV. She is author and chief of her one-and-a-half-hour Saturday show. And she is earning about $20 a month. I am working on radio now, doing my own talk show (from midnight to 6 a.m.) and I get $17 a month. A pack of less-expensive cigarettes is about one buck. I smoke two packs a day.

My mother is retired. She lives alone in my hometown. She is getting about $16 a month. Medicine she has to take every month costs about twice as much, not to mention the other. One kilogram of meat is about $5, bread about $1 or $2 . . . Jeans are between $20 and $30 . . . It is even harder if you have children (I still don't, thanks God!). One chocolate is about $1.50, a kilo of bananas $3, carriage for small children is $380 (yes, three hundred and eighty dollars).

This is second (or third?) year of war. None of your friends has become regime-lover, as far as I know.

I was fighting Milošević's police on huge riots on 9 March 1991, I was hiding demonstrates in my apartment in some nights during that period, my girl and I were on every public event against this regime, but what with it? My cousin was recruited in 1992, went to war and lost two finger there, almost bleeding to death, but what with it? I can't find any steady job since Milošević became president, all because I published some mockery on him in

1988, but still I'm hard to beat, doing any job I get to survive. I decided to stay here and fight against the regime, but now it is real fascism here (they are, less or more public–sometimes in our Parliament–threatening to all those who "don't think right"; and when I say threatening, I mean it–and they also), and everything went very far. Seventy percent of my close friends are already out of the country. Now, my girl and I decided to go, too. This summer she'll try London, and I'll try Amsterdam. We'll have to separate for some time, because it is very hard to get any visa now, if you are Serb, so we'll have to try on two separate places. I love her very much, and that will be hard for both of us, but we have to do it that way.

Very often I wish I am stupid. It would be so good, so good not to understand anything, to believe to Milošević, to believe that whole world is against Serbs (which is, now, almost true, isn't it?), and that no one at his place could do any better. It would be so comfortable not to understand what will happen in future–that Serbia will be isolated for long time (and I don't know how will anybody here survive next winter), that the economy (already ruined) will have to struggle for life for next 15 years just to get back where it had been before this war . . . that our culture (already ruined) will be completely destroyed, because one can hardly get used to war, but once you are used to it, you are half animal.

Looking from abroad, it probably looks like this is ideal situation for all kind of writers and other artists, but it is impossible to do the art when you have to struggle to survive. Art is a matter of having, not of despair. How can you write, when inflation goes 400% this month, and is expected to be 1,000% in April? How can you write about movies, when you don't see new ones? How can you paint when you don't have oil colors?

They say that inflation in Serbia in 1993 was the highest ever recorded in any economy. The official number at one time was over 70 million percent. I kept moving, looking for something cheaper, avoiding the draft, looking for a shelter from all that madness. With each new apartment I would get a new phone number, making it impossible for anyone but my very close circle to find me. There was no home anymore. Home is a nest, but there was a snake in every tree I visited.

One day, five years after Sarah had left, a female voice on my telephone introduced herself as Laura Silber, an American journalist. She said that our mutual friend Sarah Lawson had called a month before and asked if Laura could find me and deliver a present from her. That night, in Laura's rented apartment behind the Yugoslav Assembly, I heard the story: Sarah had called from New York and asked Laura if it was true that the inflation was so high and people were half starving. When Laura confirmed it, Sarah said that she would send some money and asked Laura to distribute it to her friends. I left Laura's apartment with a hundred-dollar bill in my pocket and a feeling of pure joy, but not because of the money: Sarah did not blush because of her friends in Belgrade, she believed in us.

That year of my last conversation with Sarah, my friend Dejan invited me to go with him to Germany for a weekend. His uncle, an exceptionally colorful person, wanted to buy a good car in Nuremberg (God knows why there) and they needed a third driver.

It was winter, and the snowstorms got to us on a night ride through southern Germany and Austria. We didn't want to stay in hotels, everyone was eager to go home, and so we drove slowly through the gusts of snow and wind, passing by even the mighty cross-continental trucks parked on the side of the road. An ordinary trip had turned into an Adventure with a capital A, and I felt great. I was driving the red Golf with Dejan sitting next to me choosing music, and his uncle was in his new Taurus thirty feet behind us (any more distance than that, and he would have lost our lights in the snowstorm).

Surrounded by that whiteness and with Frank Zappa on the radio, Dejan and I somehow got to the topic of friendship and death–the storm was that bad. A few days before, I'd read an interview with an old Serbian actor in which he metaphorically described death as the day when that small flying carpet beneath our feet takes off towards the sky. Stealing the metaphor, I said how, in my time of dying, I would expect on my carpet three people at the most, since I didn't believe in too many friendships. Even that number would make me happy.

That sentence has stayed in my head since then, somehow distant as if someone else had spoken it. Maybe because of the surreal circumstances under which it was said, or maybe because that was the first time I had clearly formulated my notion of friendship and what it meant to me.

I often asked myself during the war in Yugoslavia how it happened that I did not succumb to the nationalist euphoria. Why didn't I go to fight? Why did I never believe Milošević? How did I manage to keep my pride in being a Serb and not exchange it for aggressive nationalism?

It took me a while to understand that Sarah Lawson, together with the other two or three people from my metaphorical flying carpet, kept me from losing myself in all that. Trying not to make my friends blush because of me, I stayed true to my principles.

MESSAGE FROM ZVONE

At the end of 1993 Laura Silber went to Split and agreed to take my letter to Zvone with her. I didn't know his address, and I didn't know if he was still living in Split, so on the envelope I wrote only "For Zvone Krstulović, wherever he might be." When Laura returned, she called to say that she'd given the letter to a journalist from Split. He had said that Zvone was not there anymore, but he would try to reach him. By this time I had already changed three jobs and four apartments, and I didn't have much hope that it would happen, since, for all I knew, the situation in Croatia was similar to that in Belgrade.

A few months later the mail between the two countries started working again, and one day I found a big yellow envelope in my mailbox. To my surprise, the stamp was Croatian, but there was no return address. Inside was just a glossy magazine, called *Start (of the new generation).* I flipped through its pages in vain. Nothing else in there, no letter. Still, I was very happy: to get a Croatian magazine at that time felt like meeting an old friend. I went upstairs, fixed a coffee and started reading. The masthead was on the second page, and so the first thing I discovered was that Zvone was the editor-in-chief of this magazine published in Zagreb. The second thing was that not only had he got my letter, he had published it, pages four and five.

The friends that have stayed here change in slow motion, I can't notice any big difference from day to day or week to week, but if I remember the way they talked a year ago, it seems that their language is shifting towards something I don't want to speak. Chauvinism slowly enters our culture, and I guess for several reasons: those who are afraid to emigrate have subconsciously decided to become closer to the masses, to return to the Family. There is also one bad thing here: some of my friends got really fed up with CNN and Amanpour and the Western media in general. They are reacting to the kind of reporting that puts all Serbs under a big black hat, but the reaction to that means accepting the embrace of the Herd. There's no other way. Except out of this country.

I don't know if you'd heard, but I lost my job because of those nude pictures. Officially so, unofficially I think we can see the reasons more clearly now. It happened at the end of that year—the president of the company didn't even talk to me, he just sent a message for me to get lost. But, fuck, I'm glad we did it! It was the last subversion without bombs!

I don't know if you'll get this letter, but it's so refreshing to be able to tell you that you're a dirty Croat again. If I say it here, some of them will kiss me, some will leave. No jokes anymore.

On the same spread Zvone published one single photo: a street corner with a mailbox. The only thing that was intact in the picture was the mailbox—everything else was destroyed, all the houses, lampposts, all the windows. I recognized Vukovar. The photographer was Zvone. He sent me a message in code: "I've read your letter, I've seen that you're the same. I am the same, we fight shoulder to shoulder in the same cause."

If anyone had asked me on that day how I felt, I'd probably have answered that everything was wonderful, I had heard from my friend Zvone. But my own letter hit me right between the eyes. I turned around and saw that all the objects around me were found objects, that almost all the people I called friends in Belgrade now were found friends. Duchamp would have loved it. My life had turned into a Dada exhibition.

One afternoon in 1994 I started flipping through the pages of my small telephone book. I was looking for a guest for my TV talk show. Croatian artists: not available. Slovenian, Bosnian artists: not available. Tarot Barney: killed in combat, in Bosnia. Ćira: killed in Croatia. Make: in New Zealand and Sanja with him. Black: joined a paramilitary formation in Bosnia. Johnny Štulić: back in

Amsterdam. Mića the Turk: Kragujevac, recovering from a heart attack. Mila: got a visa and went to the States. Bole and Bojana: Canada. Bahus: San Francisco. Bottle: London. Dejan: in Belgrade, but was my guest last time. Jazzer: Amsterdam. Lisa: Milan. Moša: suicide by Russian roulette. Slobodan: dead. Snežana: Bonn. Momir . . .

What happened? Sure I have pictures, but I also have Photoshop, capable of making anything possible on a photo, and probably invented by J. V. Stalin. Otherwise: no tattoos, no bites, no Kama Sutran half-moons on my skin. No condoms under my bed, no lipstick on my cups, no forgotten umbrellas on my shelf.

Did I have them, did they have me? Was it a dream? Did we really play bridge? Did we love each other? Our past is a pastel in the rain. Ask not what your country can do for you, but what you can do to hide away from your country.

8

GAME: MUSICAL CHAIRS

The rules

Line up the chairs so there is one fewer than the number of contestants. The contestants walk around the chairs to the music. When the music stops, each contestant sits on the closest chair. The one without a chair leaves the game. Repeat this, removing a chair after each round, until there is only one chair left and one person sitting on it.

The reality

The contestants walk slower and slower, trying to stay close to a chair. They don't listen to the music anymore, they listen to the silence. When they finally hear it, the stronger ones push others with their butts, trying to keep the chair to themselves. Those with fat asses have the advantage.

The game ends with the winner sitting on that last chair, grinning stupidly, because he can't keep the chair, and there's no more music, and no more friends, and he knows that as soon as he gets up he won't look like the winner anymore.

NATURES MORTES

It was early winter in Belgrade, in a year between wars. Everything was still good; Tito was dead and Milošević not yet politically born. I lived in a quiet, rich part of the city, renting a basement in the same house in which a friend of mine, also a writer, lived on the top floor.

The first snow had fallen in the night, and that morning I invited my friend out to celebrate in a neighborhood café the grand white sheet, the beginning of the season of writing. It was too early for customers and only three of us were there: the bartender, my friend and me. The bartender was bored and started trying to guess what kind of music we would like, changing tunes frequently and watching our faces. As there was no reaction from us, we ended up with slow instrumentals, the kind they play during national mourning. Two *natures mortes* sitting silently by the window, watching the snow outside, while the third one was playing music for them.

A mutual friend had just left the country, one of those early birds at the end of the 1980s, and my friend, an intelligent, soft-spoken guy born somewhere in Bosnia, started talking about it.

"Where can you go when you take the same head everywhere?"

I give Bojan a call at eleven in the evening. We chat a little and I say, "What a beautiful night tonight, so quiet; too bad I can't take a walk," and we hang up. What I really mean is, "They won't knock on your door tonight." My calls to him are always coded. We have lived in Yugoslavia long enough not to trust the telephone lines.

It's 1991 and the war in Croatia has just started. I live in Belgrade and have a midnight radio show. The military police have been making night raids for some time. They pick people up with the excuse of regular training, but we've already heard the stories: for the first couple of days you stay in a military camp in Serbia, but on the third night or so they tell you it's a drill move, put you on a truck with the rest of the guys, and you wake up at the front. Officially, Serbia is not at war with Croatia, so everything is top secret. But rumors about collective mobilization are circulating, and every evening before the show I get a call from my producer, to tell me if anything is expected that night. There is a procedure I have to follow, so she has to make sure I'm ready. After I finish my talk with her, I call Bojan to pass on the news.

We had already decided not to take part in this war. He initiated our meeting one day. We sat on a patio on the sidewalk, with thick noise around us. Very difficult for spy microphones. We didn't talk long.

"I'm not going to take part in this," he said.

"Neither am I."

So we agreed to one bag each, with passport inside, some basic clothing, and all the friends' addresses we could find. We would take his car and cross the first border that came our way. That was all we said and then we shook hands. I left our meeting hoping sincerely that I wouldn't have to go. There was so much one could still do. Besides, is leaving possible?

Sometime early in 1993 a friend got hold of two albums from Croatia. They were released by the state publishing house and entitled *Rock for Croatia, Volumes 1* and *2*. At one point I borrowed them, and that was the first uncensored report about the state of mind in Croatia that I'd had a chance to get since the war started. Before the war I knew every detail on any local music scene in all of Yugoslavia, and the fact that I didn't recognize some of the performers on those records was a sure sign that the gap between Belgrade and Zagreb was widening fast.

Its title made me think it would be a selection of patriotic songs, to boost spirits and gather a younger audience around the state-proclaimed aims. I was shocked at the amount of pure hatred coming from the plastic. Although the younger performers were worse, firing insult upon insult against Serbs and calling for murder and revenge, I found especially bad one song that Jura Stublić put together.

Stublić was the leader of a very well-known band from Zagreb, one of those who climbed to fame during the early eighties boom of rock music in Yugoslavia, usually referred to as the New Wave. He and his band, Film, were popular all over Yugoslavia, and had numerous concerts in Belgrade, always sold out, and always with generous reviews. For this record Stublić took a sweet melody from one of Emir Kusturica's movies–not accidentally, as Kusturica publicly took the Serbian side in this war–and wrote his own bitter verses. It was entitled "Alas, My Belgrade Friend," and it described a friendship between the Croatian narrator and his Belgrade friend, how they loved the same women, how they sang Croatian songs together before the war.

> Alas, my Belgrade friend, we'll meet by the river Sava,
> You won't recognize me so you'll start shooting at me.
>
> I will let you shoot first, you be always first,
> I'll forgive your second bullet, and the third one will miss me.
>
> And I will not aim, and I'll pray to God to
> Miss you, but then I will shoot you.
>
> I will cry over your body, I will close your eyes.
> Oh how sad I will be when I lose my friend.

Suddenly, all we talked about in Belgrade was this song. Since the war had started people had became highly sensitive to the public opinions of their beloved authors, performers and all sorts of public personalities whose names carried any weight. Everyone searched for some support in times when no one was sure anymore what to think, and if some quote, no matter from whom, agreed with what they thought, they perceived it as a personal victory; if not, it was a betrayal of the worst kind. Stublić's song was full of irony and small, almost unnoticeable bites ("You be always first") in its lyrics, but its poison was made more dangerous by superimposing the verses on top of a melody that was, or was presented as, an old folk song: it gave the impression that this was not the opinion of one person but the general stand.

I could see a movie in my head: the large, silent river, dry branches protruding ominously from fog on its banks. Two young men in uniforms stumble from the woods, each on the opposite side of the river. One of them is this neurotic, murderous Serb, and the other one is a noble Croatian, cravat around his neck. The Croat recognizes his old friend across the river and wants to wave and say hi, but the madman on the other bank throws himself into the yellow grass and shoots–he always shoots first and never asks questions. One bullet misses, then another–and the noble Croat is still standing straight, hoping for his friend to recognize him. Alas, he doesn't, or he does, and the third bullet narrowly misses. Then the noble Croat, a knight in this dirty world, sighs, raises his pistol like in a duel, closes his eyes, says a little prayer hoping to miss, and shoots. One bullet. Blindly. Kills the bastard. Then he walks to the other side of the river–which opens before him so he doesn't wet his cravat–and kneels before his friend, closes the dead man's eyes, and cries. Every time I listened to that song I saw that movie; every time I saw the movie I needed a vomit bag.

At exactly the same time a group of Belgrade bands got together and made an anti-war song, with the simple and irreverent message, "Fuck more, shoot less."

Anica Nonveiller left Radio Politika in the meantime and went to Radio Belgrade, to continue as the music director on one of the programs. She was also struck by this song, and felt we all needed to hear it, and perhaps think about it, if nothing else. So, against the explicit orders of her superiors, who banned all Croatian music from their airwaves, she played it one day, with a few introductory comments. The reaction of the right-wing politicians and media was swift. Vojislav Šešelj, the leader of the Radical Party, called Anica a traitor and questioned her nationality. Although she was a Serb from the north and married to a Frenchman, some lunatics confronted her children on their way to school and threatened their lives if the family stayed in Serbia. Then Anica was fired from the radio, and there was nothing left for her family except to emigrate.

It all happened fast, in just a few overheated months, and this was a bitter blow to many of us. I took it almost personally: if I'd been in her position at the time, I also would have played that song (in fact, I had, but at Radio Politika–where I was at the time–Croatian music was not banned), and then probably the same thing would have happened to me.

And for the first time a thought crossed my mind that maybe we should all leave this crazy country. The number of people leaving now on a daily basis, and not hiding it much anymore, was growing every day. The state pretended it didn't know anything about it, and even if it was true–if people were indeed leaving–this exodus was good: the traitors were leaving, the true patriots staying. Fascists always like their seeds clean.

In my circle of friends everyone now talked about

leaving, one way or another: some were gathering papers, some doing research on various countries, most trying to stop the others. It wasn't happening that much with the younger generation, nor with the older–it was something with us. We were maybe the first true Yugoslav generation, and we had been raised in the spirit of brotherhood and unity. I felt that this corpse of a country–which was now falling apart before my eyes, with thousands of ugly worms eating teeny bits of it–wasn't my country. Even worse, there wasn't anything to defend anymore, because there was no attack from the outside. We were eating ourselves from within.

But I still didn't think seriously of leaving. There were still things one could do. Especially if one was with the media. Besides, where could I go with that same old head?

NESSUN DORMA

November in Belgrade, a cold and depressing night in 1993. We are under sanctions, the Yugoslav Airlines can't fly, and the closest airport is in Budapest. Our friends Eka and D.T. have just embarked on a night ark for Canada. It looked like a bus, but no one was fooled by its license plates. Even before the gentle driver slowly made the last circle for the families and friends waving good-bye on the shadowy shore of the square, we all knew his name: Noah.

A few of us decide to go to someone's apartment to throw a small party. Silvija and I don't stay long; it's late and cold and there is no heating, not in apartments, public places or on public transportation. There is no gas, not enough food, and we have a chronic fear of news. All news had been bad news in the past several years.

We leave the party and are standing at the tram station with five or six other people. Suddenly, from across the street, we hear someone yelling and then two gunshots. A man runs out of the darkness into the poorly lit street, jumps across a fence and disappears on the other side. Another man with a gun in his hand follows. He stops briefly in the middle of the street, a few steps from us, aims at the runner and shoots. He misses. Then he turns towards us, as if thinking whether to compensate right away, but decides not to.

Late that night, Silvija and I decide to go to the Canadian Embassy to apply for visas.

Months pass and I notice a slow process inside me. I'm starting to lose my fear. One afternoon in the summer of 1994, a few days after I said some nasty things on my radio show about Vojislav Šešelj, I enter the lobby of my apartment building and I hear someone coming in behind me. My inner sense transmits a piercing signal. When the guy asks for my name, I know he's going to attack me, but I'm ready. Several months before I would have been desperate and frightened, but now I'm okay; the application in the Canadian Embassy has opened a door. I am strong and I don't care. I hit him hard and fast and he runs away.

Later that summer, I have a very successful exhibition at the cultural center gallery in the heart of Belgrade. For months before the war, street vendors had been selling tapes with jingoistic songs, small figures of Chetniks with oversized penises, black pirate flags, small masked uniforms for kids and other symbols of machismo. I always thought that these tokens opened a small window for war psychology to enter our lives and prepare ordinary citizens to become tomorrow's volunteers for the battlefield. After collecting these souvenirs for a few years, I finally assembled an exhibition so people could see what was happening. By taking a closer look at this poison maybe we could come closer to the catharsis we needed so badly as a nation. It drew a lot of media attention. I gave interviews to the BBC, *De Volkskrant, The Guardian,* Reuters. Several months before it would have been a delight, but now I felt cold. The process of removal in my head was already well under way.

It is winter of 1994 and in the heart of the city a huge television screen is installed for public celebrations on New Year's Eve. I stop before it as they play the Three Tenors singing "Nessun Dorma." It's snowing, my coat is old, my friends do not live in Belgrade anymore, and Puccini hurts. I see myself in a window–my shoulders bent forward, the lines on my forehead deep, my whole body tense, I look twenty years older than I am–and I think about how the song does not belong here. It simply is not true: everyone is asleep here. You have to be, if you want to stay normal.

People leave in all directions. Some go outside and shut the door behind them; some hide inside, and forget about the door.

Early in 1995, almost ten months after we applied for Canadian papers, Silvija and I get an invitation to the final interview. I am nervous, it feels like the time of dying: I am going to God himself to be judged on what I have done with my life. My three books, are they worth something? My radio and TV shows, were they okay? My two thousand published articles, did anybody read them? Our friends had been refused several months before, and they ended up in New Zealand. But I would like to be able to choose at least something in this process of leaving, at least the place where I will land.

They are calling our names, and a woman tells us to go to the back of the building, where a special counselor is waiting for us. We're done, I think: he's discovered that I'm a scribbler and that Silvija's plays were unsuccessful attempts. But the Canadian Gabriel has glasses, his name is John, and he is friendly. He goes through our illusions: what do we plan to do in Canada, are we ready for critical situations, are our hopes too high? I describe the plans for my next book; Silvija wants to do a PhD in drama. John is serious, he doesn't laugh. At the end he congratulates us. We passed.

Suddenly I see it: I have a license to die in Belgrade and be reborn in Canada. We have our license to be forgotten and be anonymous starters in Canada. Am I happy? I don't know anymore. Is leaving possible at all?

I say quick good-byes. Some friends I don't even visit. I know what social death is, I have died several times before: when I went into the army, when I moved from my hometown to Belgrade, when I broke with some friends. No matter what they say, they always forget you. I guess that's what happens to those who travel too much: their luggage becomes so small that no memories can fit inside anymore.

I can hear the iron door closing around my emotional center. It means denial of my identity. Spit on your past, and you spit on the kisses, hugs, loves and starry nights. Stomp on your present and a deep dark hole will open below your feet. Do you know how to fly, son? Can you, dare you fly over that abyss?

THE MAP

My mother has a tin container from some imported German *bonbonnière* adorned with a romantic drawing of a happy family under a tree. Inside, she keeps our oldest family photographs, small black-and-white mementos, their edges torn, sepia setting slowly over them like a cataract. In a country that had had a war every forty years, these small pieces of cardboard covered with silver are proof of life. Armies come and go, churches burn to the ground, books disappear in smoke, friends and family die, earth soaked with blood levels fast–a small picture could be the only reminder of you.

Sometimes, when I visit Kragujevac, I open that box. Most of the faces I don't know. Although some of the pictures are inscribed on the back with what they used to call an inky pencil–one you had to lick–those tight, small letters of untrained handwriting do not say much: "Seka and I on New Year's Eve in Belgrade," or "Milun, Dara, Mileva and Boško in Novi Sad." Only an occasional date.

On one of them, my lost uncle, Dušan (was it by pure accident that my mother chose to marry a man of the same name?): tall, well built, light hair, a humorous spark in his eyes. In the end, we never learned his history. We could find neither his body nor his address. My Nana decided never to have a funeral for him, his wife never remarried, his only son, Boban, never knew if he was an orphan or abandoned. The door back to his place in life was always open.

My Nana caught in black-and-white with my grandfather Lila looks surreal. Date unknown. Judging by their wardrobe, the second half of the 1920s, but even that is uncertain, since Lila posed in traditional Serbian dress, which had been the same for the last five centuries. Nana was beautiful then, thin and tall. They'd had only another decade left of life together when they posed for the traveling photographer who came to their village and who took eggs and dry meat as payment.

When I look at that picture, I understand how she came to weigh over two hundred pounds and so immensely enjoyed all sorts of food: she was hungry. Nana had been hungry for fifty years. She and her husband never had much land, only one cow (if that), a few pigs; they had three children and their parents to feed; she and Lila would work from sunrise to sunset in the cornfields. My family didn't become rich after the communist revolution. But before World War II? My mother told me they would eat only a pair of hard-boiled eggs and leeks and there was not always bread.

Fifty years of constant hunger. Hunger for everything: dresses, scarves, shoes, socks, money, talk, rest . . . When Nana's son Mita was also taken prisoner for several days during the war, she went on foot to find him in the jail in Kragujevac. Twenty-five miles there and twenty-five miles back in one day.

I lift their picture and kiss them. My ancestors, in one of the few happy moments of their life; happy–therefore surreal.

When I ask my mother about the people in the photographs fading in her tin box, she can't remember some of them. I'm not talking about group portraits–there are some photos of single men and women, always taken in the fashion of their time, profile at forty-five degrees, look aiming slightly above the horizon (pride and hope). Some of them look appealing, some of them not. Their name sometimes on the back of the photo, but even then Ana can't tell me anything about them.

Who were they? Why are their portraits with us?

Some of these people might have been a never-forgotten first love or a best friend to some of my ancestors, and my mother doesn't want to exclude them from the box. Do these people have a family today? Would their family like to have their photo? None of us know. But I also leave those lonely people inside. There was some kind of love shared between them and some of my relatives, and I respect that. I can only hope our pictures are in someone else's box.

That box my mother always keeps in sight, on the nightstand by her bed–what is it?

The map of our genes?

ERASURE

What a magnificent interview I would give! My dignified face of a world traveler, my mild yet so decisive manners, my shining intelligence and my experience of an Atlantis survivor . . . Several cameras around me and I take my time, I maybe even drink wine . . . it has to be a 1993 red wine, I believe in a balance of pleasure: that was a bad year where I was, so it must have been a sunny year somewhere else. I could tell the audience how to recognize the slow coming of darkness, how condensed sadness can grip your chest and halt your breathing; I would instruct how to withdraw from life, how to pick friends in times of war. I would even know how to keep meat fresh out of the fridge in the summer, and how to recognize your time for leaving.

And I would say, "Some of this comes from my experience, but some, maybe even most, comes from my, from our, genes. I can't explain how I know how to treat a wound, I never learned it in school, I just know. I know how to avoid the first hit, how to use keys as a weapon of self-defense, how to kill with only one blow. Every generation in my family had at least one war. The fact that I am here says we all learned fast."

I would say that one orgasm in war counts as five in peace, that weather gets worse when the war starts, that fear is the only universal language we have, and that despair is the mother of courage. How to keep warm without heating, how to listen to the messages of the night, what to hear when one hears words, how to cut the meat for your cousin who lost his fingers on the front and joke about it.

But nobody asks me for an interview. So I write. I am a sower of this seed that doesn't grow into anything we need.

Peace culture versus war culture?

In south Slavic languages, the common word for war is *rat* (rhymes with *strut*) and, oddly, that is the anagram of *art* (which is, also, a common international word in all the south Slavic languages). The way that art is perceived in the Balkans is very close to the way war is perceived, and that is with the notion of fight: war means a destructive fight, art is a constructive fight; war is about enslaving a territory, art is about liberating a territory; war is based on the primitive, animal characteristics of the human mind, art is about achieving the refinement. Artists through the centuries have either celebrated or denounced war. There is a long list of books, paintings, poems and songs that deal with the experience of war, and mostly in a celebratory way. There is no neutral position in the history of the arts in ex-Yugoslav countries in regards to this phenomenon. There is no place there without a giant *rat* sleeping underneath.

The first story my grandmother told me about my grandfather was that he had been imprisoned by Germans and spent some time in a concentration camp. He learned German there, in self-defense, I guess, and returned to his village after the war, the only person who spoke a foreign language. A learned man of the world, he had been all the way to Germany. My father was enrolled in military school and later served three years in Tito's guard. During those eight years with the army, he learned all the basic skills that fed us later. For many generations culture came into my family either through war or through the things related to it.

War culture versus peace culture?

The first images I got from poetry in my childhood were those from the Kosovo cycle: Serbian knights in shining armor riding their big white horses against the Turkish hordes on their dark Arab studs back in 1389. The sound of the Novi Trg sword hitting the Damascus saber, the adrenaline of a fighter who forks three Turks at once with his shaft and throws them over his shoulder into the river, as described in one of the poems. The Serbian minstrels (*guslari*) kept this cycle alive for six centuries. Later, when the cycle became fashionable in Europe in times of romanticism (Goethe translated it into German), the mere fact that these poems were that old remained an important lesson in the tradition of my nation.

The war kept coming through culture at all times, even later. In those years when I started learning about the cultures of the Far East, one of the first books I read was Sun Tzu Wu's *The Art of War.* When I began taking Dylan seriously, it was *Hard Rain.* Vietnam got me really interested in the world of politics. I was ten or eleven at the time, but Yugoslav TV was full of stories about this imperialist country taking on a small nation. We all identified. The best comedy was *M*A*S*H.*

Has our war culture defined me?

Here is what it did for me:

When Slobodan Milošević brought his mixture of communism and nationalism into focus, his offer didn't work for me. I was well steeped in my religion, my culture and a millennium of Serbian history, so I didn't have to hate the Croats to define myself. The differences between us were exactly the thing that made my generation love our unity and the idea of Yugoslavia. Was I aggressive? Oh yes, fighting for this idea that was not profitable for politicians anymore but was the only roof my generation had.

My war culture gave me this will to fight against the regime in all possible ways, to stay on the streets when the clouds of tear gas were rolling, when people with their faces smashed by police batons were passing by me, when water cannons were spraying us. Was I a hero? Never. Silvija was with me all the time. Did she feel like a hero? No. But we both felt it was the only normal thing to do when you don't agree with the angels that planned your life without asking.

It's late in the evening, and I'm driving from Kragujevac to Belgrade. I know this road by heart, and, as the radio in the car doesn't work, my only fun is to close my eyes and drive blindly through the night, which I do from time to time, when there are no lights on the road ahead or behind me. There are only maybe a couple of months left of my life here, in Serbia. Tomorrow a guy will come with a van to pick up my whole music library, and I've borrowed this car to bring some of the records from my mother's apartment. I've already sold all the vinyl to a newly founded radio station in a small town in the north of Serbia. Only now it all feels final: that man will not carry records from my apartment, he will remove my condensed memories. Fifteen hundred of them. I remember why I bought each record, I remember with whom I listened to them, I remember the girls that I seduced with their help, and others who gathered the courage from my own records to leave me. Now it will all be gone.

My cousins Bojan, Zoran and Boban live on this road, but I just drive by. I'm not in the mood for sad talks. A few miles after I pass their homes the road started winding and now I keep my eyes open. The sky is clear, with thousands of stars visible in this place far from city lights. This I will miss. This old road–built by the Romans, they say–these fields on the side, tame hills, this sensual scenery that curves like a perfect body, these plum trees that bend in late summer with fruit. Was it Johnny who said how he never missed people, but smells?

I check my rearview mirror, and look ahead, and there's no one on the road. People who are in a hurry to get between the two cities take the highway, but it's without character to me, and I drive this road here whenever I can. Without thinking, I step on the brakes and pull the car to the side. I'm not sure why, but I open the door and step out. I light a cigarette and just lean against the hub. I hear the distant barking of the dogs in front of the old houses scattered across these hills like giant strawberries. I hear the night itself–its murmurs and moans and secrets. Then I'm finished smoking, and I walk to the middle of the road, open my zipper and urinate, right there, on the white line, in the middle of a curve. I'm one of the village dogs, this is my territory, and here's my mark.

A day before our departure, Silvija's parents drive us to Kragujevac, so we can say good-bye to my mom. I sold my apartment, moved out the furniture, and for the last two weeks we had been living in Silvija's parents' small space.

It's a silent trip. When we enter, I'm trying to avoid Mom's eyes, I know how they will look. She makes coffee for the four of us, and by her slow movements I can only presume how many sedatives she had taken before we arrived. Silvija's parents are trying to say some encouraging words–how we shall prosper in Canada, how it's good to start with a new future in a more normal country, how if it wasn't for the emigration we'd never get married–but it doesn't go well, since they must be devastated, too. Although they have each other, and my mom stays alone, Silvija is their only child.

After emptying my cup, I go into my old room, to see if I want to bring something else for our trip to Canada. I flip quickly through my collection of old comics, my old books, my drawings, I open my typewriter, and close it all. There's no place for any of that in my luggage. I sit in my old armchair, and I just watch my room. I'm inhaling my room. This is the place where I learned everything that counts: how to love and be lost, how to forgive and not forget. This is the place where I lost my virginity, this is the bed where I contemplated suicide that night when she was gone, the bed where another woman saved me, and then another, and another. This is the window from which I asked about Spomenka, on this chair I wrote "If Love Exists," in this drawer I used to hide my cigarettes. And someone inside me is crying, but not me, I can't do it before my mom, not now.

I return to our kitchen, it's time to go. Silvija's father is trying a joke, and it falls flatter than the *Hindenburg*. We are putting our shoes on in silence, and I hear Mom's breathing. It is uneven, and I dare not look into her eyes, because I know what I will see there: PAIN and LONELINESS and HORROR and BETRAYAL. "I love you, Mom, I love you very, very much."

"It hurts, son, it hurts so bad."

My small mother is holding me tight, my tiny mother, my baby of a mother. I am her only son who always goes farther and farther away. "I will call you, Mom, every day, I promise."

"It hurts, son, it hurts."

We leave. Thirteen steps to the second floor, this wall needs to be painted, thirteen again, these geraniums are dying, I didn't hear Mom closing the door, these slippers must be size 45, thirteen more, she must be still standing at the door, the last look into our mailbox, no fucking letters today, no fucking bills, nothing that would make me return, two steps more, we're out.

I start crying silently only while we drive by the last houses of my hometown.

Silvija and I are packing. This is not an ordinary trip, this is the Final Trip. We are emigrating tomorrow.

Our tickets say: two bags, 32 kilograms each. So, the only persons we can bring with us are the dead. The only books allowed are small books. It means limited dictionaries, appropriate for exiles. No history books, no cookbooks, no encyclopedias. No reputation. No old shoes. No heavy feelings, either. No food, no drinks, no records. No reputation. No family, no friends, no success, no failure.

What's the name for this? *Ethical* cleansing? We will arrive in Canada as what, as who? Will our memories pass through customs?

I am looking at my Yugoslav passport. It has a red cover with "SFR Jugoslavija" inscribed on the front, as in "Socialist Federal Republic of Yugoslavia." That country, my country, does not exist anymore. The passport was issued in 1991 and even at that time such a Yugoslavia did not exist.

So, what is this red booklet?

A membership card of the League of Expatriates. An ID from Atlantis. A one-way ticket to fiction.

I transfer all the files from my computer in Belgrade to floppy disks. Extra memory for the road. When we arrive, I discover that the airport magnetic frames irrevocably destroyed one-third of the disks.

MY NEW NAME

Our first month in Toronto is hectic. We rent an apartment and fill it with furniture so that it feels like home. We spend three hundred dollars a month on telephone bills. It is irresistible, it is Tom Sawyer's dream: we call our friends over there to hear how they miss us. Almost like attending our own funerals.

I try writing for Canadian newspapers. I think in Serbian and translate while writing, but it does not work the way I want. Burroughs was wrong, language is not a virus from outer space, it is a snake from hell: it whirls, it moves, it slides aside. A writer is supposed to be a toreador, but I feel more like a bull trying to nail the red cloth of ideas.

Other things work against me, too. It is the spring of 1995 and the war in Bosnia is still going on, with Serbs accused of another set of atrocities. I submit an analysis of the Bosnian situation to a local magazine, in which I claim that the war will be finished by the end of that year (it ended in September). They refuse to publish it, and when I ask for the reason, they say that I would have to be a well-known analyst to publish such a bombastic article.

But I'm a Serb. I ask myself, did they publish articles by German writers here during the Second World War?

I started publishing when I was seventeen, and since then, without noticing it, I had developed the stance, "I write, therefore I exist." Realizing that I don't publish anymore feels like an instant sunset: the night that falls is condensed, fearsome and palpable. Anxiety follows. I cannot point my finger at anything in particular, so I cannot isolate it and help myself. The symptoms are shamefully symbolic: if I go out, the fear grows with every step farther from home and weakens when I return. I can't stand the subway, it is a grave, and when I have to take it, when I force myself, I get the feeling that the platforms are slowly tilting and I will fall in front of a coming train. I also dare not look into the sky: it is so high and untouchable I get dizzy. Then there's a loop: I develop a fear of that fear, because now I know how easy it is to slip into madness.

I was half-atheist before I came here. I would go to church from time to time, but rarely enough to be recognized as a sheep. I try Serbian churches here, but they just don't feel right. The churches in Serbia are Byzantine, dignified; the buildings here look like warehouses. I cannot find God in them and he wouldn't recognize me, anyway. But Silvija had brought a small icon of the Holy Mother with her and sometimes I pray at home. At night, I turn to the west when I want to sleep. There is a big black hole of memories to the east and I dare not face it. One night I dream that the wind lifts me and carries me towards the Atlantic Ocean. I fly and expect to go home, but the wind stops and I just levitate somewhere above the huge ominous shadow in the deep. The *Titanic.*

The only thing I can do is write. But I only publish one article. Everything else stays in my drawer.

Ladies and gentlemen, please allow me to poison you tonight. To pour the sad songs of my people into your dreams, to spill the ghosts of a destroyed country into your air, let me introduce you to my dead friends, to those who are dispersed all over the world, trying so hard to learn the customs, trying to say what hurts them, may it be a thin dust of memories, a fine ash of hopes, a golden powder of lost loves, may it even be unsayable. We have no other means than to sing our sad songs to you, my dears. Everything is so slow, intolerably slow in this life, so let me show you the Speed of Pain, the only speed known to humans greater than the speed of light. Let me say thank you for all you did and even more for what you didn't do, my lovely ones. Because, we all did it together, didn't we? We were all there, we saw it all happening, but we didn't do enough to stop it. So let's take off our skins tonight, let's mix our blood, let's clench our fists into a never-ending cramp of impotence. Have you seen that Herzog film? The one where an Australian Aborigine goes to court, and the judge asks who can translate what the man says, and there's no one in the courtroom who can do it, and finally someone says that this man is the last of his tribe, and no one else in the universe speaks his language anymore, that one, did you see it? Did you feel it, did you feel how it must be to be the last one, the one who closes the doors of heaven when everyone else has already left? Did you?

I admit: I am a poisoner. Sometimes, in the summer nights, I open my window and play the sad songs of my youth with all the volume I can get from that Japanese box. I hope that this will not hurt anyone. Sad songs can kill only those who sing them.

I know it's too late. Who cares? My mutiny is impossible to control, but very killable: close the window and I'm gone. My tepee is a safe prison: there's no solid thing I could hang myself on. There is no solid thing, I say.

My language you won't understand. Once I kissed a German girl on the sand of an Adriatic beach. The night was hot and the world was mine, and not knowing German I started whispering the softest words of my language. I thought that if I said *šuma*, *ljubav*, *proleće*, *jesen*, *djeva*, *kiša*, *milovanje*, that she would not understand the meaning but would hear the whisper of centuries. She left. She got up and left.

This tobacco I keep lighting, all my relations. All my relations.

You know what? This idea about soft words is not mine. I think I stole it from somebody. We do it. All the time. It's a Byzantine thing, they say. I'll cut a piece of a virgin lamb to trick my god into the sacrifice of a virgin. A virgin is a virgin is a virgin is a chop.

I cheat. I steal. I kill. The Ten Commandments were never written in my language. Enlighten me, please! If somebody kills my brother, what should I do? If someone destroys my country . . . What was that with the bread? Did you ever feed ten thousand refugees with two fishes? Wow! And the sea opened, you say . . . If all seas open, shall we ever learn to swim?

Leave it. It's over, we can all go to sleep now. History. Nada. Nichts.

It's late summer of 1995. I am in the house of a Serbian woman who lives in the western part of town. She is a psychiatrist, and the room we are sitting in is somewhere between a traditional Serbian home and the modern office of a Westerner. Reproductions of Serbian paintings from the eighteenth-century era of national romanticism are on one wall, a big library spans the other one. The psychiatrist is not trying to help me, at least not obviously, and it feels good, since I find it difficult to think of myself as a patient. It's not like her question–my answer, in quest of the heart of my problem; it's more like a chat. She's not trying to explain my dreams, and I gladly keep my sexual snakes, mini-planes in candy coating and silent levitation to myself. Instead, we talk about trees that don't grow here, and the different smell of soil after the rain.

"Serbian roulette is the same as Russian, only you don't point the gun at your head," I say. It just came to me; I think it's funny and should present me in a good light, as a serious but interesting case.

"Aha" is all she says, and takes a note.

"Could it be agoraphobia that's bothering me?" I ask. She seems interested in this idea.

"Quite possible," she answers.

The session is over. I go out and am satisfied: my problem sounds noble. Agoraphobia. The same thing that bothered some ancient Greeks. Good for my biography.

I don't go to the psychiatrist after that. The symptoms slowly disappear. I know the name of my disease, I know its identity, and its identity is my own. Any kind of name is good when you have nothing.

In July, three months after coming to Canada, we watch Cirque du Soleil down by the lake. The benches are wooden and the tent looks like a giant blue-yellow balloon. And then they subdue the lights and characters enter from Hermann's drawings, white clowns, soaring women, weightless children, flying magicians. And then the Cirque's singer in her hoarse voice starts droning something in Babylonian, a language no one understands and everyone knows. And then the wind starts blowing from the lake and the tent closes beneath our feet and slowly lifts. And I look around and see all my friends and loves and comrades sitting with me. And so we levitate silent and funny like a metaphor. And the wind carries us and here and there someone falls out, someone in New Zealand, someone in America, someone in Holland, someone in Canada. And then the white clown makes the snow start falling, even gentler than the real one. And then there is dead silence or there isn't and I hear only wind and someone saying in Babylonian, "We are only characters whose author has died."

YUGOSLAVIA CONSIGNED TO HISTORY

Tuesday, 4 February 2003, 19:47 GMT; BBC News

The Yugoslav Parliament has voted itself out of existence, dissolving the Yugoslav federation after nearly 74 years.

From now on it will be called Serbia and Montenegro–the two remaining republics joined in a loose union.

Yugoslavia lost its other four republics in the bloody wars of independence in the 1990s, as Croatia, Slovenia, Bosnia-Hercegovina and Macedonia broke away.

Under the new arrangement, Serbia and Montenegro have the right to vote for independence in three years' time.

ACKNOWLEDGMENTS

I have resisted writing this book for a long time. After spending so much effort forgetting, it didn't seem logical to torture myself with remembering. If it weren't for several people I was very lucky to meet along the way, these pages would have contained someone else's work.

Barbara Moon worked as an editor on the piece from which this narrative evolved. Without ever losing sight of the big picture, she asked very surgical questions that opened all the important scars.

Patricia Pearson never missed a chance to ask about my progress on this project. If I stopped writing it I would have felt ashamed before someone whose friendship was always unconditional.

David Homel believed I had something to say even when I didn't. His camaraderie made this loneliest of all arts less so.

A big thank you goes to my agent Sarah Lazin for her patience and diligence.

I started working with Tanya Trafford and Anne Collins, my editors at Random House Canada, thinking that I was lucky. Soon I realized I was privileged. If I knew that this project would bring two such amazing women into my life, I would have started writing it much sooner.

Erika Varga offered her unselfish help at a point when I most needed it.

Silvija read every incarnation of this story and was with me when I felt that this book was, "What book?"

My friends, who knew this story was in the making and kept asking discreet questions, also deserve my thanks. Zoća, Žule, Dejan, Milica offered not only support, but also shared their memories of our times together, helping me write a manuscript which is true.

My mother Ana remembered the dates, the faces, and the exact words when I lost my diary in one of my many moves.

I would also like to thank the Banff Centre for the Arts, Toronto Arts Council and the Canada Council for the Arts. These institutions all do a terrific job of supporting artists, and it feels safer to have them around.

To protect the identities of the individuals mentioned in this book, I have changed their names and, in some instances, moved them to a different time and place. To all of those who recognize themselves in this story, and to those who find themselves between the lines, I owe my gratitude.

And, finally, a big farewell kiss to my beloved Yugoslavia. We probably won't meet again, dear, but nothing will ever replace you in my heart.

A NOTE ABOUT THE TYPE

The Book of Revenge has been set in Garamond BE. This font family is based on types first cut by Claude Garamond (c.1480–1561). Garamond is believed to have followed classic Venetian type models while introducing a number of important differences, and it is to him that we owe the letterforms we now know as "old style." Garamond gave his characters a sense of movement and elegance that won him an international reputation and the patronage of Frances I of France.

The subheads and "Games" have been set in DIN (*Deutsche Industrie-Norm*), a modern face originally designed for use on German road signs and license plates. Considered a "workhorse" face, DIN has become a popular sans serif due to its legibility in a wide variety of weights and sizes.